LIFE IS A HIGHWAY

LIFE IS A HIGHWAY

A Century of Great Automotive Writing

EDITED BY **DARWIN HOLMSTROM** AND **MELINDA KEEFE**

First published in 2010 by Motorbooks, an imprint of MBI Publishing Company,
400 First Avenue North, Suite 300, Minneapolis, MN 55401 USA

Motorbooks titles are also available at discounts in bulk quantity for industrial or sales-promotional
use. For details write to Special Sales Manager at MBI Publishing Company, 400 First Avenue North,
Suite 300, Minneapolis, MN 55401 USA.

To find out more about our books, visit us online at www.motorbooks.com.

ISBN-13: 978-0-7603-3858-2

Editor: Darwin Holmstrom and Melinda Keefe
Design Manager: Brenda C. Canales
Designed by: Cindy Samargia Laun
Cover designed by: Rob Johnson, Toprotype
Cover illustrated by: David Moore
On the back cover: © *Lara Barrett/Shutterstock*
On the title page: © *Hector Cademartori*

Printed in the United States of America

Library of Congress Cataloging-in-Publication Data

Life is a highway : a century of great automotive writing / edited by Darwin Holmstrom
and Melinda Keefe.
  p. cm.
 ISBN 978-0-7603-3858-2 (hb w/ jkt)
 1. Automotive journalism. 2. Automobile industry workers' writings. 3. Automobiles in literature.
4. Automobile travel in literature. I. Holmstrom, Darwin. II. Keefe, Melinda, 1982-
 PN4784.A94L54 2010
 809'.93356—dc22
                          2010008285

Contents

Introduction

THE FIRST CAR MY PARENTS EVER LET ME DRIVE to school was a red Dodge Caravan, several years old at the time and not the coolest car in the parking lot, to say the least. But it certainly got me—and quite a few other people—from point A to point B. We called it the Red Ranger, and we even had a theme song for it, reminiscent of old western TV show themes. Among its many quirks, the van had some kind of electrical issue that meant the automatic locks would really only lock the passenger-side door, the sliding door would only open from the inside, and the dome light would randomly turn on at odd moments— usually when I was driving down the highway in the middle of the night by myself, to make it all the more creepy and irritating.

I can't say I was in love with that first car, and I've definitely had better cars since, but that car was a lot more than just an old, broken-down minivan. It symbolized my newfound freedom. It had a character all its own, and it taught me how to parallel park a boat.

From the very beginning, the automobile has given man and woman a sense of independence, a feeling that the open road can lead to opportunity. The first cars—hulking, smelly, slow beasts not unlike my Red Ranger—created a real exchange between country and city, a chance to expand and to prosper. And even then, the car had its critics, both in the government and in the private sector.

But in spite of this criticism—or maybe because of it—people have developed a passion for driving that rivals their passion for just about anything else. Newer, better, and faster cars have come along in quick succession, inspiring men and women everywhere to pull out their wallets and put a down payment on a dream.

We love cars with personalities, cars that resonate with us on a deeper level. We choose cars that we can live with, and, ultimately, we drive cars that we can't live without.

Countless articles, stories, novels, and blogs have been written about this passion, and many of these pieces of motor journalism have endured well the test of time. As such a key part of everyday life for millions of people, driving has inspired some of the best writing ever published. This book contains only a small section of the highlights from the past 120 years. Featured here are chapters from well-known fiction, including Stephen King's *Christine* and Hunter S. Thompson's *Fear and Loathing in Las Vegas*.

The largest car magazines are all represented too, with pieces by P. J. O'Rourke and Patrick Bedard from *Car and Driver*; Jamie Kitman and Jean Lindamood from *Automobile*; and Zora Arkus-Duntov and Peter Egan from *Road & Track*. We've included an international contingent as well, with stories by L. J. K. Setright, Jeremy Clarkson, and Rowan Atkinson.

Some of the authors featured in *Life Is a Highway* you may recognize as respected car experts, such as Tom McCahill, Ken Purdy, and Jay Leno, and some names you may not recognize at all. Nonetheless, these stories are important too, as records of automobile history that will remain relevant for many years to come.

Auto obsession will attack when you least expect it, and it will influence every part of your life. Henry Ford felt it, as he pointed out in his autobiography *My Life and Work*: "I had to choose between my job and my automobile. I chose the automobile, or rather I gave up the job—there was really nothing in the way of a choice." Enjoy feeding that obsession with the great stories that follow.

—Melinda Keefe

CHAPTER 1 The Thrills and Spills of Car Ownership

The Storm Breaks

By Stephen King

Christine,

1983

WILL GOT UP, CIGAR CLAMPED IN HIS JAWS, and shut off his television set. He should go to bed, but maybe he would have a brandy first. He was always tired now, but sleep came hard.

He turned toward the kitchen . . . and that was when the horn began to honk outside. The sound came over the howl of the wind in short, imperative blasts.

Will stopped cold in the kitchen doorway and belted his robe closed across his big stomach. His face was sharp and rapt and alive, suddenly the face of a much younger man. He stood there a moment longer.

Three more short, sharp honks.

He turned back, taking the cigar from his mouth, and walked slowly across the living room. An almost dreamlike sense of *déjà vu* washed over him like warm water. Mixed with it was a feeling of fatalism. He knew it was Christine out there even before he brushed the curtain back and looked out. She had come for him, as he supposed he knew she might.

The car stood at the head of his turnaround driveway, little more than a ghost in the membranes of blowing snow. Its brights shone out in widening cones that at last disappeared into the storm. For a moment it seemed to Will that someone was behind the wheel, but he blinked again and saw that the car was empty. As empty as it had been when it returned to the garage that night.

Whonk. Whonk. Whonk-whonk.

Almost as if it were talking.

Will's heart thudded heavily in his chest. He turned abruptly to the phone. The time had come to call Cunningham after all. Call him and tell him to bring his pet demon to heel.

He was halfway there when he heard the car's engine scream. The sound was like the shriek of a woman who scents treachery. A moment later there was a heavy crunch. Will went back to the window and was in time to see the car backing away from the high snowbank that fronted the end of his driveway. Its hood, sprayed with clods of snow, had crimped slightly. The engine revved again. The rear wheels spun in the powdery snow and then caught hold. The car leaped across the snowy road and struck the snowbank again. More snow exploded up and raftered away on the wind like cigar smoke blown in front of a fan.

Never do it, Will thought. *And even if you get into the driveway, what then? You think I'm going to come out and play?*

Wheezing more sharply than ever, he went back to the phone, looked up Cunningham's home number, and started to dial it. His fingers jittered, he misdialled, swore, hit the cutoff buttons, started again.

Outside, Christine's engine revved. A moment later there was a crunch as she hit the embankment for the third time. The wind wailed and snow struck the big picture window like dry sand. Will licked his lips and tried to breathe slowly. But his throat was closing up; he could feel it.

The phone began to ring on the other end. Three times. Four.

Christine's engine screamed. Then the heavy thud as she hit the snowbank the passing plows had piled up at both ends of Will's semi-circular driveway.

Six rings. Seven. Nobody home.

"Shit on it," Will whispered, and slammed the phone back down. His face was pale, his nostrils flared wide, like the nostrils of an animal scenting fire upwind. His cigar had gone out. He threw it on the carpet and groped in his bathrobe pocket as he hurried back to the window. His hand found the comforting shape of his aspirator, and his fingers curled around its pistol grip.

Headlights shone momentarily in his face, nearly blinding him, and Will raised his free hand to shield his eyes. Christine hit the snowbank again. Little by little she was bludgeoning her way through to the driveway. He watched her back up across the road and wished savagely for a plow to come along now and hit the damned thing broadside.

No plow came. Christine came again instead, engine howling, lights glaring across his snow-covered lawn. She struck the snowbank, pushing mounds of snow violently to either side. The front end canted up, and for a moment Will thought she was going to come right over what was left of the frozen, hard-packed embankment. Then the rear wheels lost traction and spun frantically.

She backed up.

Will's throat felt as if its bore was down to a pinhole. His lungs strained for air. He took the aspirator out and used it. The Police. He ought to call the police. They would come. Cunningham's '58 couldn't get him. He was safe in his house. He was—

Christine came again, accelerating across the road, and this time she hit the bank and came over it easily, front end at first tilting up, splashing the front of his house with light, then crashing back down. She was in the driveway. Yes, all right, but she could come no further, she . . . it . . .

Christine never slowed. Still accelerating, she crossed the semicircular driveway on a tangent, plowed through the shallower, looser snow of the side yard, and roared directly at the picture window where Will Darnell stood looking out.

He staggered backward, gasping hard, and tripped over his own easy chair.

Christine hit the house. The picture window exploded, letting in the shrieking wind. Glass flew in deadly arrows, each of them reflecting Christine's headlamps. Snow blew in and danced over the rug in erratic corkscrews. The headlights momentarily illuminated the room with the unnatural glare of a television studio, and then she withdrew, her front bumper dragging, her hood popped up, her grille smashed into a chrome-dripping grin full of fangs.

Will was on his hands and knees, gagging harshly for breath, his chest heaving. He was vaguely aware that, had he not tripped over his chair and fallen down, he probably would have been cut to ribbons by flying glass. His robe had come undone and flapped behind him as he got to his feet. The wind streaming in the window picked up the *TV Guide* from the little table by his chair, and the magazine flew across the room to the foot of the stairs, pages riffling. Will got the telephone in both hands and dialled 0.

Christine reversed along her own tracks through the snow. She went all the way back to the flattened snowbank at the entrance to the driveway. Then she came forward, accelerating rapidly, and as she came the hood immediately began to uncrimp, the grille to regenerate itself. She slammed into the side of the house below the picture window again. More glass flew; wood splintered and groaned and creaked. The big window's low ledge cracked in two, and for a moment Christine's windshield, now cracked and milky, seemed to peer in like a giant alien eye.

"Police," Will said to the operator. His voice was hardly there; it was all wheeze and whistle. His bathrobe flapped in the cold blizzard wind coming in through the shattered window. He saw that the wall below the window was nearly shattered. Broken chunks of lathing protruded like fractured bones. It couldn't get in, could it? *Could* it?

"I'm sorry, sir, you'll have to speak up," the operator said. "We seem to have a very bad connection."

Police, Will said, but this time it wasn't even a whisper; only a hiss of air. Dear God, he was strangling, he was choking; his chest was a locked bank vault. Where was his aspirator?

"Sir?" the operator asked doubtfully.

There it was, on the floor. Will dropped the telephone and scrabbled for it.

Christine came again, roaring across the lawn and striking the side of the house. This time the entire wall gave way in a shrapnel-burst of glass and lathing, and incredibly, nightmarishly, Christine's smashed and dented hood was in his living room, she was *in*, he could smell exhaust and hot engine.

Christine's underworks caught on something, and she reversed back out of the ragged hole with a screech of pulling boards, her front end a gored ruin dusted with snow and plaster. But she would come again in a few seconds, and this time she might—just might—

Will grabbed his respirator and ran blindly for the stairs.

He was only halfway up when the revving whine of her engine came again and he turned to watch, leaning on the railing more than grasping it.

The stairwell's height lent a certain nightmare perspective. He watched Christine come across the snow-covered lawn, saw her hood fly up so that now her front end resembled the mouth of a huge red and white alligator. Then it snapped off altogether as she struck the house again, this time doing better than forty. She ripped away the last of the window frame and sprayed more splintered boards across his living room. Her headlights bounced upward, glaring, and then she was *in*, she was *in his house*, leaving a huge torn hole in the wall behind her with an electrical cable hanging out onto the rug like a black severed artery. Little clouds of blown-in fiberglass insulation danced on the cold wind like milkweed puffs.

Will screamed and couldn't hear himself over the blatting roar of her engine. The Sears Muzzler Arnie had put on her—one of the few things he *really* put on her, Will thought crazily—had hung up on the sill of the house, along with most of the tailpipe.

The Fury roared across the living room, knocking Will's La-Z-Boy armchair onto its side, where it lay like a dead pony. The floor under

Christine creaked uneasily and a part of Will's mind screamed: *Yes! Break! Break! Spill the goddam thing into the cellar! Let's see it climb out of there!* And this image was replaced with the image of a tiger in a pit that had been dug and then camouflaged by wily natives.

But the floor held—at least for the time being, it held.

Christine roared across the living room at him. Behind, she left a zig-zag pattern of snowy tire prints on the rug. She slammed into the stairs. Will was thrown back against the wall. His aspirator fell out of his hand and tumbled end over end all the way to the bottom.

Christine reversed across the room, floorboards groaning underneath. Her rear end struck the Sony TV, and the picture tube imploded. She roared forward again and struck the side of the stairs again, shattering lath and gouging out plaster. Will could feel the entire structure grow wobbly under him. There was an awful sensation of *lean*. For a moment Christine was directly beneath him; he could look down into the oily gut of her engine compartment, could feel the heat of her V-8 mill. She reversed again, and Will scrambled up the stairs, heaving for air, clawing at the fat sausage of his throat, eyes bulging.

He reached the top an instant before Christine hit the wall again, turning the center of the stairs into a jumbled wreck. A long splinter of wood fell into her engine. The fan chewed it up and spat out coarse grained sawdust and smaller splinters. The entire house smelled of gas and exhaust. Will's ears rang with the heavy thunder of that merciless engine.

She backed up again. Now her tires had chewed ragged trenches in the carpet. *Down the hall,* Will thought. *Attic. Attic'll be safe. Yes, the at . . . oh God . . . oh God . . . oh my GOD—*

The final pain came with sharp, spiking suddenness. It was as if his heart had been punctured with an icicle. His left arm locked with pain. Still there was no breath; his chest heaved uselessly. He staggered backward. One foot danced out over nothingness, and then he fell back down the stairs in two great bone-snapping barrel rolls, legs flying over his head, arms waving, blue bathrobe sailing and flapping.

He landed in a heap at the bottom and Christine pounced upon him: struck him, reversed, struck him again, snapped off the heavy newel post at the foot of the stairs like a twig, reversed, struck him again.

From beneath the floor came the increasing mutter of supports splintering and bowing. Christine paused in the middle of the room for a moment, as if listening. Two of her tires were flat; a third had come half off the wheel. The left side of the car was punched inward, scraped clean of paint in great bald patches.

Suddenly her gearshift dropped into reverse. Her engine screamed, and she rocketed back across the room and out of the ragged hole in the side of Will Darnell's house, her rear end dropping down several inches and into the snow. The tires spun, found some purchase, and pulled her out. She backed limpingly toward the road, her engine chopping and missing now, blue smoke hazing the air around her, oil dripping and spraying.

At the road, she turned back toward Libertyville. The gearshift lever dropped into DRIVE, but at first the damaged transmission wouldn't catch; when it did she rolled slowly away from the house. Behind her, from Will's house, a broad bar of light shone out onto the churned-up snow in a shape that was not at all like the neat rectangle of light thrown by a window. The shape of the light on the snow was senseless and strange.

She moved slowly, lurching from side to side on her flats like a very old drunk making her way up an alley. Snow fell thickly, driven into slanting lines by the wind.

One of her headlights, shattered in her last destructive, trampling charge, flickered and came on.

One of the tires began to reinflate, then the other.

The clouds of stinking oil-smoke began to diminish.

The engine's chopping, uncertain note smoothed out.

The missing hood began to reappear, from the windshield end down, looking weirdly like a scarf or cardigan being knitted by invisible needles; the raw metal drew itself out of nothing, gleamed steel-gray, and then darkened to red as if filling with blood.

The cracks in the windshield began to run in reverse, leaving unflawed smoothness behind themselves.

The other headlights came on, one after the other; now she moved with swift surety through the stormy night, behind the cutting edge of her confident brights.

Her odometer spun smoothly backward.

FORTY-FIVE MINUTES LATER SHE SAT IN THE DARKNESS of the late Will Darnell's Do-It-Yourself Garage, in stall twenty. The wind howled and moaned in the ranks of the wrecks out back, rusting hulks that perhaps held their own ghosts and their own baleful memories as powdery snow skirled across the ripped and tattered seats, their balding floor carpets.

Her engine ticked slowly, cooling.

What's a Poor Volvo to Do Alone in the Big City?

By Warren Weith

Car and Driver,
November 1975

OLAF THE LAZY HAS HAD IT WITH NEW YORK CITY. In seven short years, he's lost five—count 'em five—radio antennas, four grilles, three sets of parking lights, two side vent windows, one front bumper and had five sets of headlights punched out. Not to mention a hood so rumpled that it looks like a bed made by a student nurse. It's enough to make any stolid Volvo cry.

I'm inclined to agree with him. New York City has gotten too abrasive for a car built in a gentle, neutral country like Sweden. He may not own up to it, but the sulphuric acid that passes for a gentle rain in this town was just too much for his window-winding mechanisms; it turned all that fine Swedish steel into handfuls of soggy rust. And all the bumper-to-cancerous-bumper driving got him addicted to a rich diet of plugs, points, batteries, brake pads and clutch plates. There's no sense trying to get him to kick the habit, either. Whether he admits it or not, he's turned into a New Yorker living the fast, rich life. We all know what the Big Apple does to somebody from Des Moines, so you can imagine what it does to somebody from Göteborg, Sweden.

I must admit, though, he's put up a pretty good fight. The low point must have been the night someone snaked through the vent window and swiped most of the knobs off the dashboard. Now why would anybody do that? Did they own a 1968 Volvo 144 minus some knobs? Were they just itinerant knob freaks? There's a million stories in the naked city, and a knobless Volvo is only one of them. And as interesting as most.

Olaf is, in fact, a rolling barometer of what's happened in New York over the past seven years. When he was new, shiny, virginal, it was a different town. The person who backed into him and gave him his first ding kindly left telephone number and address tucked neatly under a windshield wiper. Subsequent bumps and bruises were duly reported by the various shop-keepers on the avenue, along with any license numbers they might have been able to jot down. Today, someone could put a torch to poor Olaf and the crowd would simply stand and watch. I don't even think they'd have the energy to applaud.

Of course, Olaf does have a role to play in the new city. He provides a very convenient object for the various ladies of the morning, afternoon and evening to lean against. Olaf and I are the last people in the world who would object to this sort of thing. I've been told that one of the least understood occupational hazards of being a sidewalk stewardess is sore feet, and a car you can lean on does take the weight off those tender platform-shod feet.

I guess that's the trouble with Olaf today. Everybody has leaned on him down over the years. Not that he hasn't leaned back, mind you. There was that bad case of hydrophobia early in his life. He simply wouldn't start in the rain. It got so bad that even a heavy dew would have him sitting in a silent sulk. We started to replace every electrical part we could think of, and halfway through the parts catalog, Olaf took to the wet and has been running rain or shine ever since. So much so that it's gotten to be a bit of a joke. With his rumpled hood tastefully lashed down with what used to be the jib sheets from my old sailboat, rainwater simply sluices over the engine. On any rainy day, I can collect a crowd waiting to see if Olaf is going to start. He always does, much to their amazement—and the driver's.

Passengers are enchanted with Olaf's lightweight racing window-winders. But let's be accurate: They really aren't winders. They are pieces of wood precut to various lengths. You select the amount of ventilation desired, insert the proper length of wood between the bottom of the inner door and the lower edge of the glass, and you're all set. It's rust-free, and the main component uses a renewable resource. I think it's spiffy. Jane—she's my roomy—thinks everything about Olaf is Godawful. So much so that not only won't she drive our Volvo, she won't even let me pick her up where any of her friends might see. (It's amazing how much time and trouble this saves me.)

Olaf seems to bother most of my friends too. He irritates. Just why this is so, I really don't know. Possibly my friends resent the fact that I'm not a card-carrying, monthly dues-paying member of the Consumers Club. Or it could be that *they* would like to run a ratty car and wear a sports shirt to the office but haven't got the guts. Or possibly they don't like riding in a crummy car. This last is the only reason for all the slurs cast at Olaf that I'll accept as an intelligent one.

The reaction people have to Olaf is one of the two reasons I'm going to keep him. He's my version of long hair. The other reason has to do with money. Originally, I thought I'd send him to the knacker's yard and buy myself a new automobile. Having had only one other brand-new car in my life, I thought it was about time that a man of my years and station had another new car. I changed my mind after visiting a few neighborhood dealers. $4,500 for a VW! $6,000 for a Volvo! The used-car dealers had an

even greater shock for me. One showed me a 144 two years younger than Olaf. It was polished and pretty and was about half as fast as Olaf, and all he wanted for it was two bills—two big ones, that is.

So it seems that Olaf and I are friends for life. His or mine, whichever comes first. But joy can be found in almost everything. Why not, I thought, go back to playing hot rod? Have Olaf changed into a strong road car—after all, his entrails are still in good shape—that I can use to hack my way out to the Rheingold Coast on the weekends? And then get something like a bulletproof Mini Minor to use in town.

The idea was given substance when I found out that Harry Fannelli's son had a shop in the upper Bronx. The main work at the shop seems to be putting together race cars, including the shop's IMSA Volvo. They don't win a lot, but they have learned a lot about what breaks and what doesn't on Volvos. So back to hot rodding, except this time around I'm just rich enough not to have to skin my own knuckles. I'm really not contemplating anything as drastic as some of the project cars that have graced this magazine—just a little exercise to see what can be done to make a 144 more fun to drive on a longish trip. I really don't have any concrete ideas, but I'm sure they'll come to me. And if they don't, I'm sure that Harry Jr. has a million of them.

A Fiend Goes Foreign

By Jane R. Bade

Motor Trend,
November 1955

*"I married a car fiend!" was the author's
woebegone cry to our readers 2 years ago.
Read what has befallen her now . . .*

It was one of those defenseless days when Tom sprang his newest car on me. He strode down the halls of maternity and through the louvered doors of my hospital room, with papers in hand and a grin on his face that could mean only *one* thing.

What is there about new babies that prompts men to buy cars? Maybe it's the absence of wifely restraint. At any rate, Tom was capitalizing on his week of freedom. There I lay, immobile, while he spouted his persuasive argument, documented with facts from current magazines and including a clincher about this "deal of deals." I pictured the '29 Model A roadster weathering in our backyard. It too had been *the one*. On 2 energetic Saturdays Tom had stripped it of all workable parts; now it stood, a canvas-covered skeleton. It had outlived the pipe dream, as usual, and here was *that look* again.

This deal was a 2nd-hand Volkswagen.

"Such a find!" he exclaimed, " . . . they rarely appear on lots."

"And how did this 'gem' happen to slip thru?" (I'm skeptical from grim experience.)

"Sold by a Navy man—bought it overseas. His wife didn't like it . . . that is . . . you know Memphians (this was to cover the wife-doesn't-like part), too conservative to know a good find! This guy drove it all the way back from New York, only has 17,000 miles; it's a bear for punishment."

Please understand, I had some pretty shrewd arguments stored up by then, but I let them go. This was going to be *his* baby. I had 3-day-old Susan to think about.

In the past Tom had concentrated on a Continental, a midget racer, roadsters, Model As, and had taken one regrettable fling at a current model. So this foreign business was new to me. Only once had I glimpsed a Volkswagen—and this under protest. I'd stalled successfully until one day Tom caught me without an excuse for staying home. In no time I was whisked to a foreign car shop and introduced to a blunt-nosed, goggle-eyed beetle, which I had no intention of owning. "How stupid," I thought, with all the traveling we do—2 children, the dog, and endless parapher-nalia. But now the crazy thing was ours.

I was initiated on my ride home from the hospital with baby one. Perhaps it was the sun-splashed autumn that sold me; maybe the soft bundle in my arms. Anyway, I fell in love with this machine from the start.

Tom showed me all the gimmicks: a tricky gas tank without gauge, the speedometer (in kilometers), those signal wingdings, and the motor in the rear. Before long I mastered the transmission and could double clutch in the downshift (this sounded particularly masterful to me). I could understand torsion bar suspension, quote the gas mileage, and explain gear ratios. Really I was quite proud to drive the thing and trusted its clocklike innards implicitly.

My viewpoint was not shared. Mechanics scoffed, our parents raised their eyebrows; everywhere heads turned in our direction. Children pointed, giggled, and questioned their puzzled mothers. Dignified gentlemen in Cadillacs tried to race us. One man leaned out of his rundown Plymouth and scolded, "You ought to be ashamed to drive a car like that—a big boy like you!"

So while we drove a remarkably well-built car, safely sprung and in excellent condition—a car that cut gas bills in half, never changed body style, maneuvered thru traffic and parked anywhere—we were criticized for it.

However, this was not hopeless martyrdom. Daily, curious people, from the grocery boy to society matrons, debated Volkswagens with us, pro and con. One friend sold his Triumph for a VW; another is still trying to convince his wife. We took the blue varmint on 500-mile sprints, but the big test came on our winter vacation to Chicago. When about to set forth, we tackled the problem like a keychain puzzle. Out came the right front seat, and in its place went a baby's travel bed. Three suitcases and cardboard cartons squeezed in the baggage compartment and beneath seats. Bulging duffels lay under the hood. Diapers were crammed everywhere. Baby bottles in a 6-pack cola carton sat squarely inside the spare tire. Stanley, our travel-crazy dog, assumed her position by the heater knob, where occasionally escaped a whiff of fresh air. We even managed about 6 square inches for my feet.

So we took off, in a 4-cylindered blast, while neighbors shook their heads and grandparents waited breathlessly at the end of the line. The VW sped along with the evenness of an electric commuter train. Inside we were secure and warm. We busied ourselves computing mileage (multiply by 5 and divide by 8; it takes intelligence to drive one of these things).

When bottles needed warming, we transferred them from the "trunk" to the round heater vents, and family life went on. Baby Sue lay snug in her bed. Two-year-old Carol bounced gleefully in her car seat, exclaiming about the "big cars." Her [perspective] is slightly warped!

In farm towns we caused a major sensation on every Main Street.

"What's that there frisky thing?" a weathered man inquired. Gas station attendants overflowed the tank as they peeked and probed. One proud fellow refused to speak another word after poking the hose into the rear of the car. At service stations, restaurants, motels (even in driving rain), Tom not-so-patiently explained his little oddity, permitting examination of the engine. Had we charged admission the trip could easily have paid for itself.

In Chicago the temperature hit 14 below and the Volkswagen refused to move. Such a blow to the master's ego! All night long a lamp burned beside the carburetor, and still it would not budge without a push.

This difficulty and others brought me into the hallowed bowels of the foreign car shop. Here we found sympathetic ears and mechanical know-how—at a price.

There was a tense hush as 5 men huddled over one machine. Tools lay on a scarlet cloth on the fenders. They were handled gently, then carefully locked away. This was an emergency ward. Other "patients" were parked row on row. A stripped Italian sports car 2-tone Jag coupe, a 1928 Lincoln touring car, and a custom Spohn waited silently for the specialist. Their chrome engines, burnished leather seats and lean bodies spoke eloquently to me of the dreams and heartaches entombed therein.

Of course, there was time to look around. (It's part of the plan—this opportunity to browse and whet appetites.) Tom probed the Microbus, extolling merits. He adoringly rubbed the Porsche, and deliberated "objec-tively" about a VW sunroof sedan.

A blond mechanic approached. Vut iss da matter wit her?" Tom's eyes lit up at the 1st accented words. This would be a job well done!

"Choke cable, I think." Tom lifted the hood. "She stalls and sometimes won't she won't start."

"Ve fix her fine."

"Choke cables run about a buck 50?" Tom inquired.

"Ya, but we need just a little gasket here, one there, and she be like new."

Two nickel gaskets and 3 hours' labor—that was the German economy, and no amount of talking would convince this man to discard the worn part for new. I shrugged my shoulders. Tom kept his $1.50. The expert adjusted the old cable free of charge and we went on our way, stalling at the next icy stop.

Back thru southern Illinois real trouble began. Dusk had settled, one headlight was out, and the rain came drizzling down. Once in a while a light glimmered from some distant farm. The VW moved slower and slower up each of the rolling hills. Behind me the pistons were pounding out a spasmodic rhythm. Up front Tom drove with that stern, uncomfortable look. Not only was his pride at stake this time, it was doubtful that his pride would roll another inch.

The next town, Pinckneyville, Ill., by no means a mechanical mecca. At a dimly lit station a mechanic approached us with awe. Perhaps he thought

the Martians had landed, for he'd never seen a foreign car close up, had never heard of Volkswagens, and nearly had apoplexy at the sight of the opposed 4 in the rear.

Need I say we went no farther that night? In the morning we switched directions and chanced a run to the nearest dealer, in St. Louis. Carol climbed over laps and dog, from front to back, and back to front, grinding chocolate cookies into the seat. Susan fidgeted and with gooey fingers smeared the window panes.

In East St. Louis we hunted a motorcycle shop "that sometimes had funny cars parked out front." It was closed. Someone suggested a lumber dealer who owned a foreign car. When we looked up his office, the first rays of hope shone thru. The Volkswagen shop, he told us, was across town. If we didn't make it, this dealer would gladly send his truck to tow us in.

Thru the congested city we sputtered, slower and slower. At last—there it was. Like a band of refugees we entered the place. Out came the engine, and then the verdict: due to a poorly tightened manifold, one valve had burned out. They would tear down the engine, grind all valves and replace a rusted muffler. This would take most of the day.

The shop owner (in cap and tweed jacket) sauntered over casually to offer us his unheated showroom for our stay. There among the aristocratic vehicles we cajoled, entertained, and wrestled with the children 'til they would be entertained no more. The coke and candy machines lost their appeal. Formula and dry diapers were running out. Besides, 2 leather chairs and a washroom proved quite inadequate for feedings and naps, so I took the only alternative. Back to the "bug" and up on the grease rack we went, into the stifling upper atmosphere of the shop.

Down below the men worked meticulously, dipping and cleaning, screwing and unscrewing. Momentarily they referred to the service manual, which rested in a safe, clean space as tho it were the Gutenberg Bible. Water sprayed around us; the air hose screeched. We shuttled bottles and babies up and down. Stanley muffled a growl of distrust, and my body ached in the cramped quarters.

When darkness closed in, mechanics' wives arrived, and the shop door was locked. We looked down on an impatient audience. The engine was still out, and waiting seemed unbearable. At 8 P.M. the hood slammed shut, and we paid a fat $70 bill. Free again and ready to push for home, we rolled out into a brilliant but paralyzed St. Louis, under a glaze of sleet. We crawled to the city limits, slid down a banked drive to the door of a motel room. Never had privacy and rest and quiet seemed so sweet.

Perhaps you would have given up after all this. I might have too, but not Tom. The Kraut in him was not easily daunted, especially when our dealer displayed an enticing new Volkswagen. It had synchro-mesh transmission (just for *me*), red leather upholstery, self-adjusting seats (on ours, I got out and unscrewed the bolts) and *chrome*.

It didn't matter that notes on the blue beetle remained. In the interest of "good business judgment" and "safety" we would trade this car, "the one we would keep forever," for a shiny tan model.

So now, having never owned one car more than half a year, we are on the 4th month of this new VW—and still as proud as can be. Furthermore, this foreign mechanism is stealing its way into our hearts. We've gone across country, up mountains, thru snow and dust storms; except in an Oklahoma headwind the car performs without fault. Tom vacuums, washes, and polishes it until it gleams. He keeps doors and windows closed to preserve that new smell. He parks it in the shade, avoiding "limey" trees (whatever those are) as directed in the manual. He pores over lists of accessories (there are *many*) and studies the history and manufacture of Volkswagens in myriad publications which I'd hoped didn't exist—but do!

Without doubt this car is doing strange things to my husband's ego. Before, stoplight racers, dubious spectators, and insulting remarks were routinely ignored. Now a simple glance is a personal insult to Tom, our car, and, of course, to the German *volk* as well.

I hate to admit this, but even I have endangered its European dignity now and then. The time I drove up a mountain road with the emergency on, it hurt me as much as it did those rugged brakes. Then one day I turned against traffic on a one-way boulevard. Thoroughly embarrassed, I was dodging traffic and bewildered looks when I encountered a squad car face to face. In that flustered moment I smiled weakly, waved at the officers and disappeared *with haste* at the next crossing. I presume my stupidity was attributed to womankind and not foreign cars, but each squad car I pass makes me squeamish inside. You see, in our Volkswagen we are always marked men.

All in all, we are still an oddity in this mobilized generation of Americans, but we rather like it. Those jokes about roller skates, toys in your Christmas stockings, and squirrels under the hood are all old stuff to us. Children still point, Cadillacs race, many condemn, but we think pioneering is fun! We just smile knowingly and drive economically on our way.

You've heard of conversation pieces, I'm sure. Some folks hang them on their walls, some set them on tables, but we drive ours. It's Tom's 17th car—the one, by the way, which "we are going to keep forever." I have my doubts about that, but for now (at least 'til the next "deal" comes along) my husband has gone strictly foreign.

The crazy part is this: for the 1st time in these fiendish adventures, this foreign bug has made me a fiend, too.

Come and See the Wheel Thing

By David Morley

The Age,

March 2008

THE ROT FIRST SET IN, I reckon, with the invention of the telephone. Before it came along, to bother someone you had to jump on a horse, ride through choking dust and ford swollen rivers to bash on their door.

Imagine telemarketers having to do that?

Nowadays, just about anybody who can remember, guess or buy my phone number can talk to me, whether I want to talk with them or not.

Then we got television. Oh boy!

It is now possible to "visit" faraway places and "meet" interesting people without leaving the safety and convenience of one's triple-fronted brick veneer.

But it gets worse. Pretty soon, we had the internet, which allows a whole other breed of people to, er, breed.

Thanks to chat rooms and online dating services, members of our society can, without even changing out of their pyjamas, meet, court and even propose marriage to folk half a world away.

I've seen it happen. Some of these cyber-nookies have even resulted in offspring.

"Congratulations, Mrs. Schnedd, it's a boy. Mr. Schnedd, would you like to cut the umbilical?"

"Nah, just unplug him at the USB."

Anyway, the point of all this is that I've never really been one for the pseudo experience. When I kick somebody's door down to flatten them, I like to do it with my own limbs. When I gaze out at the white cliffs of Dover, I prefer to do it standing on the deck of a boat in the English Channel. Yes, drinking warm beer, if you must know.

And when I attempt to form a relationship with another person, I like to do so over a couple of drinks, and be able to look them in the eye (it's the best way of figuring out whether they're just after my Kombi or not).

It's why, therefore, I like cars. And driving them.

Unlike all those inventions that attempt to bring the world to us, the car is the odd one out. It's the one that offers to take us to the rest of the world.

What's the difference? Well, it's simple.

The world delivered via a telephone line, a fibre-optic cable or a stream of electrons via a satellite will always be just a digitised copy of the world.

You might be able to talk to somebody in Dubbo, but you won't be able to smell their aftershave or taunt them for wearing a Hawaiian shirt despite them being hundreds of kilometres from the beach.

The same goes for the internet and the relationships it fosters. Not only are you shielded from the physical acts of shaking hands and shouting a beer, there's a risk that the 25-year-old pole dancer you think you're chatting with is, in reality, a 200-kilogram, 45-year-old truckie.

But hang up the phone, switch off the telly, throw the computer in the nearest skip and drive to Dubbo, and the world you'll see and the people you'll meet will be the real deal.

You can try the food, swim in the rivers, hang out with the locals, and even if they do turn out to be fat, middle-aged truck drivers with cheap aftershave and crook shirts, at least you'll know as much.

And—if your road trips wind up anything like mine—by the time you get home, you'll have had an adventure.

More than that, you'll have had a life. Go out and hug your car immediately.

My fear, meanwhile, is that these various forms of technology are only preparing us for the day when nobody will drive to Dubbo—or anywhere else.

Are we just being softened up for a time when driving cars is either banned or so culturally unacceptable that you'd be the social equivalent of a peddler of pornography?

Because you'd never see anything like that on the internet.

What Car Shall I Buy?

Gus Finds in So Many Autos of Merit the Problem That Confronts Us All and Puts Client's Query Up to You

By Martin Bunn

Popular Science Monthly,

February 1928

"**H**OW ABOUT GIVING THE AUTO SHOW THE ONCE OVER tonight?" suggested Gus Wilson to his partner as they were closing up the Model Garage for the night.

"I'm game," Joe Clark replied. "Stop around for me any time after eight."

"Can't you make it earlier? I'll have Bill Crowley in tow. He wants me to help him pick out a car."

"What!" exclaimed Joe. "Bill Crowley going to buy a car! Why, he's always saying he hates automobiles!"

"Yeah," grunted Gus, "that was when he was broke. But he's made money recently, so he can afford a car now."

Joe grinned. "Well, I sure don't envy you the job. No matter what car you recommend, if he has any trouble with it he'll blame you."

"No, he won't," contradicted Gus as he shuffled his muscular frame into his overcoat. "I've got a scheme to beat that. You watch how I work it."

Joe was just finishing his supper when he heard Gus's horn. Bill Crowley was already in the car.

"So the bug has stung another victim," grinned Joe.

"Yes," Crowley admitted sheepishly, "it's got me at last. I guess the only cure is to buy one; but what gets me is which to buy, they all look so good."

"Now," said Gus, as they passed into the vast hall filled with shiny, new models, "before we start going the rounds let's figure out about what type of car you want, and how much you can pay, and also let's see if you have any particular requirements that might affect your choice. How big is your family, Bill?"

"Four, the wife and I and the two kids. One of 'em is eight and the other six."

"Is your wife going to drive?"

"Yes," Crowley replied.

"Then I can see one mistake you've made right at the start," asserted Gus. "You should have brought Mrs. Crowley along. She'll have a lot to say about the type of body and the color scheme."

"That's what I thought when I first brought up the question, but she says she doesn't know one car from another and doesn't care what kind I get so long as I get a good one and get it right away."

"All right," said Gus, "now tell me how much you want to spend, and we'll look over all the cars in that class."

Crowley hesitated. "I haven't decided that either," he confessed. "I can spend up to a couple of thousand dollars, but naturally I don't want to spend any more than I have to."

"Humph!" grunted Gus. "How am I going to suggest a good car to buy when you haven't any idea what kind you want or how much you think a car will be worth to you? Well, let's get started and see if we can't pick up some good ideas."

They moved slowly from exhibit to exhibit and examined each glistening machine. Now and then Gus halted before one and briefly pointed out various mechanical and body design features.

"Of course," said Gus as they stopped to admire a particularly good-looking coach, "it isn't so hard to point out the types of cars you shouldn't buy. For instance you certainly don't want a roadster, even one with a rumble seat in the back for the kids, because you will want to use the car in rainy weather and in the winter, and the passengers in the back seat have no protection at all.

"You might want an open touring car instead of a closed model, but that would depend on how you use the car. If you want it mainly for trips about the country when the weather is good—real pleasure driving—then

an open car is fine; but if you want to combine pleasure driving with comfortable transportation in any kind of weather, you'll want a closed car. Most of the open cars sold today go to old birds like me or to families owning more than one car. Of course lots of cheap open cars are sold, but there price is the main factor."

"How many cylinders ought a motor to have?" asked Crowley as he craned his neck over the shoulders of a crowd gathered round an eight-cylinder chassis.

"That depends on what features you value most," Gus replied. "From the standpoint of reliability and general utility it makes no difference whether you get a four, six or eight. Most of the possible sources of trouble lie outside the cylinders. If the ignition system goes bad, for instance, it will stall an eight just as quick as it will a four-cylinder car, and the same applies to many other troubles."

"But the sixes and eights must have some advantages or they wouldn't sell any," objected Crowley.

"Certainly they have," Gus agreed. "The more cylinders, the smoother the engine runs and the more flexible and quiet it is. Also, it is easier to build a motor with plenty of power by using a lot of small cylinders than to use four big cylinders with correspondingly heavy pistons that would cause excessive vibration."

"What's the advantage of long wheelbase?" asked Crowley, seeing a sign listing the lengths of wheelbase obtainable in a certain model."

"The longer the car, the easier it rides, other conditions being equal," Gus explained. On the other hand, a long car is harder to handle in traffic, and it takes more space to park or turn around in."

"Well," said Crowley, as the three men stood gazing out over the sea of cars and people after they had examined every exhibit, "now that we've seen them all, what shall I buy?"

Gus revolved the question in his mind. "That's a tough one to answer," he finally replied. "Your family is about the average size. You want to use the car in an average way. You are of average size; the average driving seat will be comfortable.

"You don't seem to have formed any opinions or acquired any prejudices. I'll be hanged if I know what to advise—tell you what we'll do—let's put it up to the readers of *Popular Science Monthly*!"

A Chance to Earn $10.00

Gus, whose automobile wisdom has proved so valuable and interesting to readers of *Popular Science Monthly*, has put up to you the problem of selecting a car for his friend, Bill Crowley. What make and model would you buy if you were in his place, and why? Name the car. Do not say merely a "five-passenger sedan," if that is the type of car you think Crowley should have. Give the actual name—Cadillac, Buick, Ford, or whatever it is.

Mr. Bunn, Gus's literary sponsor, plans to publish in an early issue of this magazine the best letters of advice he gets from our readers. And he will pay $10 for every letter published.

Advice from everybody, everywhere, is welcome, whether based on personal experience, the experience of friends, or observation of the results other people get with their cars. No restrictions are laid down; it is not necessary to own or drive an automobile.

Sit down and tell us what make of car and type of body Bill should buy and give five reasons for your opinion. Keep your letter within 200 words. Address it to Martin Bunn, care of *Popular Science Monthly*, 250 Fourth Avenue, New York City. And mail it so it will reach him no later than February 1, 1928.

Cars Our Readers Choose

Sixteen Experienced Motorists Advise Bill Crowley on Picking First Machine— Contrasting Opinions Help You Find Best Auto for Your Needs

By Martin Bunn

Popular Science Monthly,

May 1928

"OSH!" SIGHED GUS WILSON WEARILY as he tipped his chair back against the wall and lighted his pipe. "I sure didn't realize what I was letting myself in for when I appealed to the readers of *Popular Science Monthly* to help me advise Bill Crowley what kind of a motor car to buy. Did you ever see so many letters in your life, Joe?"

"Most as many as Lindbergh got, I guess," chuckled Joe Clark, his partner. "I haven't totaled them up yet, but there's thousands in that stack and every single one of them has been read, too."

"All ready for you, Bill," Gus greeted Crowley as the prospective automobile buyer entered the Model Garage office. "These letters ought to make it easy for you to decide what car to buy. At any rate they'll show you what other people would do in your position. Let's go over this bunch just as I picked them out without trying to get them in any particular order. I'll read the top one. It's from B. Giegerich, of Pittsfield, Massachusetts.

"'Forget the light cars and consider your $2,000 all spent to satisfy your wife's vanity and your own. She will adore the rich upholstery and roominess of the larger car and you will admire the ease and quietness of an engine that can maintain a smooth, steady sixty miles an hour with the comfort and security afforded by added weight and larger wheelbase.

"'The ideal car for you is the Studebaker Commander Victoria. It is cozy but roomy, and you have the kids where you can keep an eye on them. The Studebaker's superiority over other cars of its class lies in lower engine speed. It is the secret of long life, smooth running, fewer repairs and minimum oil consumption. The Studebaker holds dozens of world records for endurance and speed and has all the latest features such as four-wheel brakes, balloon tires, crank case ventilation, gas pump, engine heat indicator and so on. With what's left out of your $2,000 you can buy Mrs. Crowley a new hat and coat to match the upholstery.'"

"That's one way of looking at it," commented Gus as he reached for the next letter. "Let's see what Peter Herzig, of Plainfield, New Jersey, says:

"'Bill Crowley has the money to invest in an expensive car, but his knowledge and experience in handling any kind of car amounts to plus nothing. His wife, who also will drive it, knows no more than he does. Therefore an expensive car would be a waste of money. I suggest that he buy a 1928 model Ford sedan for the following reasons:

"'It is the best value for the least money.

"'It will stand wear and tear better that the higher priced cars.

"'It is easier to operate and to care for a Ford than any other car, which in the long run will be a big advantage to the two inexperienced drivers.

"'Not only is the initial cost less but the upkeep of this new model Ford is much less than that of any other car thus far built.'"

"That," said Gus, "represents exactly the opposite point of view. Of course, the final and conclusive test of how a car stands up is in actual service. That applies to any new model of any make. Here's what R. E. Ambrose, of Verdi, Nevada, has to tell you:

"'With a six-year-old and even an eight-year-old child riding in back, for safety's sake he must have a coach. He must have a six-cylinder car because he can choose from among the best sixes within his price range and because the six gives ease of driving in traffic and is easier to park than an eight. He has missed the joys of motoring long enough to feel entitled to the added benefits of a six, yet he would not fully appreciate an eight, even if he could afford it, until he has cut his motoring teeth on a car of inferior capabilities. Four-wheel brakes are essential for the safety of his precious cargo. So for tried and true quality, size, appearance, he can find nothing better than the good old Hupmobile.'"

"I suppose he recommends the coach because the kids couldn't open the door and fall out," suggested Crowley.

"That's Mr. Ambrose's idea," agreed Gus. "The rest of his arguments seem sound enough, except the one about four-wheel brakes. All cars have them now.

"Here's one from a woman, Mrs. H. A. Thomas, of Indianapolis, Indiana:

"'I think Bill Crowley should buy a Chevrolet four-door closed model. Just because Bill has $2,000 is no reason for spending it all on a machine. This is his first car, and he should buy a dependable car—one that is easily driven and repaired at low cost. He should buy a four-door closed model so that he can drive it in any weather and because the children will not have to climb over the people in the front seat every time they get in or out. He needs four doors, not two.

"'This first car of Bill Crowley's is for use close to home—shopping, visiting, pleasure and business; and an inexpensive car is the most practical for such use.

"'On first driving a car the speed craze gets one—a light car will not tempt one into disastrous speed.'"

"Seems to be a difference of opinion on that four-door, two-door question," Crowley commented when Gus finished reading. "Which is better, anyway?"

"Being a bachelor, I can't answer that one," laughed Gus. "I never had to drive a car with children alone on the back seat, so I don't know how they act. Let's read the next one. It's from Otho A. Morris, of Kerrville, Texas."

"'Bill Crowley should first purchase a used car. It is a mistake for a person of average means, with no automobile experience, to buy a new car. We value things by comparison.

"'After Mr. Crowley has been aggravated for a year or so with an old model, he will know how to appreciate a new one, and he will know by experience just what new car will best suit his needs.

"'In his search for a used car he should not purchase too old a model, for that would disgust him with automobiles at the start. I would suggest an Overland touring 1924 model, the kind I have. It will take him where he wants to go and bring him back and be a fine little car. After he goes through a winter with it and discovers the disadvantages of celluloid curtains, he will know how to appreciate an inclosed model. Experience with an old car will make an automobile mechanic out of him by the shortest possible route. Then he will know how to take proper care of a new and more expensive car when he decides to make the change.'"

"That," said Gus, "is one viewpoint on the used car question. I remember that letter, but here's another from Ralph Cummings, of Los Angeles, California. There's no getting away from the fact that their arguments are as sound as any of the others. Here's what Cummings says:

"'There is no good reason why Bill Crowley should purchase a new car. With $2,000 to spend he can get a really fine secondhand Cadillac not more than a couple of years old and in perfect running condition. All new cars are secondhand any way the minute you drive them a few miles, so why not let the other fellow suffer the loss of the first year's depreciation—which always is the heaviest, plus the war tax, delivery and conditioning charges and so on? A good secondhand Cadillac will outlast any new car at the same delivered purchase price, and he will have a better looking and more comfortable car, a car that will do him justice in any company.'"

"So much for the secondhand car question. Now, listen to Grandison Irving, of Yale, Michigan:

"I would advise Mr. Crowley to buy a Nash six-cylinder sedan because it has the best bearing system, with seven main bearings, and full pressure oil feed. It has overhead valves with lubricated valve stems and rocker arms.

"The oil drain and radiator drain are accessible without soiling the hands. Oil can be added to the supply in the crank case through a large, handy hole in the top of the engine without using a funnel like a French horn.

"In addition to these features, Nash cars have fine bodies and the interior fittings are of the best. They don't change styles very often, so your car doesn't get to be a last year's model within a few months after you have bought it."

"Of course," commented Gus, "there are other cars on the market that have some of the features brought out in this letter. And some of them wouldn't mean anything to the owner who has his oil changed by the service station. The point is that this particular combination of features appeals to this particular owner. Here's another, from W. S. Hoover, who lives in Albion, Pennsylvania, that stresses various mechanical features:

"I suggest that Mr. and Mrs. Crowley buy a Chrysler 72 coach. There is no rear door for their youngest child to open and tumble out. Although the Chrysler has been on the market less than four years, it already holds third position in dollar volume sales. It was the first car to combine acceleration with high speed, accomplished by using a small flywheel, 4.6 to 1 gear ratio, and a motor turning 3,300 revolutions a minute, mechanical features such as the seven-bearing crankshaft, full pressure lubrication, oil and air filters, thermostatic heat control, invar strut pistons, motor supports mounted in rubber, rubber shackles, web crank case supports for

main bearings, and the new turbulence cylinder head giving a six to one terminal pressure.

"'The coach is closer coupled than the sedan and Bill won't appear lost when driving alone. Mrs. Crowley will appreciate the beautiful interior of the body and the exceptional ease of handling.'"

"Whew!" gasped Bill. "My head is whirling already. That's all Greek to me."

Gus smiled. "It represents," he explained, "the point of view of the man who takes an interest in the mechanical features of his car. Naturally, mechanical features won't mean anything to you until you have driven cars for a while and even then you may never learn anything about what goes on under the hood. And if you do, you may figure things out that other mechanical features are more important to you than the ones mentioned in that letter. Well, let's get on to the next. Another woman—Mrs. Grace H. Murphy, Melrose Park, Illinois:

"'I can't think of one reason why Bill should have a car, but I can think of fifteen thousand seven hundred and twenty-three reasons why he shouldn't!

"'First, last and always there is the matter of expense.

"'Second, think of the wear and tear on his wife's nervous system.

"'Third, garage rent alone will pay the premium on a $5,000 life insurance policy to protect his family.

"'Fourth, there's no reason in the world why Bill should pass everyone else on his way to work. Besides, the street cars are sure, safe and sane.

"'Fifth, it's easier to pay carfare than damages.

"'Sixth, Bill had better be spending Sunday in church and with his family than in the garage.

"'Seventh, with an automobile Bill and his family will be leading the life of a pack of gypsies instead of developing a decent home life.

"'Finally, I'm sick and tired of riding on the back seat of my Bill's car.'"

Gus joined in the gale of laughter provoked by this letter. "That," he said, "is a warning to show you what will happen if you get too nutty over automobiles. Now here's a letter with a totally different idea," he continued as he picked up the next one.

"'I would like to make a suggestion, in regard to that new car you are thinking of buying.' (This is from Lucile Boone, of Mantua, Ohio.) 'I suggest that you buy two of the new Fords, a roadster and a two-door sedan, in place of one larger and more expensive car. The roadster can be used in

fine weather and the sedan will be handy for bad weather and winter. You say Mrs. Crowley is going to drive, which means there will be times when you each want a car. When that happens you can let her take the sedan and you can take the roadster. Thus each of you will have the use of a car, whereas with one expensive car either you or your wife would have to go without. Then, too, if one car is temporarily out of commission the other will be available so you won't get stuck without any car."

"I never looked at it that way," observed Crowley. "Do you think much of the idea, Gus?"

"That depends on several things," Gus stated. "If you haven't a two-car garage, you'll have to pay out extra money for storage. If you don't use the car for business you aren't likely to want it during the daytime when your wife needs it. Of course, if you have room to store two cars without extra expense and you need a car for business use, two cars will be of more use than one.

"The next letter, I see, is from John P. Picco, Salt Lake City, Utah, an owner of a light six. He writes:

"'This is my third Essex coach and it is better than the other two, which is going some. I have over a dozen friends who have bought Essexes on my recommendation and to date not one of them is anything but pleased with the purchase.

"'I am an Essex enthusiast because every one of my Essex cars has shown less than seven cents a mile for operating cost, which includes every cent I have spent on operating, insurance, depreciation, interest on money invested, garage rent and so on. I can go fifty-five miles an hour all day long and feel rested at the end of the day.'"

"And here's an old timer, Jesse J. Rogers, of Miami, Florida," said Gus, proceeding to the next letter:

"'Dear Gus: I think your friend Crowley has made a mistake in waiting until he could spend as much as $2,000 for a car. It has made him more or less a cynic. Now if he had started in the automobile game about the time I did he would probably have had $360 available and there would have been no question as to what car to buy! In another way he has missed the spirit of adventure that belonged to automobiling as practiced ten years ago. Roads are so good now that it has lost all the thrills. Crossing Georgia or the Carolinas now is but a matter of a few hours' driving, while ten years ago it was a real adventure.

"'I suggest he buy a Willys Knight Model 70, painted in two shades of gray, and black above the window sills. This will give him a rich but not gaudy car that, because it has no valves to grind, will give him simplicity in operation, low upkeep cost and ample power without noise.'"

"He is quite right about the roads being better," commented Gus, "but anyone who gets any thrills out of rotten roads can find plenty to practice on!

"Here are a couple of letters that don't hold out much hope for you, Bill, as an auto driver:

"'In the first place,' writes Rube W. Davison of Holderness, New Hampshire, 'I wouldn't spend $2,000 on a car. Half that amount leaves something for doctors' bills or general repairs should Bill climb a tree while learning. A Pontiac coach would be my choice, as Mrs. Bill could easily handle it, and when the whole family is learning to drive there isn't much left of a poor car at the end of a year—so why spend so much on something you are going to spoil?'"

Then Gus read a letter from John G. Hanna, of Dunedin, Florida.

"'I advise Bill Crowley to buy a Dodge Victory Six sedan. The six-cylinder engine is the most satisfactory and the sedan is the family model. The car is large enough for comfort, but not so bulky and heavy as to increase the difficulties of a man learning to handle his first car. The price is far below Crowley's limit, as it should be, because a man's first car is bound to involve more service and repair expense, more rapid wear and depreciation, and earlier trade-in than will be expected after he becomes a skilled driver. The staunch steel body is an item the inexperienced driver cannot afford to overlook.'"

"And now here's a letter from a man who has been driving cars for twenty-five years, R. C. Jennings, of Denver, Colorado," said Gus.

"'I drove my first car, a steamer, in 1903,' he writes, 'and I haven't missed many days since. I have owned forty-five different cars—a great number of them haven't any surviving relatives at the present time. There have been the most wonderful changes the past twenty years, so that today it doesn't make much difference what car you buy, merely how much you want to spend, as all cars will return dollar for dollar if given the proper treatment. I find that cars in the $1,500 class give the best returns for the average family. I would advise Bill to buy a five-passenger Buick sedan, give it proper care, and receive in return service and satisfaction.'"

"This is the last one, from Wallace Bryson, of Cedar Rapids, Iowa," said Gus.

"Concerning what make and model car Bill Crowley should purchase, it is my best judgment that he select the Auburn 8-77, five-passenger sedan, for the following reasons:

"Comparison is the only basis of value, and the Auburn invites comparison, not only with cars in its price class, but with those costing hundreds of dollars more. In beauty of design it is years in advance of it competitors. Therefore it will be up-to-date when the owner wishes to dispose of it.

"The body construction is of the best kiln-dried wood and high grade steel. It is equipped with cam and lever type steering, especially designed for balloon tires, affording the driver sixty percent less muscular effort. The motor is equipped with vibration dampeners insuring no vibration at any speed. The chassis frame is exceptionally strong, having seven cross members, three being tubular, providing a rigid foundation. The universal joints are of hardened ground ball and socket construction, and the four-wheel mechanical brakes insure quietness and safety."

"There you are," said Gus, as he shuffled the letters into a pile and handed them to Bill Crowley. "I'd advise you to read them all over again very carefully and make a list of the various reasons for buying."

"In other words," Bill said, "you're not telling me what car to buy. You're letting me in on the secret of why other people buy cars so I will have something to go on when I pick out my own."

Benefits Conferred by the Automobile

By H. L. Barber

Story of the Automobile,

1917

THAT THE AUTOMOBILE IS ONE OF THE GREATEST boons to mankind will probably be admitted if all its benefits are fully understood.

The best teacher, it has been demonstrated, is one's own experience. In learning anything, the mind can never grasp the lesson it is told, with the same understanding it receives when the lesson is visualized by the eye.

Travel is acknowledged to be a good educator and to broaden the mind. This is because the eye sees and takes its own impressions, and does not depend on the impressions of others. Reading books of travel never instruct as does travelling itself.

The automobile is a healthful, exhilarating method of conveying people to persons, places and scenes that, before the automobile, they knew of only by hearsay, or by reading of them. To estimate the extent to which this informs and instructs, we need only go back in memory to the isolated farm of a quarter of a century ago, and vision the limited horizon of the general knowledge at first hand of the farmer's family. Practically all the current knowledge they had was from reading, occasionally going to town, or through visitors whose appearance was rare and made at long intervals. Seeing a new face in those days was a rarity.

The situation with a majority of the people in the country, before the automobile, was very much like the isolated farm family. It was like that of the entire country before the advent of the railroad.

No greater agencies for instruction in first hand knowledge than the railroad, the steamboat, and the telephone had been introduced into civilization up to the time of the automobile. Now the motor car penetrates into places where the railroad, the steamboat, or even the telephone does not go.

Medium of Distribution of Knowledge

Exchange of ideas between people is the life of wider knowledge, as the exchange of commodities is the life of world trade, and the automobile is the medium of exchanging information as money is a medium of exchange of commodities.

From time immemorial the greatest advancement of the human race has been made in groups; and the larger the groups, the higher the thought, and the more progressive the accomplishments have been. Big cities have surpassed small towns; small towns have been in advance of the country.

The reason for this is the greater opportunity afforded by numbers for the exchange of ideas and knowledge. The citizen of Rome or of Venice had the advantage of personal contact with numbers of citizens which the isolated rural Latin was denied, as the citizen of London, Paris, New York, or Chicago has, before his own eyes, the thought and achievements of millions which the citizens of the country only hear of or read about.

The railroad first enabled the resident of the country to go to the small town, and the resident of the small town to go to the big city, and by personal contact gather the fruits of himself seeing the results of community or group work, which, before, had been monopolized by his city brother.

The automobile supplements this work of the railroad, and is even more widespread as it enables more frequent visits to be made, and penetrates regions the railroad does not reach. What was a frontier is now a suburb, while the suburb has become the downtown. The motor car has opened up the far reaches as nothing else has done.

Bigotry and prejudice are the fruits of ignorance. Where knowledge is they will not abide. In enabling people to acquire knowledge in their own way—the way that most impresses knowledge on them—the automobile is changing the thought and the habits of the denizens of the entire country. It is broadening the human mind, by giving it a solid foundation to work on.

In the courts of law, among judges, lawyers, and court attendants, it is notorious that no two witnesses ever testify exactly to the same set of facts. There is a variation of detail, and many times there has been such a difference in the statement of material facts that the dispensing of exact justice has been defeated. This condition is ascribed to the fact that few people are trained observers. The automobile is correcting this popular defect more than any other one agency—by education. It is educating people to exact observation and precise knowledge.

Liberalizing the People

The automobile is a factor in creating open minds. When one travels extensively, notions and prejudices, based on false conceptions, are amended and revised by observance of the facts. In this respect the automobile is conferring on the masses a benefit which, before its advent, was confined to the classes.

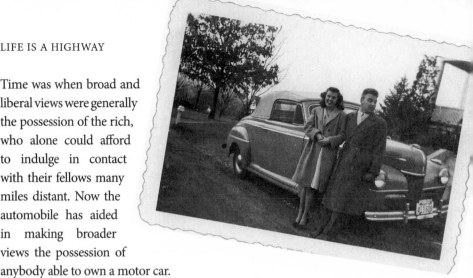

Time was when broad and liberal views were generally the possession of the rich, who alone could afford to indulge in contact with their fellows many miles distant. Now the automobile has aided in making broader views the possession of anybody able to own a motor car.

The degree in which the social life of the world has been benefited by the automobile is the favorite theme of the enthusiast on the automobile's advantage to mankind. This phase of the automobile's value is of less importance than is its benefit in informing and enlarging the horizon of the mind, but the social advantages which the use of the motor car confers are not to be underrated in an age when the most favorable mental conditions are recognized as of equal importance to a desirable physical state.

The happiness of the human race is added to by social enjoyment, and the automobile is a most important link between isolation and human intercourse. It has rendered the means of communication between people so easy and pleasant that it has encouraged and increased their association. Everybody is brought into greater accessibility to everybody else. The farmer with his family can visit his neighbor farmer and his family, many times now to once formerly.

What was formerly a long, arduous journey taken at the expense of pleasure as well as of time, is now an exhilarating spin. The farmer's wife and daughters can now go to town more frequently, and multiply the number of their visits to friends. The automobile is the emancipator of the farm woman, bringing the scope of her activities out of the narrow circle of routine drudgery and monotony into the larger circle of inspiring activities.

Farm women's clubs have been given an impetus, through the fact that a woman may attend one in the afternoon with the assurance that by the use of the automobile she can return home in sufficient time to get dinner, which she could not do by the use of the horse.

Factor in Promoting Sociability

The city man's wife in the suburbs can visit her friends oftener and more quickly, and the facility of speedy movement has given to suburbanites the benefit of the last acts at the theatre and the opera, whereas, before the automobile, they missed them in order to catch the last train.

The benefit of clergy has been immeasurably enhanced by the automobile, which, also, in addition to being itself an educational agent, has employed its speed and facilities in economizing time to increase the attendance in the schools. There are districts in the United States where children can not reach school in time without the use of the automobile.

What the automobile does for the city dweller, in enabling him to see the last act at the theatre or hear the last act of the opera, it does for the people of the farm in enabling them to spare the time to attend dances, sociables, entertainments, and motion picture shows. Where formerly the time required to drive a horse made it impossible to spare the time, now time is scarcely a factor. The change must inevitably react to the advantage and benefit of humanity, if all work and no play makes Jack a dull boy.

The health advantage of the automobile is a subject on which there is a difference of opinion among medics. The ordinary layman, however, is disposed to cast his verdict in its favor in this respect also. Some physicians have expressed the opinion that the only respect in which the automobile is noticeably not a benefit is in the matter of health. Some of them think it does not give people enough exercise, and that at the rate its use is increasing it will not be long before man loses his ability to use his legs!

It would be a catastrophe indeed if the human race, through the automobile, reverted to the condition when primitive man, according to the Darwinian theory, swung by his hairy arms from tree limb to tree limb, using his feet only as a stabilizer. But nobody, unless a writer for a newspaper Sunday magazine section, is likely to maintain this seriously, and he only pretends to be serious.

Whatever man loses in disuse of his legs by riding, as compared with walking, may be said to be made up for by his use of them on levers of automobiles and in the other exercise or operation of a car. The fresh air and the sunlight—the great outdoors—are the big health factors in motoring, and man will go on taking a chance to experience these and other delights the automobile has to give.

As an Element in Eugenics

And as still further offsetting the possibilities of decay of the human legs, which certain physicians predict, more constructive medical men have discovered that automobiling is becoming a factor in one phase of eugenics. It may not receive endorsement as a benefit in all eugenics as long as the charge can be made that since the use of the motor car the birthrate in Kansas has decreased, the discoverer accounting for this alleged fact on the theory that the expense of keeping an automobile discourages Kansans from assuming the expense of large families, but in one direction it is attempted to prove that the breed of certain Americans is being improved by the automobile, and in this way:

In certain parts of the country, particularly the Southeastern states close intermarriage is said to have been, in part, due to the inferior facilities for transportation, before the automobile came into use. Young men, it is said, courted and married their sweethearts, in the days when the buggy was king of local communication, within an average radius of five to ten miles, which accounted for people in those sections being cousins or otherwise related to one another.

Now that the automobile makes a thirty-mile or fifty-mile radius the equivalent of the five-mile or ten-mile buggy radius, the swains are seeking mates further afield, thus getting away from alliances with relatives, and there is a consequent decrease in the mixing of blood strains.

If this is true, tally one more in the score of benefits for the automobile, for it is the verdict of science that intermarriage between those of the same blood does not produce the best types, any more than does the interbreeding of other animals.

But in enumerating the benefits of the automobile its economic value easily comes next in importance to its service in imparting knowledge. Its health value may be a matter of difference of opinion, and its social benefits are comparative, but there can be no dispute about its educational value, and still less about its economic worth.

The factor time has taken on a new meaning and significance with the automobile's accomplishments in speed. Time is a vital element in the affairs of life. If the automobile's educational value can be expressed by the adage, "Seeing is believing," its economic value can be similarly expressed by the adage, "Time is money."

For Women Drivers Only!

By Jane Mitchell Clark

Motor Trend,

September 1952

ONE DAY LAST WEEK I TOOK A WALK IN THE COUNTRY. On an unfrequented lane was a Driver-Training car. An efficient instructor was teaching a *woman* how to drive.

Pretending to be collecting various stones and plants, I awaited the approach of the car, which came to a sudden halt, half-pitching the instructor and his trainee into the windshield. Imagine my surprise when I heard not one oath! Instead, the man said, "Not too bad. You're doing fine. Now just take it a little easier this time." And his voice was as calm and peaceful as a summer sunset. I had an uncanny impulse to creep into the back seat of that car, just to make sure the man was actually flesh and blood and not a hallucination of my mind. Then I heard a few more well-chosen words by him, calculated to inspire confidence as they drove away, and realized he was a *paid* driving instructor; they were all like that—so I was told later.

Well, I thought, what a difference that makes! What an advancement in social science and human relationship over the husband instructor or the boy friend. For, of all the dumb, heartless, absolutely senseless driving teachers, it's husbands, with boy friends not too far behind.

Now let's get things straight. I love husbands. I have one of these creatures and I used to have scads of boy friends whom I adored and still do to husband's secret disgust. But when I recall husband's methods of teaching me to drive the car, I simply fade away. And poor man—he's not an oddity—more's the pity—he's typical! I've interviewed some 25 women and girls who depended on their beloveds to teach them the driving art, and without exception, the pedagogy used was so similar, you'd think that all these males attended some school together and majored in profanity!

Having been a school-teacher and studied concrete methods of presenting subject matter with a psychological understanding, both of matter and student, these men seem to have perfected their teaching thrown into *reverse* gear. And I'm determined to present their method, even if I must dodge the cars of all you gentlemen readers the remainder of my life! For it's my firm belief that not one of you have looked into your car mirror and caught a glimpse of the *real* you that submerges all your cultured poise and reason when the little woman says, "Come, darling, teach me how to drive."

Discouragement is the predominating factor throughout the course. The *first* point is to make every possible effort to "talk her out of it." Now when Russia wants to break a prisoner, or get a phony confession, she uses much the same tactics—only husbands are a little smoother, and of course they're really good American citizens in practically all other directions.

"Sweetheart," they say in their most worshipful manner, "you can do so many things—sew, cook, nurse, keep house, entertain, play the piano and loads of things. But nobody can do *everything*. You just weren't born with a *mechanical sense*, dear, and without it, of course, you could never learn to drive. When I think of all the accidents by women, I —"

And right there, the little woman cuts in with, "Can you quote the statistics on that and the accidents that men have in comparison?"

Of course he can't, but while he's thinking up some liars' figures, she adds, "Thanks, honey, for all the nice compliments. But you see, in order to play the piano one must think quickly, must learn a lightning-quick coordination of head and hand—far speedier than any thinking required on a mechanical job!"

Well, he's failed on point *one*. So he proceeds to point *two*. (Heaven only knows how many gentle ladies today have fallen prey to this first point—never reaching first base on a steering wheel.)

Second Point. "Driving is a nerve-wracking business," he says, "but if you want to run the chance of a nervous breakdown and be a neurotic the rest —"

"Never mind the advice," she says, "anybody who can cook a good meal with a baby crying, a toddler pulling her skirts, and a husband yelling for the evening paper just doesn't have nerves," she argues.

Grudgingly, he opens the car door and admits her to the sacred inner sanctum, the spot under the steering wheel, while he plays up his *third* point—pity. It bulges from his sad eyes and envelopes his entire being like a shroud. His shoulders stoop and the worry lines across his forehead deepen, while she gets the idea that his heart is simply splitting in two, with anxiety for the car, anxiety for her, but most of all anxiety for himself.

"Remember, we still have a lot of payments to make on the car and our hospital insurance is only half covered," he admonishes as she tries out the throne.

"We've full insurance on the car," she retorts, "and anybody might have a wreck." (You see she's determined to be hardboiled, too—a dire necessity if she wins out.)

"That button up there is the starter. This right object is the gas. This pedal is the brake; this pedal the clutch. Here is the emergency brake. The gear is in neutral. Start your motor," he instructs—all in one breath.

She touches the starter button. Nothing happens.

"Did you expect it to start without turning the key?" he says in derision.

"But you didn't mention it," she returns.

"And you thought it would start off without igniting? Haven't you seen me turn that key every time I used the car? Women! Why, you haven't sense enough to —"

"*All right!*" she shouts back, cutting him off again. "I'll turn the key, this time."

So the key is turned and she presses hard on the starter button when he yells, "For the love of Mike—don't push it through the car! Press it gently," he advises, above the hum of the motor that has come to life.

"Okay," he says, "now shut it off. Let's see if you can do *that*. Then start again."

Quietly now, she turns the key and he shows her how to touch the starter lightly. What happens? The starter locks. It isn't difficult to guess the ensuing conversation, but after rocking the car it unlocks and they get back into it.

"I'll warm it up," he barks. "We'll drive out to some country road, if you still think you want to do the impossible." He gloats under the wheel like an ancient potentate.

Tight-lipped and tense, she nods. He's put over point *four*. He's made his trainee as taut as a fiddle string and robbed her of some of her self-confidence, but of none of her determination.

They cross a busy highway with big yellow stop signs. She watches him give the lane a look both ways, then dash across with scarcely any let-up in speed. "See how I save the gears, as well as gas and time," he boasted, "but you'd better not try it, for you wouldn't know —"

"If there were cops about, would you, darling?" she finishes.

Angry, that she can see right through him, he turns a sharp corner, giving no sign, whatever. The car behind him barely misses his rear bumper. As it pulls away, the driver glares at them and the air carries his malediction of swear words.

"Why, that blankety-blank!" husband explodes. "Can you beat that? Why doesn't he watch what he's doing?" he asks. The little woman only smiles knowingly, remaining quiet, and silence reigns until they reach the country. There, he once more surrenders his throne, after stopping and shutting off the motor.

This time, she remembers to turn the ignition key. Then she presses the starter, firmly. The motor purrs. She shifts into low gear (for this is still a standard shift car). But in releasing the clutch, she does it too rapidly, and the engine dies.

"Just what I expected," he informs her, "at this rate, we'll have a new starter to buy and they cost 25 bucks these days; but, of course, you wouldn't know." He looks down at her but she isn't paying him any attention at all. The car is moving slowly forward, and her mind and body is alert, tight and completely absorbed with her task.

In another moment, the car starts going to one side and he yells, "Gee!" waving his arms frantically like a mad-man. Naturally, she doesn't know what he means and the car heads for the ditch.

"Push down on your brake and clutch!" he shouts, while he shuts off the ignition. Now he's driven home point *five*—confusion. There's only one more point in this long scheme of discouragement he hasn't touched, and it comes next. This point, number *six*, is fear. After a lecture on how to watch the road, steer the wheel and shift gears, they're once more pulsing along. She's so mixed up and unsure of herself, she's ready to believe there must be a sixth sense—a mechanical sense. But it's locked in her heart and the only outward signs are her quivering lips and trembling hands.

Suddenly, a big truck looms up in the road ahead. "Don't let it crowd you off the road," he says. "Keep the car steady." She tries to do as he has said, but fear clutches her in a vise-like grip as she recalls all of his dire predictions. Now the truck seems to be bearing down upon them and unconsciously she veers away from it as it starts to pass. With an oath, he grabs the wheel, gives it a lurch and barely misses the tail-end of the truck while the rear wheels are nearer the ditch than they were before.

White-faced, and trembling violently, she surrenders the wheel and friend husband, believing her completely cured of "driving phobia," pats her gently, saying, "Don't worry, honey—nobody's expected to be able to do everything."

The next day, she contacts the Driver-Training Agency and learns to drive in three easy lessons. Smart girl. Smart as the new streamlined cars.

The Last Three Months

By William F. Nolan

Road & Track,
September 1963

H E SAT IN THE SILENT SPORTS CAR, FUMING, FACE FLUSHED, breathing hard. He was angry, angrier than he'd ever been in his life. *Damn!*

"What's the trouble *now*?" his wife called from the house.

"Battery," he yelled back. "Dead."

He knew what she'd say; get rid of it, Fred, she'd say. Trade it in. Get a new car. If she started that again—he'd kill her! He was mad enough. Mad. *Insane.* This car was driving him crazy.

He got out, slammed shut the garage door.

"Aren't you going to call the auto club?" she asked him.

"And get a busy signal? No thanks," he snapped. "I'll take a taxi. I don't even want to *think* about cars for the rest of the day."

"Taxis are cars," she said, but he didn't answer her.

On the way to the office he tried not to brood about the last three months. First the wheel bearing, then the water hose. Little things; always a bother, not a disaster. Then it got worse. Radiator leak, short in the dash wiring. Freeze plug out in the engine block, a defective stop-light switch. Then points, plugs, generator. Next, a new water pump. Then, fast and quick, a valve grind, carburetor rebuild, new front springs, a grease seal for the left rear wheel and a new head gasket. Then the brakes had failed—along with the fuel pump. Now, this morning, the battery. Gone. Dead.

"Dead," muttered Fred Matheson.

"You say somethin' mister?" asked the cabbie.

Fred sighed. "Battery on my car. Went dead this morning."

"Funny thing," said the cabbie. "I just had a new one put in day before yesterday myself. Not to mention the generator had trouble last week. Had to put a new muffler on her, too. Darn thing's driving me bats. Wife wants me to turn her in, but hell, she's practically new. My *car*, that is. I got only 10,000 miles on her."

Fred looked up, interested. "Yeah . . ."

At that moment the cab's engine began to spit and buck. Smoke began seeping from the hood. "Oh, hell!" said the cabbie.

Fred didn't wait to find out what was wrong; he left the distraught cab driver and walked hurriedly toward the office. Ahead of him a bus was stopped in the middle of the street, its doors open. The passengers were

shouting at the driver, but he threw up his hands, shaking his head. The bus wouldn't move.

At the office Fred ran into Eddie Fritch.

"Boy, I almost didn't make it down here today," Eddie told him. "Car conked out on the freeway. Transmission. They had to tow it in. You know, that damn car is costing me a *fortune* lately. Boy!"

"How lately?" asked Fred. He was a reporter, and suddenly his blood was up. "When did this start?"

"Well, lemme think," said Eddie. "Started 'bout three months ago. I just can't keep the thing running. The wife wants me to—"

"I know," Fred cut in. He moved through the city room, pausing at each desk. Same complaint: car's no damn good, going to trade her in. It was the same with the new car owners. Rods were letting go. Engine blocks were cracking. The auto club was swamped. Service managers were roundly cursed. Wives wouldn't speak to their husbands.

Fred Matheson's eyes blazed. He was on the trail of something—something big. He rushed into the morgue below stairs.

"Benny, get me the stats on suicide, murder, insanity and wife beating over the past 90 days. Hop!"

Benny disappeared between rows of filing cabinets.

A sick car can drive a man crazy, thought Fred. Eat up his bank balance, destroy his marriage, pitch him into senseless rage.

Benny handed Fred the stats. He checked them carefully, nodding, running his tongue over his lips. It was all here. The pattern.

Fred Matheson ran out of the building, into the street. A fruit truck was backed halfway into an alley, its hood up, the driver swearing at the engine. A cop at the corner light was trying vainly to kick his cycle into life.

Fred moved along the walk in a half-daze. Occasionally he would stop a pedestrian, asking the same question. They answered him, glad to share their troubles. Yes, their cars had been giving them a lot of grief. Why, in the last three months. . . .

Fred paused under a sign reading AUTO SERVICE AND REPAIR. He looked inside through the plate-glass window. The place was jammed full of cars, hoods raised.

He stepped inside.

"Having some trouble, sir?" The service manager smiled at him. He was a pleasant looking man in his early Twenties, but his eyes seemed almost glazed. Was it because of overwork? Three months of overwork?

"I'm a reporter," Fred told him. "I'd like to talk with you."

"Sure," said the service manager. "Come along to my office. Say, what'd I do, win the Irish sweepstakes?" Fred didn't reply. He followed the tall man to an office at the rear of the garage.

"Have a seat, and we'll—"

"I'll stand," said Fred Matheson. The door closed behind them.

"Well? What can I tell you?"

"I think you could tell me a *lot*. A lot that people should know. I'm tracing a pattern, and I think it leads to you. A nation without wheels is paralyzed. And, right now, today, it's happening to us. And it may be happening all over the world. There's some kind of . . . "

"Plot. Is that the word you're searching for?" The service manager's eyes were suddenly chilled steel.

Fred turned to scrabble at the door, but a thin purple pencil of light from the service manager's eyes killed him instantly. His body slid to the floor.

The door opened. A mechanic appeared.

"Reporter?" asked the mechanic.

The service manager nodded. "A professional snoop. Quite annoying."

The two men exchanged cold smiles. "The professionals always seem to find things out first. Which, in this case, means they die first."

The mechanic shook himself, in the manner of a dog trying to dislodge his collar. "I hate these earth bodies," he said. "This one doesn't fit me at all."

"Every planet presents its own problems," said the service manager. "And an invasion takes time. At least this one is well under way." He turned to glance into the garage area. "Did you service Mrs. Posten's Cadillac?"

"Just finished it. The master brake cylinder will fail this afternoon."

"Splendid."

The mechanic turned to leave, but the manager stopped him. "One other thing . . ."

"Sir?"

"Hide *this*." He prodded Fred Matheson's corpse with the toe of one shoe.

The mechanic quickly removed the body to the basement storage area.

Outside, an Austin-Healey sputtered and died.

CHAPTER 2

Developing a Vehicle and Developing an Industry

Slump and Be Happy

By Ken Purdy

*Ken W. Purdy's Wonderful
World of the Automobile,
1960*

A MILESTONE IN THE EVOLUTIONARY HISTORY OF *Homo sapiens* was passed some time back, quietly, almost without notice, when a Ford Motor Company engineer said that the shape of the seats in a new model were meant to conform to "the modern slump."

Heretofore there have been only two schools of thought in the design of motor-car seats: the American and the European. The European masters have favored a seat back with a soft, indented center surrounded by a firm, shoulder-gripping roll meant to brace the upper arms and shoulders. The Americans have remained true to the horse-drawn carriage maker's concept of a flat surface, upholstered to uniform tension throughout. Both have assumed the passenger to be an upright biped built around a straight, vertical spine, and therefore best catered to by a straight seat back.

But modern man does not have a straight spine, and all credit to the courageous Ford technicians for abandoning the pretense. The seat backs of the new car they talked about did not rise in an unbroken vertical line: six inches or so from the top they bent sharply forward. The round-shouldered, hollow-chested rider thus could know comfort denied his brothers in lesser vehicles. He would not need to press his shoulders into the seat back under the delusion that they belong there, nor would he have to sway in midair, his modem slump unsupported anywhere.

Now that ground has been broken, need we stop with automobile seat back? Will not the manufacturers of household furnishings, theater seats and the like have the courage to junk their comparatively puny inventories and come proudly if belatedly into line?

And who will be the first among the cutters and tailors of clothing for men to face up to reality? (The iron-handed esthetes who dictate women's wear need no urging; yearly the *haute couture* announces the shape of women to come, now hipless, now bereft of bosom, now shapeless altogether. They conceded the modern slump in the early 1920s.) What is needed now is comparable courage among purveyors to men. I look forward to the day when every three-pane fitting mirror in America will mount a sign: "Our suits are designed for men who stand *naturally*. Do *not* force your shoulders back. Slump!" Unimagined benefits will follow. Pitilessly delineated fore and aft in the all-seeing mirror, the average man pulls in his sagging abdomen, puffs his chest, forces back his brittle shoulders and holds himself so, at whatever cost, while the fitter measures and marks and pins. Naturally, when the suit is delivered and he slips into his true stance, the modem slump, the garment fits like a hand-me-down. Think of the pain, the heartache, the economic waste that would be avoided if he would stand before the fitting mirror as he stands waiting for the bus: shoulders slumped forward, chest caved in, abdomen drooping, all his weight hanging on one hip. Fitted thus, his new gray flannel would become him like something built for Lucius Beebe or William Powell the Elder.

Euphemism is horrid, disaster lies in the denial of truth, and Darwin was right. Let a deluded rear guard of gymnasts and physical education fanatics fight on, if they will, but as for you and me, let us slip our hands trustingly into the firm grasp of such as Mr. Ford's anonymous *mahatma*. They have proved that they know the True Way. Are they not even now planning for the day when the leg will be a mere vestigial appendage? Certainly. Where is the clutch pedal of yesteryear? Designs for accelerator and power-brake controls built into the steering wheel lie safely vaulted in Detroit. *Que sera . . .*

NCE UPON A TIME I LIVED IN WEST HOLLYWOOD, which is known as "Boys Town" out here because of its high concentration of homosexuals. I occupied a town house in a 23-unit condo complex, and all of my neighbors were gay except for one middle-aged lady who was a sort of den mother to us all. She drove a Toyota. I owned a Porsche. All the other cars in the vast underground garage were Cadillacs or Jeeps: either suffocatingly sybaritic Eldorado convertibles or macho-macho Renegades or Laredos, or Golden Eagles with tires the size of flotation collars, mile-high suspensions, and roll bars that looked strong enough to allow you to tumble into the Snake River Canyon and walk away unscathed.

Makes sense. Here in Tinseltown, you don't drive a particular car because it gets good gas mileage, or because you got a good deal on it, or because it never needs repairs. Here your car is your personal statement about the way you live—or the way you want your peers to *think* you live. It's not necessarily a status symbol, you understand (or even an anti-status symbol, like those college professors who vote for Anderson and drive seven-year-old Volvo station wagons, or those Libertarians in clapped-out Citroën ID-19s): it's more than that.

Driving a Jeep is as loud and clear a message as you can send: "I am tough and I am strong and you'd better not mess with me or I'll take the grease out of your candy-ass little BMW." Lately, it's not only the more trenchant gays who are trumpeting this battle cry; what with women's ever-more-militant consciousness, the biggest (or at least most visible) new market for Jeeps in Los Angeles seems to be tall, tawny, tanned females who look like *Playboy* bunnies and drive like Riccardo Patrese. The Jills drive Jeeps that don't have roll bars and off-road tires; they have winches, flame throwers, and (I imagine) built-in mounts for twin .50s. James Bond's Aston wouldn't stand a chance.

Ah, but these are just social appearances. What's a Jeep like to drive? You remember the mechanical bucking steer at Gilley's in *Urban Cowboy*? You get the idea. An amusement-park ride. Wild, uninhibited, as sexual as anything you'd ever encounter in a massage parlor. The short-chassis Jeep CJ-5 is unbearably choppy, but the CJ-7, the object of this test, while still jiggly enough to make you laugh uncontrollably on rough roads, is somewhat more civilized. It is the Jeep's most endearing—and

Jeep CJ-7 Lare

Stone Age Technology in a Microchip World

By Steve Smith

Car and Driver,

November 1980

enduring—feature. I learned how to drive in a WWII-vintage army-surplus Jeep, and loved it then as now for its rodeo ride. In those days, its visceral appeal rivaled that of a sports car. Today, sports cars ride like Cadillacs (and Cadillacs like Citroëns), so a Jeep CJ is all that's left to simulate the thrill of driving an MG TC or a Jaguar XK120MC.

Anyway, it just won't do to bounce around loose in the cockpit of the CJ—you need to be lashed down as tightly as you can stand it. The standard lap belts are totally inadequate. I'd opt for a full shoulder harness and a competition seatbelt. The seats themselves don't do much to hold you in place, either. I've driven the boss's CJ-7, the "Pig of Bronze" (David E. Davis's company Jeep, chronicled in the April 1979 issue) with its expensive Recaro seats, and they are definitely worth the extra money, although *his* pig may seem smoother because of the great weight of the engine (a six versus a four) and his fancy set of Bilstein shocks. A good steering wheel—something you can get a grip on—is another necessity. Mr. Davis's CJ has a Momo—plenty good enough.

The CJ's power steering is utterly without feeling. The only clue you get to your direction of travel is visual. With the huge Wrangler 9R-15 tires fitted to our test car, it feels as if you should be chasing the steering all over the road—particularly at freeway speeds. But it's only just tire "nibble," little feints this way and that, so if you can master your instinct to overcorrect, the Jeep will track down the highway in a reasonably straight line.

You're more likely to wander off your line of march while stealing a look at the instruments. They're unreadable, being down somewhere between your knees and the floor, and calibrated in tiny little figures that look at that distance like the Cyrillic alphabet. Oh well, you're better off driving the CJ by the seat of your Jordaches anyway.

I really like the engine: a four-cylinder, new to Jeep for 1980—although it's already seen yeoman service in the Pontiac Firebird as the Iron Duke. The original military Jeep started life as a four-cylinder, but in the years since World War II, the Jeep has grown taller and heavier, and for the past seven years it has been available only as a six or a V-8. The U.S. Army stopped buying Jeeps in 1972, preferring a sort of transistorized version, the four-cylinder M-151 Mighty Mite, which is small and light enough to be carried on airborne ops. (For the purposes of comparison, we requested an M-151 from American Motors—which bought Jeep from

Willys in 1970—for a test drive. At first, AMC denied they built M-151s; then they claimed they'd sold them all to Libya; then they said they didn't want us making any unfavorable comparisons with a vehicle that had been designed purely for the military. Huh? What was the original Jeep if not a quarter-ton army truck?)

It was the recent energy crisis that finally forced the civilian Jeep back to four cylinders. While the last six-cylinder Jeep we tested got 16 miles per gallon (*C/D*, April 1979), with the four this figure improves to 21 mpg. The Iron Duke won't run up much more than 4,000 rpm, but it feels as strong as its nickname.

Also new for 1980 is a four-speed transmission that feels as strong as a crowbar. Neither it nor the engine wants to shift very quickly, but the box drops into the next cog with a gratifying CLANG! It's fully usable, too, unlike our '78 CJ, which had a three-speed gearbox with a non-synchro creeper gear in lieu of a working first.

Despite the very loose fit of the canvas top and side curtains, the ventilation is terrible. As this test progressed, we simply removed one panel after another and finished by folding the windshield flat, combat style, and drove around L.A. in Afrika Korps goggles.

Bits and pieces rattled and fell off the test car from time to time; the CJ sheds parts with the exuberance of a man flinging off his clothes as he dashes across the beach for a dip on a hot summer day. By the time this test was over, the Jeep looked half-disassembled, and there was an untidy pile of leftover parts cluttering one corner of our garage. The day we picked up the CJ for the test, the four-way emergency flashers were stuck . . . on. Rather than scrub the mission, we attempted to fix the problem in the parking lot, with the PR man looking on anxiously. After thoroughly mangling the column-mounted switch, we yanked the flasher relay out by its roots and drove off, smiling in triumph. But thereafter, every time we hit the brakes, the parking lights flashed on.

So who cares? It's a Stone Age vehicle in a microchip world. You have to love a machine that makes everything in your path scramble out of your way. The Jeep CJ has the feel and heft (and technology) of a cave man's club; only the driver of a Kenworth eighteen-wheeler carries a bigger, ah, stick. Nor do you have to be gay to find happiness in a CJ-7. Even Anita Bryant wouldn't look out of place.

Auto of the Air . . . Why Go thru Traffic When You Can Go Over It?

The Helicar Can Create a New Dimension in Private Transport

By Henry Keck

Motor Trend,

August 1951

ONE OF THE DREAMS OF MEN HAS ALWAYS BEEN complete freedom of transportation, to travel any place in any media whether air, water, land or vacuum. Today, technological advances in materials, structure and power plant design make practical many new possibilities for adding to this freedom. One of these is a configuration which I arbitrarily call the Helicar, a combination helicopter and normal passenger car.

The helicopter as it now exists is the most universal unit of transportation ever devised by man. The addition to this unit of ground transportation for short trips would add greatly to its universality.

One experiment involving land-air transportation was made by Consolidated Vultee following World War II in the form of an airplane-car. This work attracted wide attention and was successful technically. However, enthusiasm for the project waned when, on one of its first test runs, the plane crashed into a marsh. The ignominy of the crash was that fuel supplies had not been checked; the plane simply ran out of gas. One sidelight of interest—the pilot's life was saved by the impact-absorbing qualities of the car body (plastic impregnated Fiberglas).

From a merchandising standpoint this car was suited only to Rolls-Royce pocketbooks. The requirement of an airport for take-off and landing, the difficulty of removing the flying superstructure, and this initial high cost (approximately $10,000) stripped it of its appeal. At the time of this work the price of a helicopter too was not exactly at the common man's command (approximately $25,000).

But this picture has changed radically. In 1947, McDonnell Aircraft of St. Louis and a little later Hiller Helicopters Inc. of Palo Alto began experimenting with jet type propulsive units to power the rotor blades (the rotary wing). The successful application of jet principles to helicopter design which grew out of this work marks the beginning of an era when the man who can own a Ford can own a helicopter. It also marks the time when it has become practical to combine the virtues of a helicopter with those of a car.

The simplified power supply of the jet helicopter eliminates much of the impedimenta associated with previous design: a complicated mechanical transmission, engine weight, the structure necessary to support this weight and the need for torque correction. In most helicopters the force required to turn the blade in one direction reacts on the fuselage, tending to turn it (the fuselage) in the other direction. This must, of course, be compensated for by a tail rotor, counter-rotating props or some similar device. The jet helicopter eliminates all this by supplying its power at the most advantageous place, the blade tips. The only tendency there is to rotate the fuselage is the very slight bearing friction of the rotor hub.

For safety's sake, ignition of the helicopter power plants would be made impossible unless the blades were securely in place and the doors of the vehicle were shut. Car ignition would require removal of the blade end sections and the locking of the remaining section of the rotor in place in line with the long dimension of the car. Although for the sake of simplicity and low cost the present design specifies removable blade sections, retractable blades are a definite possibility and would require considerably less driver inconvenience. Although this would involve some mechanical difficulties, a great deal of work has already been done on the problem by a man in England, Vittorio Isacco.

I fear that enthusiasts for the low slung approach in car design will cast a rather baleful glance at the height inherent in this proposed vehicle. The driver is purposely perched in a position which will permit him to command all views including up and down—it might be well for motor car manufacturers to follow a similar proportion of window-to-metal area.

The ram-jet engine developed by Hiller gives an idea of what can be expected in low cost helicopters. It weighs 11 pounds, develops 31 pounds of net thrust (equivalent to approximately 34 horsepower), has no moving parts, permits the use of extremely simple controls, and will cost less than $50.00 per unit in mass production. One of these power plants is attached to the end of each blade with two screws. Fuel is fed through the blades from a central tank. A tested helicopter of this simplified type combined with a lightweight car is certainly not stretching the facts of today. Proposed basic specifications for the design illustrated are as follows:

Gross weight of Helicar: 1,000 lbs. (without passengers)
Payload: 450 lbs. (two passengers)
Helicopter power source: Two ram-jet engines developing a net
     thrust of 70 lbs. each
Single Rotor: Two blades, overall diameter 25 ft.

Helicopter Controls: Overhead cyclic control for the rotor combined
with throttle for regulating speed, forward, backward, up and
down flight.

Helicopter fuel: Kerosene or low grade automotive gasoline

Car power plant: 25 hp, four cyl., aluminum engine head

Car drive: Front wheel drive, engine placed parallel to front
suspension

Wheelbase: 95 ins.

Width: 60 ins. front, 48 ins. rear

Height: 68 ins. (not including rotor hub)

Underbody: Completely enclosed

Rotor blade storage: Space for two 6 ft. end sections of the blades,
including power plants, in the rear of the car extending forward
between the two front seats

Cost of Helicar (preliminary estimate): $2,200.00

Although the case for the Helicar is strong, all is not roses. The ram-jet engine at present uses too much fuel. By its very nature the engine is most efficient at supersonic speeds. At these speeds, however, present day helicopter blades give very poor lift characteristics. A corollary to this high fuel consumption is relatively short range since a large supply of fuel becomes a load problem. The Helicar deserves further investigation as transportation of unprecedented versatility.

New Anger-Powered Cars May Revolutionize the Way We Drive

Anonymous

The Onion,

February 2004

ETROIT—With gas prices approaching $2 per gallon in some areas and gridlock on the rise, Detroit's three major automakers are stepping up development of their newest brainchild: the anger-powered car.

"By drawing a significant percentage of its motive power from the unbridled temper of the American motorist, the new anger-powered car will change, or at least take mechanical advantage of, the way Americans drive," General Motors vice-chairman Robert A. Lutz said. "We plan to have these furiously efficient machines careening down America's highways, byways, and sidewalks within two years."

Lutz said automakers have been researching fury fuels since the mid-1970s. As early as 1984, they began to look for ways to take advantage of the limitless supply of bad temper generated daily by American drivers—outrage currently vented wastefully into dashboards, steering wheels, and passengers.

An engine burning clean, white-hot hatred will release few harmful byproducts into the atmosphere—bad vibes and a small amount of water vapor will combine to be released in the form of human spittle. In addition, anger technology will turn the standard fuel-economy paradigm on its head: An anger-powered engine is actually more efficient in heavy urban traffic.

"The theory behind the anger-powered engine is actually quite simple," said Keith Cameron, chief engineer on General Motors' Project Instigator until January. "The average motorist traveling a clogged American highway produces hundreds of kilowatt-hours of negative energy per infuriating drive. The Instigator motor converts this emotional energy into kinetic energy by a process most drivers—people too goddamn stupid to use their goddamn blinkers when they change goddamn lanes—will never be able to understand. Just trust me, dumbasses, it works."

Cameron, who is currently serving a seven-year prison sentence for vehicular manslaughter and high-efficiency battery, added, "In the white-knuckled hands of the average American driver, it's an extremely powerful tool."

GM is currently developing two anger-powered cars, the entry-level Chevrolet Tantrum coupe and the larger, pricier Buick Umbrage. Ford has announced a multi-tiered move toward anger power, with plans to introduce anger/gasoline hybrid engines in the popular Lincoln Frown Car in 2006, to offer a de Sade option for its classic Mercury Gran Marquis in 2007, and to unveil a line of Acrimony family-sized cars and wagons in 2008. Daimler-Chrysler will resurrect the defunct Plymouth brand name with the reintroduction of the Plymouth Fury.

Anger power was first explored by Daimler-Chrysler, whose concept car, the Plymouth Violent, caused an uproar upon its introduction at the 1989 Detroit Auto Show. The Violent, more a seething showcase of technology and rage than a workable production car, achieved a remarkable 89 miles per gallon and hospitalized 19 auto-show attendees.

The anger-powered car will be aimed solidly at the middle of the market. Options such as semi-tinted glower windows, auto-locking brakes, and a baffling array of randomly blinking warning lights will be standard on all models.

"Production models will have angry-punch-absorbing energy-conversion pads in the dashboards, steering wheels, and driver-side doors," Chrysler Group chief executive Dieter Zetsche said. "Sound-sensitive materials in the cars' interiors will convert livid outbursts into motive power. And, because an angry driver is, in this case, a better driver, literally hundreds of anger- and performance-enhancing options will be available, including loud, ineffective mufflers, talk-station-only radios,

truly intermittent wipers, steering wheels which imperceptibly tilt forward over the course of an hour, and excruciatingly well-heated seats."

Early consumer tests of the cars indicate that they perform beyond designers' expectations. The automotive press has been particularly enthusiastic about anger power.

"This bitch's bastard's whore went like a goddamn raped ape with me at the wheel," said *Car and Driver*'s Brock Yates, who test-drove Daimler-Chrysler's Dodge Rammit pickup. "The vitriolic-assist brakes barely worked, the rear-view mirror found my bald spot every time, and the voice-response OnStar system mocked me for writing the script for *Cannonball Run*. I was getting 107 miles to the gallon when I T-boned that bus."

Car manufacturers have yet to determine a price for the rage-fueled vehicles.

"We have a delicate balance to strike," Ford Motor Company president Nick Scheele said. "The middle-income customer should be able to afford the car, but in order to increase engine efficiency, the price should be high enough to eat away at him the entire time he's driving. We're considering wildly fluctuating interest rates or a monthly payment rate that's pegged to the basketball standings."

Added Scheele: "I can assure you that there will be a model priced so that middle-class Americans who spend hours each week commuting between mid-level office jobs in the city and noisy, demanding families in the suburbs can afford it."

Fully anger-powered cars are expected to begin hitting American showrooms and other cars in summer 2006. If successful, the venture may vindicate the auto engineers still smarting over their brief and disastrous flirtation with love-and-happiness power, a trend that failed commercially and eventually petered out during the positive-energy crisis of the 1970s.

The Real Story Behind the New Ford Car

By Edwin Ketchum

Popular Science Monthly,

March 1928

OWN A MICHIGAN ROAD, NOT LONG AGO, RATTLED a dilapidated "tin lizzie." Over the steering wheel crouched a tall, gaunt, gray-haired man, a small boy at his side.

Henry Ford was the man. The car was a new Ford, secretly built and disguised under a body of ancient vintage. The small boy had been picked up along the roadside because Henry Ford wanted from his lips an unbiased opinion of his new car—an opinion he could get in no other way.

Ford's new cars, already dotting the highways, are the climax of the most spectacular drama in the history of the automobile. One man, by sheer driving personality, dominated it. Success, wealth, fame were his, yet he would not sit idle and let others build his new car. Ruthlessly he scrapped men and machines and started over again. At sixty-four he undertook the hardest task of his life, harder even than the production of his first car more than a quarter of a century ago. He was everywhere at once, passed on every idea, tested most of them personally. Never before has there been such a story of an emergency autocratic control of a mammoth industry—of inventive persistence, and inventions made to order on a huge scale.

Ford seized the first new model as it came from the assembly line at the great Fordson Illinois factory. "Is this the best you can do?" he asked his engineers. "Yes," they told him. "I'll represent the public, then," he said; and a second later the car, with Ford at the wheel, leaped out upon a near-by field. When he returned, after bumping over stones and logs, he declared, "Pretty good, but it bounces. Put on hydraulic shock absorbers."

And so, day after day, the new Ford was changed and modified and improved. Ideas for integral parts came from chance remarks of his aides, sometimes on country drives far from the designer's room. Frequently Ford would enter his factory, already engaged on production, and say, "This part is not right. Let's try it this way!" A part would be built and tried. If it didn't work, the idea was scrapped and a new one developed. Trial and error on a titanic scale!

I went out to the great Ford experimental laboratory near Detroit a few days after the new car was announced to the public to find out the unpublished details of the gigantic new start of the Ford Company. Yet at that great plant few people really knew anything about the things I wanted to

know. But Sorensen knew—Charles E. Sorensen, Ford's right-hand man, in charge of production. And it was to him I went first.

Better steel at lower cost would be needed for a better car. That was decided several years ago when the new car was first discussed. Mr. Sorensen and a few others, a very few others, knew, therefore, just why Ford purchased obsolete vessels from the Shipping Board and acquired a glass factory and new timber lands. Henry Ford was going to produce a new car from his own raw materials in his own factories.

That was the program Ford outlined for himself in 1922. To carry it out he had to scrap the costly machinery of the largest and most successful automobile factory in the world. For weeks great machines had to stand idle. Thousands of men had to be thrown out of work temporarily. Ask any business man what it means in dollars and cents to stop such a plant for even a day, and you will have some idea of the courage it took Ford to determine to build a new car whose success no one could foretell.

First there was talk of making the momentous shift after the ten millionth "lizzie" had been made; but "there never seemed to be an opportunity to get the new car started," Ford said, so the fifteen millionth Ford was set as a tentative turning point.

Meanwhile Ford laid down his fundamental orders. "Build a car designed for a need, not any definite price," he told his engineers. Specifically, he demanded a machine that could go sixty miles an hour.

A mile a minute! That called for a forty-horsepower motor. Shall it be a four-cylinder car or a six? Ford demanded a low speed motor. Such an engine, spinning its crankshaft 2,600 times a minute can develop forty horsepower with four cylinders. A four it was to be, then. "Better make the cylinder chambers about as wide as the distance the pistons travel up and down," Ford directed, explaining that he favored the "square" engine, with bore and stroke nearly equal.

So Ford, master engineer, had his ideas built into the motor that was to drive his creation—an entirely new motor from the ground up. Strength! That must be the keynote of the crankshaft—the sturdy, looped, whirling shaft through which power from the aluminum pistons flows to spin the car's wheels.

Was it balanced? In action as well as at rest? Ford wanted to know, for if it was even a trifle unevenly weighted, it would vibrate and shake the whole car. A precision testing machine proved its balance.

The engine was satisfactory. "All right," Ford said. "Build a compact car around it. A light car, but one that will hold the road." Some of those engineers may have told their wives that the task was impossible, but they didn't tell Henry Ford.

It is the "unsprung weight" of a car, the weight of the wheels, axles and everything not hung on springs, that jolts and bounces when it strikes holes in the road. Ford found unsuspected ways to eliminate unsprung weight—a rear axle housing of spun steel, steel-spoke wheels, changes in the front axle and the new four-wheel mechanical brake system, all lighter without loss of strength. Even the springs themselves, usually attached by their heavy end, were reversed so that their own weight would be "sprung"!

Now an up-to-date gear shift was required—a break with years of Ford precedent. The frame itself, forged throughout, for strength. Colors, too, for the body—Edsel Ford chose for his father the two shades of blue, the gray, and the sand-color that became the new finishes. Accessories? "The best," Ford said. Even the old familiar "squawker" horn was scrapped.

There was the car—on paper, but there were no machines in existence that could make, in quantity, some of the things that Ford had put in it—a gasoline tank electrically welded of steel covered with anti-rust lead alloy, for example. "We'll invent our own machines," Ford decided.

Ordinary electric welding machines couldn't make the gasoline tanks because the current sputtered and failed momentarily as it flowed through the bearings to the welding disks. One of Ford's men hit upon the scheme of running the bearings in mercury, a good conductor of electricity, and that problem was solved.

To spin hot metal into rear axle housings, a device like a huge potter's wheel was invented. Instead of clay, it whirls a red-hot forging; a special forming tool pressed against the metal flattens it into the dish-shaped housing. Now that machine makes three a minute.

Thus new machines were invented. Existing ones were modified. Ford found that he must scrap and replace a quarter of all his machines, valued at forty-five million dollars! Half could be made over, the remaining quarter could be used as they stood.

The secret of the Ford success has been mass production, developed to a degree that left men of lesser imagination gasping. Now he would make them gasp again. He would not only make the cars, but make the materials that went into them. Besides his own steel plant, he built a factory to manufacture unbreakable, three-ply glass for his windshields. Fuel for his plants came from his coal properties in Kentucky and West Virginia. His Michigan timber lands supplied him with wood. Obsolete vessels went into his furnaces and emerged as metal for his cars.

Then Ford faced the greatest decision of his life. Should he stop the plant in the midst of production and go ahead with the new model? Or play the safe course; stick to the old familiar car and the parts business? Millions were at stake.

"We'll make the new car now," he said, and one spring day of 1927 he drove the fifteen millionth old-type car off the Highland Park assembly line. Then the plant shut down.

Out came the old machines at Highland Park and Fordson. New machines sprang up—among them forging presses that shaped frames of cars at one mighty blow.

Then came the Fordson plant's gala day. Down the assembly line rolled a shining new car with Sorensen at the wheel. Behind it came a second, a third. Here was the new Ford!

And yet Henry Ford wasn't satisfied. He disguised a few of these first cars and started picking up small boys around Dearborn to get their verdict. He got it and gave the machine to the public.

How much did it cost? No one knows. A staff of accountants could easily find out, of course. The point is that they don't. Ford apparently doesn't care how much it cost and obviously he isn't worried about those engineers who say he can't make money on the new car.

"When we began work on the new model, we had $350,000,000 in the bank. Now we have $250,000,000," he said.

That is the story of how one man built a car that set the world talking.

Thos. A. Edison's Views on Motor Carriages

Author Unknown
The Horseless Age, December 1895

"The horseless vehicle is the coming wonder.

"The bicycle, which ten years ago was a curiosity, is now a necessity. It is found everywhere.

"Ten years from now you will be able to buy a horseless vehicle for what you would have to pay to-day for a wagon and a pair of horses. The money spent in the keep of the horses will be saved, and the danger to life will be much reduced. . . .

"It is only a question of a short time when the carriages and trucks of every large city will be run with motors. The expense of keeping and feeding horses in a great city like New York is very great, and all this will be done away with, just as the cable and trolley cars have dispensed with horses.

"You must remember that every invention of this kind which is made adds to the general wealth by introducing a system of greater economy of force. A great invention which facilitates commerce enriches a country just as much as the discovery of vast hoards of gold."

With the main drift of Mr. Edison's remarks we most heartily coincide, but when he postpones the day when a motor carriage can be bought at a price now paid for a carriage and pair of horses until the next century, he forgets the recent wonderful development of electrical science, in which he himself has played so important a part, and shows that he is not aware of the amount of intellectual energy that is being concentrated upon the motor vehicle problem in America to-day.

Had Mr. Edison read the first number of *The Horseless Age*, he would have said ten months rather than ten years.

Bugatti Type 57SC Atlantic Coupe

By David E. Davis Jr.

Automobile Magazine,

August 1991

"A technical creation can only be perfect if it is
perfect from the point of view of aesthetics."

—Ettore Bugatti

Essex, Massachusetts—

IT IS TWO O'CLOCK ON A SUNNY WINTER AFTERNOON. The road is anything but deserted. We're rolling along through the Massachusetts countryside in the incredible black Bugatti you see on these pages—every raised seam, every exposed rivet reflecting the sunlight like the facets of a jewel. The small cabin is filled with sounds nobody ever hears anymore. Every mechanical process has a voice and every voice joins in a lovely muted chorus, a hymn to the fundamental automotive verities. Paul Russell steers us onto the roadside and opens his door. This is it. Jeez. I've been wondering for a week whether or not they'd actually let me drive this car . . . what's it worth? Twelve million dollars? Fourteen million? Does anybody know? *It's only a car, for God's sake.* But it's a car I've been admiring in pictures since I was a teen-ager. It was sapphire blue then—painted, so the story goes, to match the stone in the engagement ring the owner gave his wife. But who knew? The pictures were always black and white. It's a car that Paul Russell and his people labored over for nigh on to two years. It's the car that won best of show at Pebble Beach last year, the third and last of Jean Bugatti's Bugatti Atlantic coupes, Ralph Lauren's car. It's not just a car. It's an *automobile!*

Nonetheless, I'm an adult with a high-school education and normal reflexes, and I can do this. Paul is not so sure. We're not even moving yet, and Paul is already beginning to hyperventilate. The mirror is tiny. Visibility to the sides and to the rear is hopeless, like turning your head inside the hood of a parka. I can feel each tooth on the gears as I bring them together with a grumbling rattle, but first gear is finally engaged. I flip the little trafficator signal out in warning, hoping that I haven't overlooked an onrushing transit mix concrete truck in the minuscule mirror, let the clutch pedal rise from the floor, and we're off! Each shift is agony. I pride myself on being good at this, and I don't want to look like a klutz. The steering is positive, and amazingly low effort, partially because of a very large steering wheel. The brakes are smooth and progressive. Handling and roadholding are about what you'd expect from a 1938 car with skinny tires and positively cambered front wheels. It might have been fun to drive in the Thirties, when it was a great automotive bargain for its British owner, but today, with its value way out there in the auto-motive ionosphere, it is intimidating as hell.

We trundle tentatively up and down the two-lane road a couple of times for the benefit of the photographer, and then, seeking a place to turn around, I inadvertently turn onto a parkway on-ramp and find myself and the gorgeous black car out there among the civilians at seventy miles per hour, getting farther away from the photographer—who has no idea where I've gone—with every revolution per minute. Guys in crummy pickup trucks zoom up alongside to stare. A twelve-year-old solemnly gives me the finger from the rear window of the family station wagon. Madonna would get less attention if she were out here jogging naked with her hair on fire. After thirty minutes or so of this, I've made no mistakes worse than the turn onto the parkway, but Paul is about to implode. The 3.3-liter straight-eight engine has begun to cough through the supercharger pop-off valve. Somebody back at the shop is going to have a little soot to wipe away from the engine and the wire mesh hood panels (known as "gauze" to Bugattistes). "Would you be more comfortable if you were driving?" I ask, innocently. "YES!" snaps Paul, and I stop the car. Shucks, just when I was learning how to manipulate that long, whippy shift lever. To be honest, I'm a little relieved to be out from under the responsibility.

The Atlantic (pronounced At-lan-*teek*) coupes have been described in loving detail by dozens of writers, but here's a little background. The prototype, called the Aérolithe, first appeared in 1935 on a standard Type 57 chassis, fitted with a magnesium body. The unique raised and riveted seams that give the Atlantic its one and only identity apparently grew directly out of the great difficulty in joining that material. Due to that difficulty, and the related costs, subsequent versions were built of aluminum, but the cars are still sometimes called "Elektron" coupes, that being the commercial term for magnesium in Europe at that time. They were built on the Type 57S chassis, which lowered them by allowing the rear axle to pass through large oval holes in the frame rails. Only two cars were delivered as Type 57SC (supercharged) models. Most often, cars were returned to the factory sometime after purchase for the supercharger installation. An SC of the quality of the Lauren car is probably capable of 120 to 125 mph, with a 0-to-60-mph time of less than ten seconds.

To appreciate the special character of the automobiles built by Ettore Bugatti, we have to understand something about the man and the times in which his creative genius flowered. He was born in 1881 to an artistic, well-to-do Milanese family that divided its time between the salons of Milan and Paris. His father, Carlo, was a painter, a silversmith, a sculptor, and a designer/manufacturer of fine furniture who insisted that his sons, while training as artists, should also learn to work with their hands. Ettore learned cabinetmaking in his father's studio, while studying painting and sculpture. At age sixteen he announced his intention to "give up art" and shifted his interest to industrial design, but industrial design uniquely skewed by his artistic training and inclinations. Underscoring the point, he said, "A technical creation can only be perfect if it is perfect from the point of view of aesthetics."

At the end of his 1910 catalog we read, "I have tried to put on the market a car that its owners will enjoy working on." A clear warning. Later in his career he would become more high-handed and autocratic. To a customer whose car wouldn't start, he suggested that Bugatti owners should have heated garages. Later, when someone complained about poor brakes, he sniffed, "My cars are built to go, not stop." He was an artist, not an engineer, and practicality was not a particularly high priority. He once refused to sell a car to a prospective customer because he disapproved of the unfortunate man's table manners. He lived like royalty, surrounding himself with châteaux, blooded horses, hunting dogs, beautiful things of every kind, yet the great French champion René Dreyfus—himself a Bugatti team driver—tells us in his autobiography, *My Two Lives*, that Bugatti was always broke. Car sales alone could not support Bugatti, the man or the marque. The firm nearly went under in 1929 and 1930 as a result of his obsessive commitment to the enormous Royales, and was only bailed out by his son, Jean, who engineered a government contract to power railway cars with the thirteen-liter Royale engines.

His factory at Molsheim in northeastern France turned out exquisite sports and racing cars and utterly pedestrian sedans. It was also his personal atelier, the place where he created lovely pieces of cabinetry, and horse tack that would rival anything ever done by Hermès or Gucci. René Dreyfus recalls that it was not unusual for the racing cars to be shunted aside, despite approaching deadlines, so that the Bugatti workmen could be pressed into service on some special job for the Bugatti household.

If you were Ettore Bugatti's friend, or a very good customer, you might be invited for lavish driven-bird shoots. An impeccably tailored Ettore would conduct these outings from atop a horse as elegantly turned out as himself, and the quality of the birds, the hospitality, and your fellow guests would knock your hat in the creek. He built a sort of inn/clubhouse next to the Bugatti works, called the Hostellerie du Pur Sang, where customers and shooting guests and team drivers stayed.

If you were the fiend of his son, Jean—who designed the Type 57SC on these pages—you might also stay at the Pur Sang, but you were then more apt to be involved in wild midnight revels, drunken chases through the halls, bizarre and dangerous practical jokes, and hair-raising midnight rides to distant venues that promised more wine, better-looking women, more outrageous jokes. Other car companies, even the French ones, didn't operate this way.

Obviously, a company run like this could not produce ordinary cars, nor would it attract ordinary customers. Thus, Mr. Ralph Lauren is probably the perfect owner for Atlantic coupe number 57591. His car collection—which includes a breathtaking array of other Bugattis, historic Ferraris, Mercedes-Benzes, Porsches, Alfa Romeos, and one Blower Bentley—has been thoughtfully assembled and lovingly restored. Ralph Lauren represents style, in an era that has been consistently misled by the dictates of mere fashion. Bugatti's taste, his sense of style, his unwillingness to allow current trends or mechanical difficulties to deflect him from his chosen course, would all find a sympathetic reception in the idealized environment where Ralph Lauren's clothing and home furnishings are meant to be seen.

Mr. R.B. Pope, the original owner of this car, would also find himself right at home there. The Atlantic was his tenth Bugatti, painted, as noted above, to match his lovely wife's engagement ring. He was a British attorney and successful amateur tennis player, and he enjoyed driving his Bugattis between London and Monaco. Mr. and Mrs. Pope could easily be gazing back at you from the elegant pages of the next Lauren Polo insert you see in the *New York Times Sunday Magazine*. Mr. Pope took delivery of this car in 1938 and returned it to the factory in 1939, where it was upgraded from Type 57S to Type 57SC by the addition of a supercharger like the one fitted to the same basic engine in the

Type 59 Grand Prix cars. This was probably when the roof was modified to give Mr. Pope an extra inch of headroom. It's not difficult to imagine an agitated R.B. Pope firing cables off to Molsheim in 1939, begging them to finish modifying his car and get it out of there before the onset of World War II and the subsequent German invasion of France.

Because of a pound/franc exchange rate that was increasingly in Great Britain's favor through the Thirties, Brits could buy Bugattis very inexpensively, and, because of those favorable prices, Brits became the backbone of Bugatti's new-car business. They were, until quite recently, the backbone of the cult that grew up around old Bugattis. More than any other group of vintage-car enthusiasts, except perhaps the Bentley Drivers' Club, Bugatti owners used their cars, and used them hard. Now, Japanese and American speculators are buying Bugattis and parking them out of sight, waiting for the next major price escalation.

This is tragic, and we're fortunate indeed that Ralph Lauren admires cars as machines for human enjoyment first, and only secondarily as works of art, or investments. Like any discriminating Bugatti buyer, he was very specific in his instructions to Paul Russell and his technicians

at the Gullwing Service Company. The car's engine and chassis and performance had to be restored to original Bugatti specification, but the interior and exterior had to meet the rather exacting Lauren aesthetic standards. Mr. Pope's blue car with tan goatskin interior and exposed wire wheels became Mr. Lauren's black car with black garment-leather interior and authentic Bugatti metal wheel covers. The result is a joy to behold and an epiphany to drive.

Our Most Cherished Possession

By James Dalton

MoToR Magazine,

October 1940

WITH DEADLY DANGER TO OUR DEMOCRATIC institutions lurking just around the corner, the thoughts of all Americans are concentrated upon national defense and modern engines of destruction—airplanes, tanks, armored cars, mechanized artillery. All these weapons will be designed to turn back potential enemies. We have the men and the money to fashion them but while we are doing it we must guard against one enemy which can bore from within while we are preparing. We must have no "war of nerves" to sap our morale.

Every real American will be glad to make material and spiritual sacrifices for his country's good. He will cheerfully yield luxuries, comforts, even necessities, if the need arises. He will not begrudge a penny for defense and will want the spending speeded. He will tolerate no needless delays and he will not smugly tell himself that our citadel of democracy is in no danger because an ocean lies between us and the totalitarian masters of Europe who want the world under their heels.

Readiness to yield all else, if need be, to preserve the United States as a land of opportunity is merely common sense. Happily, however, our national resources are so vast we can make ourselves impregnable without seriously dislocating our normal way of life unless the menace to our safety becomes more acute than now seems likely.

Ours is no nation of "panty waists." From the day our forebears dumped British tea into Boston harbor, through 167 years, we have demonstrated that we can take our tribulations along with our successes but it is not the American creed to accept hardships needlessly. That was not the way we made our standard of living the highest in the world. We fight first for what we cherish and then for what we want.

Like the British we will submit to voluntary regimentation if temporary surrender of our liberties is the only way we can hope to make them permanent. Unlike the British we have not waited until war is upon us before beginning to prepare for it and for that reason we probably shall escape the necessity for regimentation.

National defense will not be expedited and our country's welfare will not be served by prematurely denying ourselves the necessities and comforts to which we have become accustomed as a people. We owe it to America to prove that we can raise our standard of living while at the same time standing resolute guard over the ramparts of democracy. That will not denote decadence but rather will it be a manifesto to the world of our tremendous might and virility.

Those who prate of transforming automobile plants into airplane factories may be well-intentioned but their reasoning is puerile. Airplanes are vital in modern war but any limitation upon the use of motor vehicles would throw into hopeless confusion this nation of more than 130,000,000 people. Individual transportation will continue to be the first essential, the mainspring, the spark plug, of our workaday and holiday lives in war or peace.

The motor car ceased to be a rich man's toy when Henry Ford sold nearly 200,000 of his Tin Lizzies in 1913 with a price of $525 on the runabout. Because of that benefaction he still is a national idol although he long ago surrendered to competitors his position of absolute dominance. When hard times gripped our throats 10 years ago, millions of families clung to their cars after all else was gone. Individual transportation was their most cherished possession.

MoToR believes that anything which interferes with armament at top speed should be crushed ruthlessly but we hold, by the same token, that anything which limits the use of motor vehicles will slow down the preparedness program. We are convinced, also, that the American people should be permitted to lead their normal lives in every way which does not militate against defense.

Even in times of stress or crisis everyone who can should be permitted to acquire those treasures counted most desirable. We know that motor cars are the most prized belongings of millions of American families and we are thankful that many of those upon whom adversity has pressed hardest in lean years of unemployment soon will be able to buy them again in a new era of prosperity.

To families of moderate means—and that takes in most of us—a motor car is as dear as a casket of pearls to a dowager. The motor cars of 1941, now making their debuts, are entitled to their hour upon a stage free from the panoply of war and we are proud to give it to them in this—our 36th annual Show Issue—as we dedicate ourselves anew to the service of a great industry which has kept its proud traditions untarnished.

PMD Unplugged

The "Old Broken-Down Piece of Meat" Edition

By Peter M. De Lorenzo, autoextremist.com

The Autoextremist,

March 2009

DETROIT. Now that we have been blessed with a visit from President Obama's auto task force, we can just feel the rush of Shiny Happy adrenalin running through our veins. *Not.* Unfortunately, there's no amount of fact-finding and due diligence that's going to get these people up to speed in order to save the domestic auto industry, no matter how well intended they claim to be.

With countless auto suppliers on the verge of total collapse, GM and Chrysler teetering on virtual bankruptcy, auto dealers closing left and right, and the car business veering close to coming to a complete standstill, it is difficult to see anything positive that we can grab on to, especially while we're waiting for a plan from people who are trying to compress 35 years of recent auto industry learning on top of a century of auto industry history in a little more than eight weeks' time in order to make an "informed" decision about the industry's future. In other words: notevenremotely-gonnahappen.com.

Of course added to all of this is the growing national gloom-and-doom offensive that's threatening to swallow this country whole. The relentless din of negativity in the media is infiltrating every nook and cranny of our society, and it is taking its toll, to the point that Brian Williams of *NBC Nightly News* has been getting slammed from viewers via email demanding that he come up with something, *anything* positive to say about our country right at this very moment. (And to his credit, each night this week he's closing the program with a positive story.)

As for the doom-and-gloom thing, it's something that people who live around these parts are unfortunately very familiar with. This state and region have been in a serious recession for three years now, and I think it's safe to say at this point that we've now graduated to being in a full-blown depression.

The Motor City Meltdown and the ongoing economic calamity have absolutely decimated this region, with thousands upon thousands of people losing their jobs and their homes. And their minds are probably not far behind, too, for that matter. And in a state already widely known for its dangerously crumbling infrastructure—our roads are simply legendary around the country for their shocking state of disrepair—the reduced funds that go hand in hand with the declining tax revenues of a plummeting economy and the fact that there's no money to repair them have left the citizens of this state simply begging for mercy, or some kind of respite of any kind, even though there's no relief in sight. (How bad is it? Some major thoroughfares are approaching the impassable stage unless you have a vehicle with substantial ground clearance. Even the local traffic reports have switched from being primarily about the usual traffic tie-ups and such to a relentless stream of road-crumbling alerts. Grim doesn't even begin to describe it.)

Several years ago, I called Detroit and the declining U.S. auto industry "the canary in the coal mine" for the rest of the nation. The lack of a national health care program, the nation's growing uncompetitiveness in the face of a burgeoning global economy, the steady erosion of this country's manufacturing base and so on were issues that were going to catch up to the rest of the country eventually. Add in the real estate fiasco and the egregious and rampant Wall Street misbehavior, and it's no wonder "we the people" are finding ourselves in dire straits today. (I will leave that flat-out embarrassment masquerading as the "City of Detroit" for special commentary in this week's "On The Table.")

But all of that being said, I say enough already.

I'm tired of the auto industry being treated like an old broken down piece of meat or something that should be taken out back and shot. Our so-called "leaders" in Washington—particularly certain senators and representatives who should know better—have relegated an entire industry to the dust heap. And why? So a few idiot southern senators can tout their states as the "new" center of the auto industry? Or is it because Detroit and the center of industrial America don't quite fit into the new "Green" world that Northern Californian politicians want to shove down our collective throats?

I'm tired of this "Green" sickness that's spreading due east from California like an out-of-control virus that there's no known antidote for. With Nancy Pelosi and Gov. Arnold Schwarzenegger—those quintessential manifestations of vapidity—leading the charge and insisting on projecting their relentless lack of common sense and glaring inability to differentiate facts from outright fiction as the environmental platform that this nation must adhere to going forward, even if it means prolonging the national recession and darkening this country's manufacturing future, it's no wonder the rest of the country is finding it difficult to be optimistic about the direction we're heading.

Memo to the Green Horde (and you, too, Mr. President, since you seem to fuel these blowhards): You will not have an auto industry to "reinvent" after you finish dismantling this country's manufacturing base and crippling its ability to innovate because of your Byzantine declarations and manifestos.

Do I want cleaner air? Of course I do. We *all* do. Believe it or not there are citizens all over the country—not just in California—who embrace the notion and want to get there for the well-being of *all* Americans. But it won't come by way of a simple *voila!* and a "finger snap" or by cramming increasingly ridiculous rules into law that will turn huge swaths of this country into vast wastelands of unemployment and futility. If the "Green" vision for our nation—at least as brought forth by Pelosi, Schwarzenegger and Co.—consists of a so-called idyllic future featuring a Shiny Happy populace peddling our way around in balsa wood smiley cars while whistling our way to work that we can't find, well, then, *you can include me out*, as Sam Goldwyn once said.

The domestic automotive industry—much to the chagrin of its critics—is home to some of the most advanced technological expertise and innovative minds in the world today—yes, equal to if not better than any car maker from any other country too—and I am absolutely confident that they have the talent and the know-how to move this country forward when it comes to meeting the goals of environmental responsibility. It will take a serious commitment and incredible amounts of research and development time and money to get where we eventually want to go, but we will get there.

We won't get there, however, if we leave it up to the people who have little or no understanding of concepts like production feasibility or the idea that a car company must deliver vehicles a.) that people actually *want to buy*, b.) that they can actually afford to buy and c.) that the company producing it can actually make real money in the process. That last part is the real kicker for the Green Horde. Not only is profitability a dirty concept to them—after all, someone might actually *make* money by taking risks and delivering a desirable product (how radical is that?)—but I get the idea that after all of their pronouncements and hard and fast rules that they're so quick to throw around they'll feel "entitled" to paying less than ten grand for a car that will allow its passengers to walk away from a

60 mph crash into a bridge abutment while emitting nothing but the faint whiff of Pacific sea breezes going down the road.

For that and several other reasons I have zero confidence in the politicians from Northern California and other states and their green-tinged acolyte-activists when it comes to moving this country forward, and unless the din of misinformation that's emanating from this environmental cabal is countered with common sense and reality—and soon—then this country is in for a horrendous period of mediocrity and ultimately a second-rate future.

As for the rest of what's ailing this nation, not much of anything is making sense these days, frankly. Banks being gifted government money that they refuse to lend out; blatant, malicious dimwits with the title of "U.S. Senator" not even pretending to be "for the people" anymore while pushing their particular egregious agendas to the detriment of the rest of the nation; and our so-called government "leaders" standing around paralyzed waiting for something to happen as the U.S. auto industry's infrastructure and supplier and dealer networks continue to crumble.

And now that we've all been brow beaten and scolded for months for being bad, wasteful Americans for using our credit cards and living our lives—and we all actually listened for once and stopped doing *anything*—our esteemed leaders are now telling us *not* to go into duck-and-cover mode, that it's fine to spend a little bit of money, that it's all going to be okay.

Oh, *really*? When is *that* going to be, exactly? The end of the fourth quarter? When our Green Snuggies are aligned with Nancy Pelosi's emerald chakras just so? When the grand pooh-bah, aka Warren Buffett, declares victory and says it's okay for us to play outside again? When Arnold and Nancy do a two-step on the ashes of what's left of the domestic automobile industry? Judging by what passes for public discourse in Washington and around the country these days, let's just say the nation won't be collectively holding its breath.

While I'm at it, since when did Americans turning on fellow Americans become a sport in this country? The abuse that the domestic auto industry and the people who work tirelessly in it has received from the legions of two-bit pundits and instant auto "experts" out there over the last six months is unconscionable and despicable. Even those words don't come close to describing the kind of out and out hatred that has been aimed at our own automobile industry over the last 12 months. Hell, even Bernie Madoff has gotten more of a break than the U.S. auto industry, and that's just disgusting.

Why is it okay for thousands of Americans and their families to become expendable for being aligned with an industry that not only forged this country's manufacturing base and to this day is responsible for much of this nation's technical innovations, but fueled our country's ability to meet global military challenges throughout history while powering the emergence of the American middle class?

Why is okay to dump on an industry that still either directly or indirectly employs one out of every ten Americans?

Why is it okay for some asshole in a New York TV studio to pontificate about an industry he knows absolutely nothing about, and then have his unmitigated bullshit be taken as "gospel" by another hundred TV pundits who know even less?

I say enough. Enough to *all* of it. I say enough to this country's mass embracing of this collective "mope-a-dope" mentality as I like to call it. And I say enough to the media's crucifixion of our own domestic automobile industry as if it and all of the hard-working people in and around it somehow deserve to be put on trial for war crimes.

We can do better. *Much* better. And we will get better, too, individually *and* as a country. As more Americans discover that fear mongering and negativity for negativity's sake is not a good look for us—and that waiting for our esteemed politicians in Washington to adjust our attitudes, or waiting for them to do *anything*, for that matter, is a fool's errand—I absolutely believe we will rise above this.

In the meantime, thanks for listening.

A Message from Our Chairman

By Ted West

Road & Track,

December 1986

WE HERE AT INCREDIBLE MOTORS, Detroit's largest builder of Incredible Cars, are proud—just plain proud. We're proud of our cars. Proud of our TV commercials. Proud of the new yellow paint on the front gate. We're proud of *everything*.

We're even proud of the little people who try to criticize us. They have their place. And we need to know what they're thinking, make no mistake, for if we ever find ourselves thinking as they do, we're in trouble—real trouble.

Besides, they can't be right—that's what our Marketing Dept is for. And if Marketing isn't sure what's right—it's never happened yet—we can always turn to our Futurist Division. These savants know everything that's going to happen from now until the Great Third Famine, which ends in 2034 with the triumphal rise to power of George F. Clemens of Billings, Montana.

So we're not worried. We've seen the future and it's ours—a world jammed with "formal" rooflines, onboard cable TV, so-so performance. Dr. Mindfinger and his Futurists can prove it.

Still, the little people persist in yammering. They say we're out of touch, clumsy, in bad taste. They even have the insolence to say our market share will decrease, our profits drop.

What do they know! They're not professionals! We've analyzed the matter backward and upside down!

Besides, who do these midgets applaud—a bunch of Germans and Japanese? Why, they can't even choose between people who charge too much for a car and people who charge too little! In candor, though, we must admit there have been unsettling signs. For the first time since gold, we're *number two*. In late summer, our market share was down from 42 percent to 36 percent. We have a 79-day supply of cars, while the competition's supply is 54 days. We may have a slight crisis of confidence out there.

Therefore, we at Incredible want to reassure you, our faithful buyers— *we're not wrong*. We know what we're doing, you're lucky to have us and what I'm here to disclose today will prove it.

Here, then, is Incredible Motors' top-secret "Market-Endogenous Sales Strategy"—or MESS—for the Nineties. In normal circumstances, of course, we wouldn't divulge this sort of material, developed at a cost of billions—and we know the minute we do, the Germans and Japanese will use it against us.

But let 'em try. It takes decades to start thinking the Incredible Way.

On to the meat of the matter, then. It seems the bulk of the complaints against us concerns the faulty notion that we're selling dumb cars.

Impossible. Our studies can prove it. No company on earth has a broader array of methods for proving its cars are *not dumb* than we here at Incredible.

First, we buy an example of every competing car. Now, normally at this point, other companies have their engineers and stylists go over each car with a fine-tooth notebook. Not at Incredible. We consider people who wear mechanical pencils and talk about drag coefficients to be little more than quiet servants of the system. Likewise with stylists. In the Fifties, these light-footed prima donnas were central—indeed, crucial . . . though back then, the little people were just as busy criticizing us. (We wonder if people who criticize us aren't just sick. We're doing a study.)

Anyway, having locked the engineers and stylists in the next building, safely away from the competition's cars, we now summon the *experts*. Some are what our critics call "beancounters." Most, however, come from that fount of all wisdom, our Marketing Dept.

Indeed, to be truthful, if the Germans and Japanese are so all-fired smart, we wonder why they don't know that a *truly* wise marketing decision is one you've proven successful *beforehand*! Our Marketing Dept can do that. Except for a brief anomalous period since 1950, during which our market share has steadily slipped 20 percent, Marketing can *guarantee* us quarterly sales figures year in and year out. Presto.

Relying on Marketing exclusively, then, we remove *all risk* from selling. More important still, we're no longer saddled with stylists and engineers blubbering about building "The Great Car." We no longer even *care* about "great" cars—we'll leave that sort of elitist arrogance to the Germans.

To the contrary, Marketing's strategy is simplicity itself. They locate the median American mouth-breather, expose him to "product"—"clinic" him, as we say—until he's wall-eyed with boredom . . . then build a median mouth-breather car to suit.

It works—it has worked for years. It's genius!

Frankly, we don't understand all the whining against us. Why, only six years ago we introduced a whole new look—a look so stylish and sleek that even glamorous Volvo imitated us. Now they say we're awkward and dull!

And they claim our five divisions—which are really only two divisions, but in another way, very definitely five divisions—need more differentiation. Preposterous! For 1987, each of our five Q-cars got its very own gill-slit motif. The mid-range Identiac has a unique power ashtray. The luxury Simillac has *triple reading lights*!

Our patience is running thin. We're doing everything right, including moving inventory with our brilliant 2.9-percent financing plan—and even *this* draws sneers! Come on, little people, we're *making money* losing money!

Say what you like, Incredible Motors is still America's greatest car company—it's just that, now, we're America's greatest *smaller* car company.

In fact, only Incredible is *great enough* to be Number Two . . . and if the American buying public doesn't come around to seeing things our way darn soon, we're just going to ignore them completely.

Future of the Automobile

Soon Its Position Will Be Reversed and It Will Be the Conveyance of the Laborer

By Arthur Brisbane,
of the *New York Evening Journal*

Popular Mechanics,

February 1903

I N LESS THAN FIFTY YEARS FROM NOW the working man, the mechanic and the laborer will go to their work from their cottages in the country in automobiles.

You smile at this?

Don't smile too confidently.

Do you remember when the present model of bicycles first came into fashion?

Who used and paid for the first bicycles, at one hundred dollars or more each? The rich men and women.

Who made fun of the first bicycle riders, laughing at their sensible costumes, throwing tacks on bicycle paths, doing everything to delay the manufacture of the cheap bicycle by discouraging those who paid for the first experiments?

You did, you who now laugh, or throw tin cans at the fast automobile, did the same for the bicycle, not so many years ago.

And who uses the bicycle now? Get up early in the morning, especially in the country, and you will see the bicycle carrying the mechanic to his work. The cheap bicycle is almost exclusively used by working men. It is used exclusively by people of moderate means.

The rich have long since tired of it. The bicycle at Newport used to fill the foolish "society" columns. It now carries the butcher boy to and from work. It enables the workman to save his carfare, to get cheaper rent and fresh country air for his children by living far from his task. It gives these advantages, in addition to fresh air and daily exercise to thousands of clerks with small salaries.

Suppose that public jeering, sprinkling of tacks, etc., had prevented the development of the bicycle. The rich would simply have been deprived of one toy. They would never have missed it. The great loss would have fallen upon the poor, to whom the bicycle now offers many economical advantages, and their sole chance of reaching the country and of knowing nature's beauties.

What's a Good Name Worth?

Its Preservation for Post-war Opportunities May Be Worth Sacrifice During the Conflict

By Alfred P. Sloan Jr., Chairman,

General Motors Corporation

MoToR Magazine,

October 1942

WHAT IS TO HAPPEN TO US AND TO OURS is a question which I believe dominates the thinking and arouses the fears of the great majority of all the peoples of the world. It applies to our national life, to our business and to each of us as an individual, both economically and socially. There are really two parts to the question: First, the near future, or the duration, let us say; and second, the more distant future.

Many of us believe that the war effort should occupy the entire field of our thought and effort, involving as it ultimately must sacrifices such as we have not yet even commenced to visualize. Expressed otherwise, it is felt that there should be no consideration nor discussion of the tremendous problems of reorganization and reconstruction which we must finally face, nor even our current economic planning in relation to the post-war adjustments.

Certainly the war is the prime and vital problem. Nothing should be permitted to stand in the way of complete victory. Certainly if we do NOT win the war, WHAT happens then will be of little consequence and NOT for us to determine. I subscribe fully to that expression of our war responsibility. At the same time I believe we should and can, without prejudice to the war effort, begin to think and to plan and to discuss what is to come after. We should do this in a business way, as a nation and as individuals. It is, I believe, entirely a matter of relativity involving a definite responsibility for effective action in each sphere—each without prejudice to the other.

Perhaps we fail to realize that war differs fundamentally from other contests. The war objective is NOT to win the contest as such. We make enormous sacrifices of lives and wealth only in the hope and belief that we will dominate in the great issues involved. Too frequently those issues remain obscured and poorly defined, far in the background. The contest itself absorbs our complete attention. Too little do we keep in mind the real objective and too few have any clear conception of what the objective really is.

I have faith that sooner or later—and I sincerely hope sooner rather than later—we shall realize, through the process of trial and error, the absolute necessity of a truly effective administration of the war effort from the standpoint of a sound organization, supported by experienced personnel with clearly defined responsibilities. In such a scientific approach must be embraced intelligent management of the entire economy. Only by so doing can we fully capitalize our resources, both human and economic, in a coordinated and effective whole. By so doing, with courage and efficiency, victory is assured. To win the war is one thing but to win the peace is another. I have faith in our ultimate ability to win the war. I fear as to our ability to win the peace. Preservation of democracy and an economy of free enterprise and the perpetuation of our civilization are, to an important degree, in the balance.

The contribution of the automotive industry to the war effort is a matter of record. It is a highly commendable record. As new plants come into production and the conversion of existing plants is completed, it will become recognized as a remarkable accomplishment of engineering and production, especially with respect to time. All who are taking part have reason to be proud.

Looking backward down through the years, the automotive industry can view with satisfaction its contribution to industrial progress and to a higher order of living. It can well take pride in the fact that the technical evolution of its products, its methods of production, its scheme of distribution and service to the community, have resulted not only in attaining first place among all industries in the domestic field, but in addition, American motor cars have dominated, through their technical superiority, every market where they were competitively sold. That is likewise true of the products of the great majority of American industries.

The social impact of our performance was to revolutionize the American way of life, to raise our standard of living and to afford employment for millions at the highest rates of pay ever attained. The industry's war contribution has been possible only because of such an unusual background.

The policy of promoting continuous technological progress, as exemplified by the yearly new car models, is now being reflected in a very aggressive attack on the technology of war. American technical and production genius is called upon for the first time to concentrate its ingenuity, experience and ambitions toward advancing the effectiveness of all implements of war. Whatever our relative competitive position may have been at the start, it is inevitable that in the final analysis American industry will dominate technically and by a wide margin of superiority, just as it will dominate quantitatively.

The relative value of these two qualifications is difficult to measure. It might well be said that technical superiority will go far to offset quantitative superiority. We should have both. Thus American industry now stands out most dramatically as the keystone of the American war effort. Its great aggregation of workers, technicians, administrators, its superb production facilities, unrivaled techniques, constitute the foundation of the structure that will make possible the preservation of our institutions and the American ideals of living.

In this all-out war effort in which we are engaged, however, we must not overlook the civilian economy. It must be effectively maintained, the morale of our people supported and their physical well being preserved. It is far more dramatic to operate a bomber than to repair a motor car but both are demanded. We can not achieve victory unless we recognize all the component parts of the problem. It must be a well balanced, coordinated effort.

It is generally accepted that the maintenance of our 20,000,000 passenger cars and our entire present complement of trucks is essential to the war effort. This part of the industry's war responsibility falls upon the automotive dealer. At the moment the problem may not appear impressive but as our war effort increases in intensity, more and more existing surpluses will become shortages. Then the part each plays, and its responsibility to the whole, becomes more clearly defined. We may well visualize each unit within our great system of automotive transportation having ultimately its duly appointed task.

To discharge the dealer responsibility, under existing limitations, presents real difficulties. But war is an aggregation of difficulties as well as sacrifices. It has been said that it is also a great accelerator of progress because it usually involves the question of self-preservation, in some form or other, and that is the greatest of all human incentives. Each dealer must reorganize his activity in harmony with such an intensive war economy. In each economically self-contained dealer unit, serious difficulties must be faced sooner or later unless income closely balances outgo. Revenue normally accruing from new car sales—the most important part of the dealer's activities—has already been curtailed sharply. In all probability it will be entirely eliminated during the coming year.

Two Objectives

The new objectives of the dealer appear to fall within two broad classifications. One involves the duration and concerns the war effort with its responsibilities while the other involves what follows afterward. Among the first might be mentioned: The responsibility of service; the distribution of new merchandise, as available; the redistribution of existing automotive transportation in the form of used cars in order that what we may have may be used most effectively. The second objective is to maintain at the same time as virile and effective a position as possible, economically and otherwise, so that the responsibilities and opportunities of the post-war era may be most effectively capitalized.

Here is a double challenge. It involves many difficulties but they can be overcome. Most automotive dealers have been in business for many years. They have established enviable reputations for honesty and integrity. And, after all, the most important business asset is a good name. Without it permanent business success is impossible. The value of a good name is a vital factor in appraising any balance sheet, even though it cannot be indicated in cash. It can easily be lost unless constantly defended.

Today there might appear the urge to accept lower business standards. Shortages of materials or personnel offer good excuses for poor service. Difficult economic conditions might well act as an incentive to adopt practices that ordinarily would not be countenanced.

Challenge and Opportunity

Here is a challenge and an opportunity for every business man who is earnestly striving to discharge his duty to the war effort to maintain at the same time the position he has earned through many years of constructive effort and thus to insure for himself a place after the war is over. Those who accept such a challenge will find it will pay large dividends. For a position sacrificed or forgotten, something not difficult in a period such as this, involving dramatic changes and a rapid evolution of events, is hard to regain. This is true of the producer as well but it particularly applies to the dealer.

Whether we look at the problems as a nation, as a business organization or as an individual, I believe we should accept the philosophy that we should discharge our duty as we see it to the very best of our ability, without reservation, and in doing so determine our course in such a way that we will be as well prepared as possible to carry on after victory has been won. For only after the war is won does the problem of the real victory arise. Sacrifices in the meantime are not of such great consequence with such vital issues at stake.

Automobile dealers as a group and the automotive industry as a whole are to be congratulated on the manner in which they are accomplishing the most important job of reorganized distribution in line with the changed conditions. It is true to the form that has characterized the accomplishment of the industry from the beginning. It is a remarkable tribute to the business capacity of the dealers. Facts have been faced, as they must always be faced if we are to keep in line with the rapid evolution of circumstances—in this particular instance a revolution.

Organizations have been reconstructed, expenses reduced, consolidations effected, and all without any sacrifice of war responsibilities. The results so far achieved, both as to operating technique and in an economic sense, have been far more satisfactory than seemed possible a few months ago. We have reason to hope that, from the dealer's standpoint, 1942 may rank among the good years of the industry's recent history. Let us hope it may be possible—and it might well be—to continue this same general trend, even if modified.

I have tried to emphasize the fact that winning the war does not insure winning the peace and that only by winning the peace can we really win the war in fact. A discussion of the issues that arise in the problem of peace is far too complicated and involved to come within the scope of these observations. Again, there are two distinct periods of time, which must be considered. They might be termed the periods of shortages and surpluses. The first involves the two or more years

DON'T

1. **Don't use a motor car or motor cycle for pleasure purposes.**

2. **Don't buy new clothes needlessly. Don't be ashamed of wearing old clothes in War time.**

3. **Don't keep more servants than you really need.**

In this way you will save money for the War, set the right example, and free labour for more useful purposes.

Your Country will Appreciate Your Help.

immediately following the suspension of hostilities and the second the long term following. What we may expect in the first period is rather definitely outlined. What follows in the second period involves great uncertainties—too many to consider at this time.

Limited Stockpiles

We entered the war with a certain investment of automobile miles represented by the motor cars available for use at the time. The aggregate amount was a measure, even if crude, of our standard of living. The same applies to the inventory of electric refrigerators and the whole array of appliances in almost infinite variety upon which we so much depend for both our comfort and the luxury of our living. The use of such things cannot be extended because they are no longer in production. The existing use cannot be wholly maintained because depreciation and depletion and other losses will take their toll.

After-War Demand

The war is developing a demand that will accelerate in volume as we pass through the duration. The aggregate of all this may well be expected to tax our facilities when production is resumed. History indicates that following a great conflict comes a period of great industrial activity. Its length and intensity depend upon circumstances. We can, I believe, definitely depend on the record as indicating what we may expect. Thus we will have a sound demand for consumer durable and semi-durable goods and all others, as a matter of fact, to make up for the then existing shortages.

Post-War Demand

I believe we should have more purchasing power available, relatively, than in similar periods that have gone before. Wages of the masses who, in the aggregate, constitute what might be termed the Mississippi River of purchasing power, are at an all-time high. The bank of purchasing power contained in the installment plan of purchase has been replenished by liquidation of all past indebtedness. Forced savings, available for use after the war, are probable. General personal indebtedness will have been importantly liquidated through the pressure of war-swollen income and perhaps even encouraged by governmental action. And it is hoped that

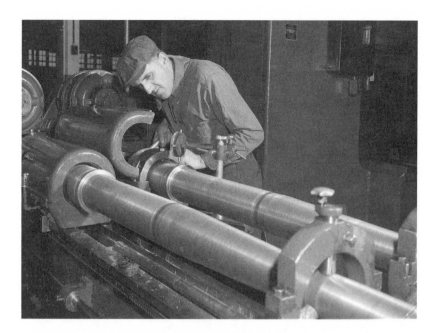

before it is too late adequate steps will be taken to *prevent* a runaway of prices which would prejudice what otherwise might be possible.

Thus, as we in the great automotive industry look forward, we recognize the problems we face in the all-out war effort to which the nation has dedicated its economic as well as its human resources. We accept our responsibilities and the sacrifices that must be made. We look forward with confidence to the belief that VICTORY can be won if we have the determination to win and are willing to face the issues involved in a truly realistic way. THAT'S the real question and upon it depends both the VICTORY of War and the VICTORY of Peace.

Noise, Vibration, and Harshness

The Big Three American Auto Companies

By Jamie Kitman

Automobile Magazine,

September 2008

GAME OVER.

AFTER ALMOST HALF A CENTURY OF FIGHTING BATTLES, America's Big Three—the Moderately Large Three, if you prefer—have at long last lost the war. Yes, it's official. From this day forward, fuel economy matters. From now on, judicious use of fossil fuels trumps road-hugging weight. Too bad Detroit carmakers weren't prepared. They only had fifty years to get ready.

Of course, many said the same thing—mileage is the new, eternal bogey—during the energy crises of the 1950s and the 1970s, and they were wrong. They failed to recognize that, given enough encouragement, Americans would use too much fuel again. The captains of Detroit professed their blamelessness: Americans love big, thirsty machines. Gas is cheap. What could we do?

But now that gas isn't cheap, this is the part that's important to remember. Detroit didn't have to encourage profligacy, it chose to. And some will argue that the power of advertising dollars could and should have been used to encourage efficiency. The American industry could have played the same patriotic card it deployed following 9/11 to advocate fuel conservation instead of throwing around billions of dollars to make sure there were large SUVs in every garage. It didn't have to spend some four decades fighting safety, emissions, and fuel-efficiency standards.

By way of justification, the men from the Motor City have maintained that America's large cars—virtually unique in the world for their heft—were safer. This didn't explain the big spike in deaths in single-car rollover accidents that accompanied the shift to SUVs. Or why these same companies were selling all those unsafe small cars to Europeans and Third Worlders. (Don't their lives count, too?) And it ignored the hazard large SUVs posed to occupants of normal cars, cyclists, and pedestrians. In a war between a Ford Excursion and a Focus, the Excursion wins. But only sometimes. The Focus can outmaneuver an Excursion, and it takes up less room, two keys to avoiding accidents in the first place. The truth is, if you're going to get hit by an 80,000-pound Peterbilt running late and full up, it makes no difference whether you're in a 7,000-pound Excursion or a 2,600-pound Focus. It's kind of like asking whether you would rather die in a fire at 1,000 degrees Fahrenheit or 2,200. Myself, I think I'd go with the 2,200-degree fire.

Unlike rough patches in the past, Detroit isn't making any money now—and that's after it's closed plants, squeezed suppliers, slashed waste, jammed the union, and laid off workers. Excepting executive salaries, more generously supersized than ever, what's left to cut? (Alongside a bold $38.7 billion loss in 2007, General Motors turned over a new leaf by approving a 64 percent increase in chairman and CEO Rick Wagoner's annual compensation, to $15.7 million, among other raises it handed out to top execs. Imagine if the company actually turned a profit.)

It is chilling to remember that GM spent a fair part of the last century fighting to keep its market share below 50 percent for fear of triggering antitrust intervention. And it seems like only yesterday that GM executives wore "29" buttons on their expensive lapels. That represented the percentage of market share GM was going, as their bold exhortative prophecy indicated, to reclaim. Whoops. GM's market share has just sunk below 20 percent, its lowest showing since the 1920s. Will we see "19" buttons this year? Or should we go straight to "16"? Recently, the company announced plans to close four factories, lopping a substantial 35 percent off its light-truck production capacity—about 700,000 units—in one fell swoop.

Just as grave, GM says it's thinking of selling the Hummer division, on which it has surely lost billions and its dealers millions. Or perhaps the company will just shutter it. GM has a point. Who would be foolish enough to buy Hummer? Besides GM, that is. It probably shouldn't bother. Unless what's in the cards is a radical recasting of Hummer as a maker of low-volume, high-tech, alt-energy off-roaders. But GM is too broke to make Hummer relevant, much the way it's too broke to aggressively market the desirable cars it does sell. May's disappointing total of 1,091 Saturn Astras sold is a picture worth 1,091 words.

How violent is the sea change for Detroit? In May, Ford's F-150, which hadn't been outsold by a car since October 1991, skydived to fifth spot behind a couple of Hondas (Civic and Accord) and two Toyotas (Corolla and Camry). The Civic is now the best-selling car in America, with 53,299 sold in May alone. By contrast, Chrysler sales are off 25 percent, and as I sit down to write, Dodge has just announced plans to darken its Ram facility in Saltillo, Mexico, for what it said would be only two weeks.

We'll see about that.

Clearly this is not just a down year, it's a total paradigm shift. Honestly, it's hard to think about cars in the same way anymore. Cars that seemed like pretty good ideas—say, Pontiac's six-cylinder G8, headed in the right direction with 25-mpg EPA highway mileage—suddenly seem less inspired with only 17-mpg city. Cars that appeared bad ideas before now seem like the worst ideas ever. The Hummer brand, for instance, is on target to sell fewer than 35,000 units this year, or about twelve percent the number of Oldsmobiles GM was selling when it decided to shut that venerable brand to concentrate on . . . Hummer.

Mercifully for our domestic makers, they're not the only ones whose affection for American gluttony is reflected in suddenly ridiculous products and plans. Audi has been talking about setting up a factory in the States. But instead of building the A3, the second-highest-mileage model in its lineup, Audi talked about building large SUVs, possibly to share with Volkswagen. It goes without saying that VW has been given a golden opportunity by the oil potentates—not to sell Americans more crap-mileage, me-too SUVs, but rather a production version of its tempting Up! show car, the one with the two-cylinder, rear-mounted engine that promises to be both highway-ready and incredibly green. It would be perfect for marketing to Americans at a semipremium price, with currency-exchange woes excised if the car is built in the United States. Porsche, reclaiming the old formula, should conjure something wondrous based on it.

The point is, the peace following the war that the carmakers have lost doesn't have to be a bad thing. Let the new game begin.

CHAPTER 3

Dream Cars and Dream Trips

Excerpt from Part 2

By Jack Kerouac

On the Road,

1957

WHAT IS THAT FEELING WHEN YOU'RE DRIVING AWAY from people and they recede on the plain till you see their specks dispersing?—it's the too-huge world vaulting us, and it's good-by. But we lean forward to the next crazy venture beneath the skies.

We wheeled through the sultry old light of Algiers, back on the ferry, back toward the mud-splashed, crabbed old ships across the river, back on Canal, and out; on a two-lane highway to Baton Rouge in purple darkness; swung west there, crossed the Mississippi at a place called Port Allen. Port Allen—where the river's all rain and roses in a misty pinpoint darkness and where we swung around a circular drive in yellow foglight and suddenly saw the great black body below a bridge and crossed eternity again. What is the Mississippi River?—a washed clod in the rainy night, a soft plopping from drooping Missouri banks, a dissolving, a riding of the tide down the eternal waterbed, a contribution to brown foams, a voyaging past endless vales and trees and levees, down along, down along, by Memphis, Greenville, Eudora, Vicksburg, Natchez, Port Allen, and Port Orleans and Port of the Deltas, by Potash, Venice, and the Night's Great Gulf, and out.

With the radio on to a mystery program, and as I looked out the window and saw a sign that said USE COOPER'S PAINT and I said, "Okay, I will," we rolled across the hoodwink night of the Louisiana plains—Lawtell, Eunice, Kinder, and De Quincy, western rickety towns becoming more bayou-like as we reached the Sabine. In Old Opelousas I went into a grocery store to buy bread and cheese while Dean saw to gas and oil. It was just a shack; I could hear the family eating supper in the back. I waited a minute; they went on talking. I took bread and cheese and slipped out the door. We had barely enough money to make Frisco. Meanwhile Dean took a carton of cigarettes from the gas station and we were stocked for the voyage—gas, oil, cigarettes, and food. Crooks don't know. He pointed the car straight down the road.

Somewhere near Starks we saw a great red glow in the sky ahead; we wondered what it was; in a moment we were passing it. It was a fire beyond the trees; there were many cars parked on the highway. It must have been some kind of fish-fry, and on the other hand it might have been anything. The country turned strange and dark near Deweyville. Suddenly we were in the swamps.

"Man, do you imagine that it would be like if we found a jazz-joint in these swamps, with great big black fellas moanin guitar blues and drinkin snakejuice and makin signs at us?"

"Yes!"

There were mysteries around here. The car was going over a dirt road elevated off the swamps that dropped on both sides and drooped with vines. We passed an apparition; it was a Negro man in a white shirt walking along with his arms upspread to the inky firmament. He must have been praying or calling down a curse. We zoomed right by; I looked out the back window to see his white eyes. "Whoo!" said Dean. "Look out. We better not stop in this here country." At one point we got stuck at a crossroads and stopped the car anyway. Dean turned off the headlamps. We were surrounded by a great forest of viny trees in which we could almost hear the slither of a million copperheads. The only thing we could see was the red ampere button on the Hudson dashboard. Marylou squealed with fright. We began laughing maniac laughs to scare her. We were scared too. We wanted to get out of this mansion of the snake, this mireful drooping dark, and zoom on back to familiar American ground and cowtowns. There was a smell of oil and dead water in the air. This was a manuscript of the night we couldn't read. An owl hooted. We took a chance on one of the dirt roads, and pretty soon we were crossing the evil old Sabine River that is responsible for all these swamps. With amazement we saw great structures of light ahead of us. "Texas! It's Texas! Beaumont oil town!" Huge oil tanks and refineries loomed like cities in the oily fragrant air.

"I'm glad we got out of there," said Marylou. "Let's play some more mystery programs now."

We zoomed through Beaumont, over the Trinity River at Liberty, and straight for Houston. Now Dean got talking about his Houston days in 1947. "Hassel! That mad Hassel! I look for him everywhere I go and I never find him. He used to get us so hung-up in Texas here. We'd drive in with Bull for groceries and Hassel'd disappear. We'd have to go looking for him in every shooting gallery in town." We were entering Houston. "We had to look for him in this spade part of town most of the time. Man, he'd be blasting with every mad cat he could find. One night we lost him and took a hotel room. We were supposed to bring ice back to Jane because her food was rotting. It took us two days to find Hassel. I got hung-up myself—I gunned shopping women in the afternoon, right here, downtown, supermarkets"—we flashed by in the empty night—"and found a real gone dumb girl who was out of her mind and just wandering, trying to steal an orange. She was from Wyoming. Her beautiful body was matched only by her idiot mind. I found her babbling and took her back to the room. Bull was drunk trying to get this young Mexican kid drunk. Carlo was writing poetry on heroin. Hassel didn't show up till midnight at the jeep. We found him sleeping in the back seat. The ice was all melted. Hassel said he took about five sleeping pills. Man, if my memory could only serve me right the way my mind works I could tell you every detail of the things we did. Ah, but we know time. Everything takes care of itself. I could close my eyes and this old car would take care of itself."

In the empty Houston streets of four o'clock in the morning a motorcycle kid suddenly roared through, all bespangled and bedecked with glittering buttons, visor, slick black jacket, a Texas poet of the night, girl gripped on his back like a papoose, hair flying, onward-going, singing, "Houston, Austin, Fort Worth, Dallas—and sometimes Kansas

City—and sometimes old Antone, ah-haaaaa!" They pinpointed out of sight. "Wow! Dig that gone gal on his belt! Let's all blow!" Dean tried to catch up with them. "Now wouldn't it be fine if we could all get together and have a real going goofbang together with everybody sweet and fine and agreeable, no hassles, no infant rise of protest or body woes misconceptalized or sumpin? Ah! but we know time." He bent to it and pushed the car.

Beyond Houston his energies, great as they were, gave out and I drove. Rain began to fall just as I took the wheel. Now we were on the great Texas plain and, as Dean said, "You drive and drive and you're still in Texas tomorrow night." The rain lashed down. I drove through a rickety little cowtown with a muddy main street and found myself in a dead end. "Hey, what do I do?" They were both asleep. I turned and crawled back through town. There wasn't a soul in sight and not a single light. Suddenly a horseman in a raincoat appeared in my headlamps. It was the sheriff. He had a ten-gallon hat, drooping in the torrent. "Which way to Austin?" He told me politely and I started off. Outside town I suddenly saw two headlamps flaring directly at me in the lashing rain. Whoops, I thought I was on the wrong side of the road; I eased right and found myself rolling in the mud; I rolled back to the road. Still the headlamps came straight for me. At the last moment I realized the other driver was on the wrong side of the road and didn't know it. I swerved at thirty into the mud; it was flat, no ditch, thank God. The offending car backed up in the downpour. Four sullen fieldworkers, snuck from their chores to brawl in drinking fields, all white shirts and dirty brown arms, sat looking at me dumbly in the night. The driver was as drunk as the lot.

He said, "Which way t'Houston?" I pointed my thumb back. I was thunderstruck in the middle of the thought that they had done this on purpose just to ask directions, as a panhandler advances on you straight up the sidewalk to bar your way. They gazed ruefully at the floor of their car, where empty bottles rolled and clanked away. I started the car; it was stuck in the mud a foot deep. I sighed in the rainy Texas wilderness.

"Dean," I said, "wake up."

"What?"

"We're stuck in the mud."

"What happened?" I told him. He swore up and down. We put on old

shoes and sweaters and barged out of the car into the driving rain. I put my back on the rear fender and lifted and heaved; Dean stuck chains under the swishing wheels. In a minute we were covered with mud. We woke up Marylou to these horrors and made her gun the car while we pushed. The tormented Hudson heaved and heaved. Suddenly it jolted out and went skidding across the road. Marylou pulled it up just in time, and we got in. That was that—the work had taken thirty minutes and we were soaked and miserable.

I fell asleep, all caked with mud; and in the morning when I woke up the mud was solidified and outside there was snow. We were near Fredericksburg, in the high plains. It was one of the worst winters in Texas and Western history, when cattle perished like flies in great blizzards and snow fell on San Francisco and LA. We were all miserable. We wished we were back in New Orleans with Ed Dunkel. Marylou was driving; Dean was sleeping. She drove with one hand on the wheel and the other reaching back to me in the back seat. She cooed promises about San Francisco. I slavered miserably over it. At ten I took the wheel—Dean was out for hours—and drove several hundred dreary miles across the bushy snows and ragged sage hills. Cowboys went by in baseball caps and earmuffs, looking for cows. Comfortable little homes with chimneys smoking appeared along the road at intervals. I wished we could go in for buttermilk and beans in front of the fireplace.

At Sonora I again helped myself to free bread and cheese while the proprietor chatted with a big rancher on the other side of the store. Dean huzzahed when he heard it; he was hungry. We couldn't spend a cent on food. "Yass, yass," said Dean, watching the ranchers loping up and down Sonora main street, "every one of them is a bloody millionaire, thousand head of cattle, workhands, buildings, money in the bank. If I lived around here I'd go be an idjit in the sagebrush, I'd be jackrabbit, I'd lick up the branches, I'd look for pretty cowgirls—hee-hee-hee-hee! Damn! Bam!" He socked himself. "Yes! Right! Oh me!" We didn't know what he was talking about any more. He took the wheel and flew the rest of the way across the state of Texas, about five hundred miles, clear to El Paso, arriving at dusk and not stopping except once when he took all his clothes off, near Ozona, and ran yipping and leaping naked in the sage. Cars zoomed by and didn't see him. He scurried back to the car and drove on. "Now Sal, now Marylou, I want both of you to do as I'm doing, disemburden yourselves of all that clothes—now what's the sense of clothes? now that's what I'm sayin—and sun your pretty bellies with me. Come on!"

We were driving west into the sun; it fell in through the windshield. "Open your belly as we drive into it." Marylou complied; unfuddyduddied, so did I. We sat in the front seat, all three. Marylou took out cold cream and applied it to us for kicks. Every now and then a big truck zoomed by; the driver in high cab caught a glimpse of a golden beauty sitting naked with two naked men: you could see them swerve a moment as they vanished in our rear-view window. Great sage plains, snowless now, rolled on. Soon we were in the orange-rocked Pecos Canyon country. Blue distances opened up in the sky. We got out of the car to examine an old Indian ruin. Dean did so stark naked. Marylou and I put on our overcoats. We wandered among the old stones, hooting and howling. Certain tourists caught sight of Dean naked in the plain but they could not believe their eyes and wobbled on.

Dean and Marylou parked the car near Van Horn and made love while I went to sleep. I woke up just as we were rolling down the tremendous Rio Grande Valley through Clint and Ysleta to El Paso. Marylou jumped to the back seat, I jumped to the front seat, and we rolled along. To our left across the vast Rio Grande spaces were the moorish-red mounts of the Mexican border, the land of the Tarahumare; soft dusk played on the peaks. Straight ahead lay the distant lights of El Paso and Juarez, sown in a tremendous valley so big that you could see several railroads puffing at the same time in every direction, as though it was the Valley of the world. We descended into it.

"Clint, Texas!" said Dean. He had the radio on to the Clint station. Every fifteen minutes they played a record; the rest of the time it was commercials about a high-school correspondence course. "This program is beamed all over the West," cried Dean excitedly. "Man, I used to listen to it day and night in reform school and prison. All of us used to write in. You get a high-school diploma by mail, facsimile thereof, if you pass the test. All the young wranglers in the West, I don't care who, at one time or another write in for this; it's all they hear; you tune the radio in Sterling, Colorado, Lusk, Wyoming, I don't care where, you get Clint, Texas, Clint, Texas. And the music is always cowboy-hillbilly and Mexican, absolutely the worst program in the entire history of the country and nobody can do anything about it. They have a tremendous beam; they've got the whole land hogtied." We saw the high antenna beyond the shacks of Clint. "Oh, man, the things I could tell you!" cried Dean, almost weeping. Eyes bent on Frisco and the Coast, we came into El Paso as it got dark, broke. We absolutely had to get some money for gas or we'd never make it.

We tried everything. We buzzed the travel bureau, but no one was going west that night. The travel bureau is where you go for share-the-gas rides, legal in the West. Shifty characters wait with battered suitcases. We went to the Greyhound bus station to try to persuade somebody to give us the money instead of taking a bus for the Coast. We were too bashful to approach anyone. We wandered around sadly. It was cold outside. A college boy was sweating at the sight of luscious Marylou and trying to look unconcerned. Dean and I consulted but decided we weren't pimps. Suddenly a crazy dumb young kid, fresh out of reform school, attached himself to us, and he and Dean rushed out for a beer. "Come on, man, let's go mash somebody on the head and get his money."

"I dig you, man!" yelled Dean. They dashed off. For a moment I was worried; but Dean only wanted to dig the streets of El Paso with the kid and get his kicks. Marylou and I waited in the car. She put her arms around me.

I said, "Dammit, Lou, wait till we get to Frisco."

"I don't care. Dean's going to leave me anyway."

"When are you going back to Denver?"

"I don't know. I don't care what I'm doing. Can I go back east with you?"

"We'll have to get some money in Frisco."

"I know where you can get a job in a lunchcart behind the counter, and I'll be a waitress. I know a hotel where we can stay on credit. We'll stick together. Gee, I'm sad."

"What are you sad about, kid?"

"I'm sad about everything. Oh damn, I wish Dean wasn't so crazy now." Dean came twinkling back, giggling, and jumped in the car.

"What a crazy cat that was, whoo! Did I dig him! I used to know thousands of guys like that, they're all the same, their minds work in uniform clockwork, oh, the infinite ramifications, no time, no time . . . " And he shot up the car, hunched over the wheel, and roared out of El Paso. "We'll just have to pick up hitchhikers. I'm positive we'll find some. Hup! hup! here we go. Look out!" he yelled at a motorist, and swung around him, and dodged a truck and bounced over the city limits. Across the river were the jewel lights of Juarez and the sad dry land and the jewel stars of Chihuahua. Marylou was watching Dean as she had watched him clear across the county and back, out of the corner of her eye—with a sullen, sad air, as though she wanted to cut off his head and hide it in her closet, an envious and rueful love of him so amazingly himself, all raging and sniffy and crazy-wayed, a smile of tender dotage but also sinister envy that frightened me about her, a love she knew would never bear fruit because when she looked at his hangjawed bony face with its male self-containment and absentmindedness she knew he was too mad. Dean was convinced Marylou was a whore; he confided in me that she was a pathological liar. But when she watched him like this it was love too; and when Dean noticed he always turned with his big false flirtatious smile, with the eyelashes fluttering and the teeth pearly white, while a moment ago he was only dreaming in his eternity. Then Marylou and I both laughed—and Dean gave no sign of discomfiture, just a goofy glad grin that said to us, Ain't we gettin' our kicks anyway? And that was it.

A Ferrari among Friends

By Jean Lindamood

Automobile Magazine,

December 1988

*There's one way to explain to friends
and neighbors what we do for a living:
Give forty-nine of them rides in a Testarossa.*

Ann Arbor—

THE SKY WAS PACKING UP WITH SOME pretty nasty-looking clouds when the Testarossa came to town. Snow, no doubt about it. I was feeling sorry for myself. A Testarossa for the weekend, and a killer winter storm was on the way.

I got to drive a Testarossa once before, for about twenty miles. Here my once-every-five-years driving opportunity had come up again, and I was trying to figure out how much of that precious time it would take to drive it somewhere warm and sunny. From the look of the weather map on the evening news, I wouldn't be able to get past Ohio without a snowplow.

This was one problem I wouldn't be able to share with my friends, who have come to the conclusion that I don't deserve to have anything good happen to me for the rest of my life. I'm talking about my *real* friends: the ones I drove taxis with. The mechanics and test drivers from the Chrysler proving ground. The guys at the local bar. The butcher, the baker, and the local doughnut maker. My neighbors. The ones who always say, "Where are you jetting off to *this* weekend, turkey? Rio? Do you need someone to carry your bags?" and then buy me a beer. Most of them had never *seen* a Ferrari.

And then it dawned on me. If I couldn't turn this into a test drive, I could at least share the spectacle of the car itself. I might never need anyone to carry my bags to Brazil, but with the Testarossa, I sure as hell could take my friends with me. All of them. Or at least as many as I could round up in three days. For me, it would be like reliving my first ride in one of the world's most coveted and exotic machines.

It took ten rides on Friday morning to clear out 120 East Liberty Street, which accounted for most of the local nonwriting staff of *Automobile Magazine*: managing editor, receptionist, production assistant, editorial assistant, business manager, secretary, advertising assistant, art assistants, and gopher. It was a great rollicking production, with someone on deck in the lobby waiting for the car to return, a hasty passenger transfer, and the next person running down to take up the wait by the lobby door. In the face of all this commotion and excitement, it seemed a little odd that no one had much to say inside the car. Basically, they laughed a lot and then said, "Thank you." Come to think of it, I think that's what I did when I first rode in a Testarossa.

My duty to the office done, I headed for Stockbridge, a farm town thirty miles northwest of Ann Arbor, where mechanic Danny Houk was watching his one-year-old twins before he headed off to the afternoon shift at Chrysler. I wiggled down his snow-covered drive and parked next to his old Plymouth Belvedere GTX and his Dodge SnoCommander pickup/snowplow.

"Get out the snowsuits!" I hollered, as I burst into the big farm kitchen. "We're going for a ride."

"*Damn*," said Danny, looking out the window over the kitchen sink. He went out onto the porch in his flannel shirtsleeves, stared hard at the world's reddest car blazing against the snow in his yard, then looked at the farm across the road. "*Damn*," he said again. "Donny ain't home. Boy, is *he* going to be bummed out."

We whooshed down the highway and into the village, ringed the town square, and paid a visit to another Chrysler second-shift mechanic. Danny laughed a lot. Back at the farm, we put the twins behind the wheel and took pictures for the family album. He said thanks.

I had to race to get to Saline Middle School in time to pick up Erin Maki. She's my favorite twelve-year-old because she can make her tongue look like a fluted candy dish. By the time she made it out the school door, there was already a knot of excited kids around the Testarossa—and you know how excitable twelve- and thirteen-year-olds can be. They were hopping up and down, spinning like tops, and striking rock-and-roll poses around the car. I checked their back pockets for pens, combs, and knives and then let them sit behind the wheel. They, at least, had *lots* to say.

"I got Ferrari dust on me! I got Ferrari dust on me!" yelled one, dragging his fingers through the Testarossa's side strakes. And then they were all wiping their fingers over the car and waving their fingers in the air.

"You should get an F40," said another. "It goes 201, and it comes with extra cams." I raised my eyebrows.

An unsuspecting 944 drove by. "A Porsche!" one kid screamed. "Race the Porsche! Race the Porsche!" they yelled, some of them grabbing my arm.

"Porsches suck! Porsches suck!" they all took up the chant, doing a little kid dance in the parking lot. Erin, ever cool, rolled her eyes. "Get away from my car," she said imperiously and got into the passenger's seat, her social success now guaranteed.

Next stop was four o'clock shift change at the proving ground, a fairly speedy affair on Friday afternoons. In fact, on Fridays people actually run from the garage to their cars when the whistle blows. The Ferrari slowed them down. A little clump of die-hard car freaks gathered around and peered under the hood at the lovely fender-to-fender expanse of engine, their lunch buckets held carefully behind their backs.

"Somebody's been burning the clutch," said transmission expert Sonny Benson. The group of mechanics leaned forward and sniffed. They looked at me.

A few rides brought me eventually to the Wolverine Bar in Chelsea, to the table of my good friend Leva Norris, age seventy, who was having an early evening nip with Frank Klobuchar, age eighty-two. She was clearly in no mood for thrill rides.

"Can't you just say I went?" she asked. "How about if I just looked?"

"Leva, this is a *Ferrari*," I reasoned. "You *have* to take a ride."

"Well, let's get this over with," she huffed, pulling on her coat and grabbing her handbag.

"You're gonna love this," I promised. She groaned when she saw how low the seat was, but once we got under way, she started laughing and didn't stop until we'd returned to the bar.

"Now wasn't that worth it?" I asked smugly.

"I'da liked it a lot better if you'da been Don Johnson," she replied and hauled herself out.

Friday's total: eighteen rides.

THE SATURDAY SKY WAS PURE BLUE, the snow clouds having blown down to Ohio. I started at the South Main Market in Ann Arbor, hauling Ginny the butcher out from behind the counter, followed by her son Tom, bloody apron and all. Next came Washtenaw Milk and Ice Cream, home of Ann Arbor's best coffee and the world' s best friedcakes, and a place where the problems of the day are solved every morning by the regular clientele. They moved outside this morning to admire the Testarossa.

"Hell of a car. Jesus!" said Jim Smith, the owner.

"Heh-heh-heh," said young Jim, the owner's son.

"I thought my pickup was nice," said one of the regulars. "Now I'm embarrassed that I'm parked in front of it."

"Well, did you see *my* car?" asked Jim junior. "I got hit by a hearse. Wiped out the whole side. He was carrying cargo, too. The guy driving said, 'The way I figure it, everyone who went into this alive is coming out of it alive.'"

They were warming up.

"Go on, Jimmy. Get a ride," they said to Jim senior.

"Nah, no way," he said, putting up his hands. "I like the lying down part, but not in cars."

They all laughed. "Aw, go on," they insisted. "All right, all right, let's go," he said. He got on his knees and crawled over to the door as they cheered him on.

He didn't say a word as I wheeled it around a few blocks, hard on the throttle so we could hear the mighty rip of the engine and snapping the shift lever through its metal maze.

"Next time you get another good one, drive it on down and I'll go for another ride with you" was all Jim senior had to say when it was over.

As the day wore on, I realized that the Testarossa was having the same effect on all my normally talkative friends. It was a fairly overwhelming piece of machinery—all red and low and leather and noise and power and Ferrari and they were trying to somehow fit this one rare moment into the fabric of their everyday lives. It was a mental task that left them with almost nothing to say about the experience.

Paul Hyssong, paramedic: "God, I'd hate to cut one of these apart after a crash."

Michael Stander, computer wizard, to his waiting wife: "Hold on to your hat."

Gail Stander, artiste: "I feel like I'm in Macy's Thanksgiving Day parade."

Howard Krausmann, engineer: "This is no way to live, Jean. You ought to quit your job and grow roses."

John Norris, electrician: "That's what I like. Just a couple of gauges, no bullshit."

Mike Lower, mechanic: "This is the only car I've been in that's exciting from the passenger seat."

Linda Lower, school teacher: "We're going to have to pave our driveway for when you come over."

Saturday's tally: nineteen rides.

I WENT BACK TO THE KIDS ON SUNDAY, starting with Jenny and Lorelei, two teen-agers from across the street. Lorelei sat on Jenny's lap, and they screamed and waved at the local gas station as we rumbled by.

"Yoo-hoo! Yoo-hoo! It's just us! Ha-ha-ha!"

"My dad is just going to *crap*!" said Lorelei. "I really mean it."

Then came Larry, age sixteen.

"Oh, God!" yelled newly licensed driver Larry when he answered the door and saw the Testarossa behind me. And with barely a pause, he said: "What's the next car you're getting? When are you getting a Countach? Bring it over, okay, 'cause I *have* to ride in that. The Countach will blow this away." We hadn't even left his driveway. This was more like it. Some unbridled enthusiasm. I should have had this car when I was a high-school geek, I thought. What would have happened?

Maybe this . . .

"Who's the coolest guy in school?" I asked my friend Kristen as we drove around her small country town.

"He doesn't know I exist," she answered, in the same way that any other sixteen-year-old girl would say such a thing.

"He will after today," I told her, and I turned the Testarossa toward our unsuspecting hero's rather upscale subdivision.

"I can't believe you're doing this!" squealed Kristen as I turned into His driveway and shut off the car.

"I'll do all the talking. Don't worry," I assured her. She stood behind me as I knocked on the door.

"Oh, I just *love* your car!" said his mother at the door when I explained who we were looking for. "I'll go get him." She never asked me my name, which proves that you can steal people's children if you have the right car.

The heartthrob in question wasn't sure what to make of the older woman standing in his kitchen with the young girl he thought he maybe recognized from school.

"My friend Kristen says you like Ferraris and might like a ride in ours," I explained. "I have a Testarossa outside your door. Get your shoes on. Hurry up." He bolted for his shoes.

I arranged her on his lap and took off like a shot out of the drive, raced to the end of the cul-de-sac, pulled the handbrake, and shot down to the next cul-de-sac, continuing through the subdivision until we'd finished them all off. People were standing on their front porches in the frigid air, waving.

"Oh, God, *thanks!*" he said when we gave him back to his mother.

Kristen slid down onto the floor.

"I don't believe you did that!" she wailed. Her phone was already ringing when she hit the front door.

But I didn't have a Testarossa in high school, so who knows what would have happened?

My husband took the last ride of the weekend. He, of everyone, knew exactly what it all meant, these two old cab drivers honking around southeastern Michigan in the dead of winter in a Ferrari Testarossa. He watched me at the wheel for a while, clearly amused at our lot in life, then chuckled. "Heh-heh-heh," he said. "*Sick.*"

Old Caddy, Big Muddy

The Mother of All Cruisers Takes on the Father of Waters in a Search for Delta Blues, Cajun Food and New Orleans Jazz

By Peter Egan

Road & Track,
November 1996

A SHORT TIME AFTER MOVING TO RURAL WISCONSIN, I realized it was theoretically possible to put a canoe into the small stream that flows right past the front of our house and float all the way to New Orleans. From Badfish Creek to the Mississippi. Simple as gravity.

And every time I walked down to the fast-moving creek last spring and tossed a stick into the water, I had the same thought: That stick is going to New Orleans.

The Big Easy, where they have crawfish *étouffée*, French Market coffee, beignets, blooming magnolias, great music and warm weather. No snow, no salt on the roads, no freezing fogs and bitter winds.

Stick envy may seem a pathetic state for a full-grown human being, but you have to bear in mind that this past winter was one of the longest and darkest in Midwestern memory.

All of us searched our souls for a dream to fight off cabin fever, and mine became a trip down Highway 61, along the river into that sun-warmed part of the imagination where Delta blues and Spanish moss live with filé gumbo and pirogues on the bayou.

The germ was planted when R&T Executive Editor Rich Homan called and asked if I'd like to join him and a couple of friends at the New Orleans Jazz & Heritage Festival in April. Rich, who is a huge music buff, goes to this event every year, much the way a good Muslim goes to Mecca or a good Catholic goes to public school, as I once did, because there are more girls.

"Fine idea," I told Rich. "I'll be there. Maybe ride my motorcycle down, like I did 18 years ago, or find some appropriate old car . . . "

The appropriate car, of course, appeared as if by magic that very week, in the form of a dilapidated royal maroon 1963 Model Sixty-Two Cadillac 4-window sedan that was languishing behind the repair shop of my friend Chris Beebe.

I've already written about this car twice before at dizzying length, so I'll keep the history short: Chris acquired the Cadillac last year from our friend Libby Livermore, who in turn had inherited it from another mutual friend, Suzanne Ames, whose mother had given her the car.

I know this all sounds rather biblical ("Japheth begat Meshech who begat Reebok," etc.), but the point is, no one knew exactly what to do with a slightly dented old Cadillac, so it got passed hand to hand with a mixture of awe and dread, like a large handgun at a PTA meeting.

The car had sat for 15 years in a cold, damp garage, so it needed rebuilding of all its systems: brake, cooling, fuel, exhaust, etc. About $2,000 worth, altogether, and many hours of work. One other basic problem was the Cadillac's smell. A rich, moss-green layer of mildew covered the white vinyl seat tops, so it smelled like a basement mushroom farm.

A weekend of scrubbing and disinfecting brought the interior back to immaculate showroom condition, visually speaking. Yet still there was a slight aroma of mold, mixed with a new, heady bouquet of chemicals and perfume. Now it smelled, as one friend delicately put it, "Like a French whorehouse with a mushroom farm in the basement."

Open windows, hot sun and lots of fresh air, I decided, would do the trick. The car needed the same things I did.

As a last step, my friend Dennis Marklein unleashed the full force of Marklein Auto Body on the Cadillac's many door dings and badly weathered paint. Two weeks later it was done. And it looked stunning when I picked it up, resplendent in its original royal maroon. Not quite burgundy, not quite brown. More like the silt in the bottom of a burgundy bottle. A rich, organic color with perhaps a little French roast coffee in the mix. Perfect for a blues pilgrimage. Chuck Berry would approve.

And so did I.

The car came from the 1961–1964 styling era, a period when GM design vice president Bill Mitchell and Cadillac design chief Chuck Jordan were up against the exquisite new Lincoln Continental, whose chiseled, old-money look had suddenly made the late Fifties' finned Caddys seem too flashy.

They toned it down, but still kept some of the sweep and glamour that said "Cadillac" to the American public. The earlier, fish-tail Cadillacs may be prized these days for their sheer, unrestrained flamboyance, but a '63 is (to my eye) simply a handsome large car for the ages, irrespective of nostalgia and general kitsch. Never was so much sheet metal wrapped around such a large chassis with so few mistakes.

So I drove my gleaming 18-ft., 6-in., 4,720-lb. beauty home and began to pack.

Toolbox, suitcase, sleeping bag, Gibson J-45 guitar, hat, sunglasses, Chesterfield Kings, box of lead additive to help the old 390 V-8 ingest modern fuel, and several cans of Marvel Mystery Oil, a top lube to help free sticky valves and keep the rings happy. My luggage filled about a third of the trunk, which is larger than some apartments I've lived in.

I also took along a transmission rebuild kit, in case the old Hydra-Matic coughed its cookies and blew its ancient, time-hardened seals. A distinct possibility, I was told by many doubters and naysayers.

D-day.

I LEFT EARLY ON A BRIGHT, COLD Saturday morning, April 27. The big V-8 fired up, and the Cadillac swept out of our driveway, rumbling like a Chris-Craft.

Having once owned a rather loose 1962 Lincoln Continental that changed lanes just for fun, I was surprised to find the Cadillac's steering to be remarkably tight and precise. I have the original sales brochure that came with the car, and it says the Sixty-Two Sedan "threads its way through traffic and into parking spaces at the gentle command of its driver."

Not a bad description. The car can be hustled down a winding road, effortlessly, with two fingers on the steering wheel (don't try this in Driver's Ed, kids), and its front anti-roll bar keeps it relatively flat in corners. The long wheelbase and coil springs give you a supple, unjarring ride, and the huge, vacuum-assisted finned brake drums stop the car right now, with light pedal pressure.

Power? The 390 is not neck-snapping quick, but the car picks up its skirts and moves easily with modern traffic, cruising along at 70–80 mph with no effort. The old Hydra-Matic does its work silently and unnoticed.

A fine motorcar. Civilized.

It threaded its way through the hills and old Welsh lead-mining villages of southwestern Wisconsin and headed for the restored brick river town of Galena, Illinois, home of many antique stores and Ulysses S. Grant.

Grant was a Mississippi Valley man himself, fought his first great battles up and down the river and made his reputation here. I've always admired Grant for his slouching, informal determination and often-underrated genius for command.

Speaking of massed troops, when I got to Galena, there was a Boy Scout Jamboree in progress and the streets were filled with more scouts than I thought existed. I toured Grant's home, which was also thronged with uniformed youth. When I got back to the Cadillac, the windows and doors were covered with several hundred small nose and hand-prints.

A scout leader and his troop were standing by to hear the car start and drive away. "How much would you sell that for?" someone asked.

"Can't sell it; just restored it," I said.

"Yeah, but how much is it worth?"

"About seven thousand dollars," I replied.

The boys looked confused and troubled. Perhaps their scout leader had told them much more. Or much less.

Better not to ask.

Dropping down the winding, lovely ridge of the Great River Road, Highway 84, I hit the riverbank at Palisades State Park, then drove along the saturated flood plain, plowed farm fields glistening like wet coffee grounds. I crossed over the Mississippi at Fulton on a narrow, elegant suspension bridge with twin towers and did not hit anything while sneaking looks at the river.

"Welcome to Iowa. You make me smile."

Nice sentiment, suggesting a slow, smoldering kind of pleasure.

I whipsawed the car off Highway 67 to look at the Buffalo Bill Cody family homestead—a small 7,000-acre parcel of prime bottomland—then cruised through the Quad Cities (Quick, name all four. You forgot Bettendorf!).

Rain clouds were building, and the cool sunny day grew cold and dark. By the time I stopped for the night at Hannibal, Missouri, boyhood home of Mark Twain, it had been pouring like the end of the world for three hours. The Cadillac wipers had a bad motor switch, causing a 3–4-minute delay after switching them on. Once in motion, however, they swept the entire windshield clean in rhythmic, overlapping strokes.

Engineering Award No. 2: Best wipers I ever saw.

I awoke to a gray, misting day, then drove over to the preserved block of buildings that formed young Samuel Clemens' universe. I bought a copy of *Life on the Mississippi* at the Becky Thatcher bookstore, then took an upstairs tour of Becky Thatcher's house (real name, Laura

Wright), residence of Twain's childhood sweetheart and heroine of *Tom Sawyer*.

When I read—and reread—that favorite book as a kid, I never imagined I would one day be looking out Becky Thatcher's window, admiring the roofline of my Cadillac, with Tom Sawyer's famous white fence across the street. It's no wonder archeologists can't untangle a culture, three centuries later. Makes no sense even now.

On the way out of town, I cruised up Cardiff Hill, where Tom and Huck used to watch the river, then drove down the famous Highway 61 toward Wentzville, west of St. Louis. There I made my mandatory stop at the sprawling, fenced-in rural estate of Chuck Berry.

I photographed the Cadillac outside the front gates, fostering a faint hope that Chuck himself would walk out and say, "Hey, nice Caddy! Want a beer?"

When I was here 18 years ago, the Man himself pulled into the driveway as I stood beside my motorcycle. He smiled wanly and waved. He was driving a Seventies'-vintage coffee-colored Cadillac.

No sign of Chuck this time, so I rolled south in a heavy downpour ("rainwater blowin' up under the hood") and finally hit clear, warm weather at Memphis. I checked into the historic Peabody Hotel, then went down Beale Street to B.B. King's club, for a quiet Monday night of listening to a good local blues band.

In the morning I drove out to Graceland for a look at Elvis' car museum to see if he had any good Cadillacs.

He did. A purple '57 Eldorado convertible (legend says Elvis crushed a handful of grapes on the fender to show the dealer what color he wanted it painted) and a pink 1956 Fleetwood he gave to his parents.

I was going to eat lunch at the Fifties' redolent cafe and shopping mall across the street from the Presley home, but the crowds and the heavy commercial nostalgia of the place suddenly overwhelmed me and I bolted.

Time to head for the Delta.

The Mississippi Delta is a broad flood plain that begins just south of Memphis and ends at Vicksburg. Dull, flat cotton country, it has somehow produced more great blues musicians than any place on earth—Robert Johnson, Son House, Charlie Patton, Muddy Waters, Howlin' Wolf, Sonny Boy Williamson, B. B. King. . . . The list would fill this page, if I let it.

The epicenter of this tradition is Clarksdale, Mississippi, and the sprawling cotton plantations around it—Stovall Plantation, Dockery Farms—whose many laborers provided both audience and talent.

I rolled into Clarksdale late on a sunny afternoon and checked into the legendary Riverside Hotel, a onetime black hospital where Bessie Smith died after her car accident on Highway 61.

It was converted to a hotel in the early Forties and became a traditional residence for traveling musicians. It is now run by a gentle old black woman named ZL Hill (not initials; "ZL" is her first name).

The Riverside turned out to be a clean but rickety place on Sunflower Street, a main building flanked by small, separate units, all furnished with an odd assortment of garage-sale furniture. Clean sheets, hot water, window air conditioner; everything worked. An authentic old place, rich in history. Forty dollars a night.

I had a nice long talk with ZL Hill. She remembered all the great bluesmen and women, and said Ike and Tina Turner had lived at the hotel for some time. She had grown up in Port Gibson with Bessie Smith and knew her well. Clarksdale had gone downhill, she said sadly. "Used to be a lively place, people dancing and jukin' around, but now kids want to fight and clown all the time and use that bad language. They don't respect older people. It's the crack and drugs . . . "

I sat outside that evening on a lawn chair in front of my room, sipping a little rye and playing a few Robert Johnson songs on my Gibson J-45. It seemed like the right thing to do. Maybe the aura of the place would infuse my guitar, or my clumsy hands.

Robert Johnson is probably the greatest bluesman who ever lived—the rock upon which the church of blues is built. He died young, after only a couple of recording sessions, given a poisoned drink by a jealous husband at a country juke joint near Quito, Mississippi.

There is a legend that he started out with no talent, but went to the crossroads at midnight where (as everybody knows) you can trade your soul to the devil for musical talent. There was no other explanation. Suddenly, he showed up at local clubs, playing as if possessed.

Maybe this would work for me.

Blues fans have been debating for years, however, over which crossroads he had gone to. One of the candidates was right in Clarksdale, at the junction of the two great blues highways, 49 and 61.

I went there and found a busy intersection flanked by gas stations and fast-food joints. If the devil showed up there now, he'd be hit by a truck about every 3 seconds. Or a Japanese pickup pulsing with rap music. Or my Cadillac.

Maybe any crossroads would work, the lonelier the better.

The next morning, on my way out of town, I stopped at the small but nicely conceived Delta Blues Museum and ran into a group of blues fans from Norway, no less. They told me they had thought of staying at the Riverside Hotel, but drove by and thought the neighborhood looked too rough, so they stayed at a new motel out on Highway 61.

Too rough?

To my eternal credit, I did not say, "Perhaps this is why Muddy Waters did not come from Oslo."

Authenticity is a scary thing. Almost always.

That day the Cadillac and I set out with two goals: to find the grave of Sonny Boy Williamson, the greatest blues harp (harmonica) player who ever lived, in my opinion, and the grave of Robert Johnson.

I found Sonny Boy's grave at the ruins of Whitfield Church, a few miles outside Tutwiler, Mississippi, with the help of a local retired carpenter who was hunting for arrowheads. Williamson's neat marble headstone sat in a small oasis of mown grass in an otherwise overgrown cemetery. The names of his best-known songs were chiseled in the stone. "One Way Out" remains my favorite. Our garage blues band plays the song, and I have a picture of Sonny Boy and his own band on the wall of our living room.

Robert Johnson's grave was not so easy. He was murdered at the Three Forks Store, off Highway 7, and his death certificate says he's buried at the nearby Payne Baptist Church in Quito. An ex-girlfriend, however, claimed he was buried at Mt. Zion Baptist Church, 3 miles south. Blues fans have erected monuments at both places.

At the Payne Baptist Church, a 75-year-old gent named Miller Carter stopped to talk to me. He was pushing a lawnmower along the road. He remembered when Johnson was killed in 1938, but never heard him play. "Black folks had a 10 o'clock curfew then, so if you went to a juke joint, you couldn't get home. You had to stay there all night, and I had to work in the morning. Those cops caught you on the road after ten, they'd tear you up good."

Carter said he thought Johnson was buried 3 miles south, at Mt. Zion.

"Why?" I asked.

"They got a nicer headstone there," he said, smiling.

Indeed they did. I found the place, and the stone was a large obelisk with inscriptions on all four sides, also with a list of famous songs: "Love in Vain," "Sweet Home Chicago," "Cross Road Blues," "Rambling on My Mind," "Walking Blues," "Come on in My Kitchen," "Stop Breaking Down Blues," etc.

What a guy.

I sat on the fender of the Cadillac for a long time, toasted Johnson with a sacramental nip of Old Overholt and wondered at the fragile thread of chance and eccentric scholarship that allowed these powerful, almost-lost songs to resonate so clearly for later generations.

We humans have our faults, but we are, in many ways, a great species. "Here's to us," I said, raising my brown paper bag toward Johnson's tombstone.

SO I LEFT THE TWIN TOMBS of Robert Johnson and drove south, through many lonely crossroads, evening approaching with a full moon counterbalancing a huge setting sun on the horizon, shadows growing long. Though the Delta is largely flat and cultivated, the road occasionally dips into small pockets of swamp and shaded bayou, the remains of the old panther-infested forest that was cleared for cotton farming, cool spots where people fish off bridges. You see abandoned sharecropper shacks, forgotten churches and failed country stores—what V.S. Naipaul called the "southern landscape of small ruins."

As I drove south through the Delta that evening, I tried to think of the correct word to describe the Cadillac's mode of progress. An old Citroën 2CV I once drove cross-country "trundled" down the road, my co-driver and I decided, while my Lincoln Continental "walooned." What did the Caddy do?

It felt somehow nautical, but not in that sloppy, pitching and rolling sense. I finally decided that the Cadillac "cuts," as a Coast Guard cutter does. Or a naval cruiser, nicely making way and slicing through waves untroubled by all but the largest swells.

Sunset found me docking in Vicksburg, at a motel right near the gates of the battlefield of that once-besieged hilltop city. Some of Grant's work again, along with his friend Gen. William Tecumseh Sherman—two men for whom almost no streets are named in Mississippi, I noticed. I toured the battlefield in the morning and stopped for gas, doing my usual chemistry experiment with Instead-O-Lead and Marvel Mystery Oil.

The Cadillac was doing better than I'd expected with fuel, getting between 12 and 15 mpg, depending on the amount of city driving. It liked open, fast roads and steady cruising. It was running like a watch and had used no discernible oil or transmission fluid.

In the warm southern weather, I was driving with all four windows down and had discovered that the wind flow through the Cadillac's interior was almost perfect. No buffeting or wind noise, but a sense of being cooled by a light, pleasant breeze. Serene cruising.

My Mustang (or almost any current sedan) felt like a cave by comparison. In the Cadillac, you feel as if you are sitting in the shade of a wing supported by glass—or in air—rather than in a dark room with windows cut out of the walls.

I suddenly felt a little sheepish about all the "land-yacht" jokes I'd made about these cars over the years. It did them a disservice. They were superbly engineered and beautifully thought out in detail. Big, yes, but you might as well make fun of a Beach Staggerwing because it's not a Cessna 150.

Following the roller-coaster, kudzu-shaded highway, I took a short side-trip to the famous Windsor Ruins. Windsor was a grand mansion that burned down in the 1890s, leaving behind nothing but a massive collection of pillars. Mark Twain once used its bright party lights as a guidepost on the banks of the Mississippi.

From there I crossed into Louisiana at last, with roadside forests ever more towering and dark, pools of swamp water greener, Spanish moss thicker. Real bayou country. Ignoring a chance to visit a hundred beautiful old River Road plantations (someday, perhaps), I pressed on to New Orleans.

Ah, New Orleans. Ain't nothin' like it nowhere.

A big tourist town, but, like Paris, it's larger and grander than all the generations that pass through and live there for their fleeting hour. It's an opera set of a city, full of life and color and the aura of eternal decay and renewal, water everywhere. It always feels like the morning after the best day of your life, which is about to start all over again . . .

You come in on the Eighth Wonder of the World, the highway on stilts that crosses Lake Pontchartrain and drop down into the French Quarter, which smells like raw oysters and garlic and the river. Then you drive your '63 Cadillac all over the place on one-way streets trying to find the Quarter House, your hotel for the week, cruising through thick, slow-moving pedestrian traffic as bystanders heap praise and shouts of joy on your car: "Oh, man! Great Caddy!" and "I *want* it! Give me a ride!" At a stoplight a young man in sunglasses leans into the passenger window and gives me the okay circle of thumb and first finger. "This," he says quietly, "is a fine Cadillac."

The town is full of music people, and music people love old Cadillacs. I feel like a hero, all but showered with tickertape, before I find our hotel. And there is my good pal Rich Homan, and his two friends Mark Phelan and Kevin Patterson, who gather here every year for the Jazz & Heritage Festival to share expenses on a hotel room and hear music. I throw my sleeping bag on the hotel room floor and we hit the town.

My three friends have shifted over to New Orleans Vampire Time. They sleep until late afternoon, then get up in search of food, drink and music, returning to the room at sunrise. We walk the Quarter, have coffee and beignets at the French Market Cafe at 3:00 a.m., hear my favorite band, the subdudes (small "s"), at Tipitina's and go see Van Morrison and Allen Toussaint (knockout show) at the Fairgrounds.

One night we sit on a second-floor porch cafe overlooking Bourbon Street, eating oysters and drinking beer, with a warm gulf breeze blowing lightly and music pouring from the bars and clubs below, and I realize this is it:

This is the night I dreamed about in midwinter, the evening containing all the good things one might find at the other end of the river. The floating twig has made it from Badfish Creek to New Orleans. It can really be done.

All you need is gas money, a river to follow, gravity and a good long car.

It was raining when I got home, but that was okay. It took me four days to get there, with a one-day stop in the lovely old college town of Oxford, Mississippi. There I visited the home and environs of William Faulkner, whose beautiful juggernaut of words had carried me deep into the South long before I ever saw it.

At the end of the trip the Cadillac had 77,186 miles on the odometer, having gone 2,701 miles on the round trip. It used two quarts of oil, one quart of transmission fluid, no water and averaged 13.6 mpg.

Repairs? I burned out a headlight in Vicksburg and replaced it at an auto parts store. No other trouble or adjustments.

Every other old car I've driven across the country has exacted some toll for its age, penalized you with some crankiness or difficulty of operation for its character or sportiness. Not the Cadillac, though. It is probably the most owner-friendly car, new or old, I've ever taken on a road trip. And it's certainly the most graceful and elegant. But then it was built in the Sixties, which was a very good time for American cars. Most problems had been worked out and they were pretty reliable by then. They stopped and handled reasonably well, and they were good-looking, powerful and easy to repair. Cars got better and safer in small increments after that, but they often gave something up, traded something in. Usually a little bit of soul.

The Cadillac was built in that short period of history where style intersected with science and neither overwhelmed the other. A car, you might say, from the crossroads.

A Private Letter to Henry the Second

Wherein Our Man Smith Goes for a Furtive Joy Ride around Carroll Shelby's Parking Lot in One of Henry Ford II's Le Mans Cars

By Steve Smith

Car and Driver,

April 1967

DEAR MR. FORD:

Anyway, I wanted to thank you for letting me drive one of your race cars. You probably didn't know about that, but we were out at Shelby's testing one of his GT 500s, and somebody figured it'd be a *great* idea to roll out one of your Ford Mk. II 427s—the big red number 3 car Gurney drove at Le Mans—to use as a prop. You know, to show how the scoops on the Mk. II look so much like the scoops on the GT 500.

Anyway, Mr. Ford, nobody exactly said I could drive it, but nobody exactly said I *couldn't*, either. I mean, it was just sitting there after the mechanic had driven it over, so it was all nice and warm and ready to go. It had to be moved, and the mechanic had his back turned, so I just kind of pulled open that big wrap-over door and sat down on the door sill. I don't know what came over me, Mr. Ford. All I meant to do was push it out of the way a little, but why walk when you can drive, right? I mean, it was pretty difficult trying to wiggle my legs around and under that steering wheel and ease myself into that long hammock of a seat, so I must have known what was in my mind.

Anyway, I just couldn't *help* myself. I didn't need to adjust anything, because Dan is only a few inches taller than I am, and I could get a good grip on the wheel and reach the pedals and the switches and the gearshift lever. I'd seen the mechanic flip off a switch on the left marked "BAT." and another one over on the right marked "IGN." so I just flipped them back again. Everything might have been all right even then. I might just have sat there grinning like an idiot and listening to the fuel pump clicking and feeling how the seam in the leather covering on the steering wheel was coming unstitched where Dan had wrenched it back and forth at Le Mans, but the starter switch was on the ignition toggle, and I must have pushed a little too hard, because the engine fired right up. Not at all like your usual fussy racing engines, Mr. Ford—more like a regular passenger car engine. But it sure didn't sound like a passenger car engine—more like a hibernating bear who just happens to be a light sleeper. Boy, that mechanic must of been *deaf*. By the time he heard all that bellowing and turned around to see what was happening, I had already doped out that shift gate. Just took a piece of sheet metal and snipped an H-pattern in it, eh, Mr. Ford? Doesn't look too pretty, especially with that one piece crimped over to lock out reverse, but it sure gets the job done.

Anyway, I probably would have shut it down right then and there, except that when they washed down the car (for the photos, remember?) a lot of water seeped inside and soaked the seat. I guess all that water doesn't leak in when you're going down the Mulsanne straight at 21.5 mph—maybe the body doesn't even get wet—but the bottom of my pants where I was wedged down into that tight bucket seat was *soaked*, and if I'd been hauled out of there, everybody would have thought I'd wet my pants from all the excitement. I'll admit I was pretty nervous at that point; I mean we had this girl model and all.

Anyway, I just pushed on that old clutch there and snicked it into first gear. That clutch is a *bear*, Mr. Ford. Really fights back at you, don't it? With a clutch spring like that, I thought for sure it'd grab too quick and the engine would stall and it'd be all over. But do you know what, Mr. Ford? That's the smoothest darn clutch I've ever driven. I wasn't sure I was giving the engine enough gas. You know how your usual racer, you have to peg the tach and try to feather a dog clutch while the engine goes *wheep*-blubba-dubba-*wheep-wheep*-cough-blubba-*wheer*row-chirp-*screEE-VAR-OO-OO-OOM!*, well, nossir, not *your* racer. Just as smooth as you please from 1,500 rpm, like a diesel tractor-trailer in compound low.

Anyway, I'm sorry, Mr. Ford, but I was up to here in it anyway. Might as well be hung for a sheep as a lamb, right? That mechanic was holding onto the tail for dear life, I can tell you, with sparks shooting out from under his shoes as I towed him around in first gear. I mean, the acceleration was so *strong* that I didn't even feel it when he finally let go. I tugged the gearshift knob back toward second—easy as a finger through whipped cream—and floored it. Oh, don't worry, Mr. Ford, I didn't take it over 5,000 rpm. Well, maybe 5,500. And boy, talk about your funny cars at the drags! It just chomps down on the asphalt and tries to jump out from under you. You have to grit your teeth and ginch up your face just to remember which way the world is pointing. I mean, you know you're not going to black out or anything, but you hold on real tight—just in case—even when it's you yourself holding the throttle open.

Anyway, that's when I found out you'd disconnected the brake. I can't say as how I blame you. If I had a $50,000 car like yours, I'd probably disable something too, just to keep guys like me from driving off in the thing. I mean, how far can you get without brakes? So the only way to stop it was spin it out. I'd used up all the space I'd had, and it was either spin it or drive it through the Anchor Chain-Link Fence and out onto the runway of the Los Angeles International Airport ("LAX;" you've probably seen it on your baggage tags, Mr. Ford).

Anyway, I shut my eyes tight and cranked that steering wheel around for all I was worth, and gave it the gun. *Holy G-Loads*, Mr. Ford, if that darn racer of yours didn't make a U-turn in about its own length. In fact, I was so surprised, I made two or three U-turns before I realized it wouldn't spin out. There I was, whipping around in a 60-foot circle, with that big Galaxie engine thumping away behind my left ear and the cockpit filling up with oil blow-by, rubber dust, and confusion.

Anyway, by the time I'd got it straightened out, I felt kinda weak and dizzy, and I must not of seen those guys running out in front of me, trying to wave me down. They were all in shirt sleeves—Shelby's executives from upstairs. They must of seen me from the window and wondered what in heck was going on down there in the parking lot. They were pouring out of that administration building like it was a Red Alert.

Anyway, I guess you hadn't told them about disconnecting the brake, eh? Because they wouldn't get out of the way, and I had to veer around a lot to miss them. Making your car as wide as a houseboat is long didn't help any, either, Mr. Ford, or maybe it just seemed that way because of sitting down so low on the wrong side of the car. I tried to warn them about the brakes, but I guess they couldn't hear me over the bellow of that great big engine.

Anyway, when they saw I couldn't stop, they tried to run away. Boy! Shelby's executives sure can run when they have to, Mr. Ford. I don't know if you do anything like this, but you ought to give Shelby a medal for hiring

Olympic track stars to manage his company. But me chasing them finally seemed to get them *mad*, and they turned around and started chasing *me*. I was doing a pretty good job of zig-zagging between them, but they fooled me by throwing up a solid wall of human flesh around me. I was trapped.

Anyway, I figured I had enough strength left for one last stab at the brakes. You never know, right? So I leaned on that pedal like I was gonna press about 650 pounds, and whaddaya know? I hear this little click! Maybe that's a brake light switch, I say to myself, and I push even harder. Sure enough, the car shudders a little, and the engine slows down a smidgeon. Well, I never did get to find out how good the brakes really are, because by that time, Shelby's guys had fingers stuck in just about every crack, slot, vent, scoop, and louvre—and who knows better than you, Mr. Ford, how many of those there are on that car of yours—and were dragging me to a stop. But you really ought to do something about those brakes, sir. Not even Burt Lancaster could push on those binders without rupturing himself.

Anyway, the point is, Mr. Ford, Shelby's guys threw me out of there so fast I think my wallet fell out in the car. I mean, I know it's *your* car, because Shelby's guys pointed that out to me (and the photographer and the model) in no uncertain terms. So what I'd like to say is thanks for letting me drive the smoothest, easiest, nicest goshdarn race car in the whole world, and I'd like to ask you if you could spare a little time—to go over to Shelby's with me. It'll only take a minute. I'll just walk straight up to the car and kinda slide down in there to look for my wallet and . . . hey, sir . . . maybe we could go for a quick ride around the parking lot?

Anyway, sincerely yours, Mr. Ford,

Steve Smith

It All Boils Down to This

By Tom McCahill

The Modern Sports Car,

1954

BY NOW, IF YOU HAVE READ ALL THE MUMBO-JUMBO that has gone before, you must realize sports car people are just a few notches different than the dyed-in-the-wool, conventional mugwump. In a sentence or even less, a word, it all boils down to one simple fact—sports car people have the "feel." Maybe it's an appreciation for the better things of life, or a normal revolt against regimentation on a commercial scale.

One thing is certain, the true sports car man revolts against taking to the highways like a duck parading with millions of other ducks in vulgar creations created to catch the eye of vulgar people.

As this book is being put to bed, the writer has noticed an increase of idiotic Sunday newspaper supplement articles slanted to soothe the Detroit ad buyers by condemning all types of sports cars and sports car owners. These are generally written by intellectual delinquents with no mechanical, and very little family, background. These Union Square soap-box editorialists usually have the literary talent of a Borneo gorilla and usually only succeed, I am glad to say, in interesting more people in sports cars.

Unless you have the "feel," sports cars definitely are not for you. The man who doesn't feel that his MG, Austin-Healey, or Jaguar is a sporting and adventure companion just doesn't have it. I realize many sports cars are bought primarily for show-off purposes, but this is only a small part of what the sports car man knows about the sport.

Let's take a hypothetical trip in a sports car, all alone. Actually, although you never tell this to your wife, sports car driving on a trip is more fun alone. You don't need your wife or a close friend to keep you company—your sports car is your good companion. It is impossible to get this feeling with a cold, Detroit commercial stamping.

Let's say your car is a little Austin-Healey. Everything about it is top quality of the very finest material. Unlike your Cadillac, Lincoln, or Chrysler, you have a *feeling* for this little car, an affectionate regard almost like one you have for that good dog you own. When on the highway, you often talk to the little car as if it had warm blood running through its veins. Well, it *is* a friend, and warm liquid *is* running through its veins, though in this case it doesn't happen to be blood.

After the car has given you exceptional pleasure on a fast 100 or 200 mile jog, which may have been a business trip or to another friend's for a weekend, you often, as you get out, give the fender a friendly pat of thanks. (How long since you've patted a Cadillac?) The man who does this has the "feel." He may never race, enter a hillclimb or a rally, but he has the "feel." Let's say you work in New York and live in New York, and garage your little jewel in a not-too-tidy auto hotel where it is continually surrounded by unaesthetic iron. You find yourself often just before you turn out the lights at night wondering how they're treating your pal over in the garage and whether dirty hands have been marring its highly polished finish.

Our hypothetical trip, and it actually happens every day to thousands, starts in your office. Old Joe Blow, the firm's wealthiest client, wants you to come down to his plantation near New Iberia in Louisiana for some late fall duck shooting and the possible discussion of future plans.

Your secretary checks the air schedule and trains. By plane, it's just an afternoon's hop, but you elect to do something that has the other men in the office slightly suspecting your sanity when you announce that you're going to drive down in your Austin-Healey.

You don't get mad at the many questions, such as, "Supposin' it rains, can you keep dry in that bucket?" or remarks that it would be a lot safer and cheaper to fly. You don't try and explain—these fellows have all the adventure in their souls of a meek ribbon clerk and couldn't understand if you told them. So you just say goodbye when the time comes and leave the office ignoring a wisecrack or two about walking back or hitchhiking.

It is exactly four A.M. when your alarm clock lets go like a furious rattlesnake and, with high adventure ahead, you're out of bed and wide awake in the first jump. Twenty minutes later the sleepy night elevator man in your apartment building eyes you suspiciously as he takes your gun case, duffel, and kit bag. You leave these in the lobby and make the two block brisk walk to the garage. The night garage man openly looks at you with suspicion as he shufflingly leads you over to junior, parked way in the back between two man-made mountains of chrome. You give it a fond pat on its left flank and slip behind the wheel.

The top is up and the passenger side curtain is on. With the adequate heater and your big greatcoat you won't need the other side curtain as the temperature outside is a mild 40 degrees. You turn the key and instantly the engine roars awake. You let it idle for several minutes and then pull up to the gas pumps. The tank filled, you drive back to your apartment for the bags and your gun and, with these in place in the trunk, you head for the Jersey Turnpike.

The speed limit is 60 mph and in overdrive the engine is happily loafing at 70, a speed you calculate will not attract John Law. You are just settling down to the trip when a turnpike all-night restaurant-service-station looms, reminding you you haven't even had your coffee. After a good, solid breakfast (the driver on a long trip needs plenty of fuel just as the car does), you emerge from the diner and find that it's just daylight.

Now you're really on your way at your steady 70. The car wants to go faster, but you hold off, the cops are thick on this throughway (in more ways than one). As the sun comes up over your left shoulder, signs indicate Philadelphia somewhere on your right.

The engine is purring a song that no symphony could compare to. As they say in the Ozarks, boy, you're *really* livin' it up!—and you know it. Ever since you pulled out of the tunnel back in New York, there's been a tingle in your spine, a real, perpetual, underplaying thrill that seems continuous. In a short time you're over the Delaware Memorial Bridge, a short shot through Delaware into Maryland and onto the great Chesapeake Bay Bridge.

As you cross the bridge you slow down, noticing several flocks of canvasbacks trading back and forth. The fact that you're going all the way to Louisiana for duck shooting momentarily strikes you as a little silly when right now you are over some of the greatest duck shooting water in the world. Around Annapolis and over to U.S. 301, and then the high Potomac Bridge and more ducks.

Now you are in Virginia. At Port Royal you pull up for a second breakfast and re-fueling.

It's only a quarter of eleven, the day's young. A fast trip through the City of Richmond, and then a s-l-o-w drag through Colonial Heights and Petersburg. Once clear of Petersburg you snap back to life quickly and head for South Hill and Raleigh.

At three o'clock you're not even tired, though you've been driving ten hours, at moderate speeds for the Healey—which made the trip effortless. In Raleigh you get yourself a late, late lunch or an early dinner and head for Southern Pines on U.S. 1, 70 miles further south. In the outskirts of Southern Pines you find a beautiful motel with a restaurant and a vacancy, so you pull in.

It is five o'clock and you've covered just under 600 miles. The year before when you made this same trip in your Detroit car you were pooped, but tonight after a quick shower and shave (so you won't have to do it in the morning) you feel like a million dollars.

Of course you had to answer with a smile several times in the restaurant when the motel manager and one or two other friendly people asked, aghast, "You mean to say you came all the way from New York in *that* little thing today?" Then they'll usually add, "Why, that would even be a long trip for my big Buick [or DeSoto]."

You smile back friendly enough, but don't try and explain. Ignorance knows no limitations and your mission in life is not the education of the multitude.

Happily, you find the motel coffee shop open at six the next morning. After a big breakfast of flapjacks and grits, you're on your way once again, bowling down U.S. 1.

On the way back you'll come by way of Atlanta and the Piedmont Trail, but this time you'll stay on U.S. 1 until just south of Augusta where you head west for Macon and Montgomery. Down to Mobile and along the Gulf on #90 to New Orleans. Then the short run to the plantation on Vermilion Bay where the mallards come up like thunder just at the break of day.

By nine o'clock you've taken the passenger side curtain out, and by ten, when you stop for a second breakfast and re-fueling, down comes the top itself. It's late November, but the temperature is in the high sixties.

Just after eleven o'clock you make the swing west a few miles south of Augusta. The deeper you penetrate the South, the more attention your car gets, especially from the children on the roads, who wave and yell gleefully as you pass.

That afternoon, after leaving Montgomery, you head south toward the Gulf and at night you pull into another motel near Mobile. At noon next day you are in New Orleans and stop off to see your old friends at La Louisianne, that fabulous restaurant, for a meal that no king has been able to buy for some time.

By mid-afternoon your little gem, tooling along under the moss-laden trees, sounds just as solid as when you left the garage many miles back. You are now driving in your shirt sleeves and are feeling pretty smug about yourself and life in general since you've just blown off a couple of Louisiana hot-rodders with ease.

As you pull up to the plantation you give the instrument board an extra-friendly pat for a job well done—but your host won't let you leave the car. He has to feel the seats, kick the tires and touch the paint, then the old routine again, "You came all the way from New York down here in *that*?" By now you're feeling so good about everything, so superior to most of your fellow earth-dwellers, you almost tell Old Joe Blow to go climb a tree—in fact, you do, but you're smiling.

Three days of wonderful duck shooting and another big order from Joe and you're on your way home. You find as you are tooling over the highway some of the roads in the south are long, fast and deserted. You pass 100 mph on several occasions and cruise at 80 or 85 much of the time. You're all alone, and you sing to yourself as you haven't sung in years, and whistle off-key as much as you please; the car doesn't protest, and you never have to slow for a corner but just keep bowling along.

Old Betsy, your prize double barrel gun, did you proud, and you suddenly realize that the deep affection you have for this gun that was given to you before you entered college is similar to the feeling you have for this car. Both fine pieces of sporting equipment and both good companions.

You understand this, you have the "feel." Those realists can have their reality, this is for you. A man's gun and a man's car.

As you unload in front of the apartment you realize a great adventure—nothing really much, no lions, no tigers, no rescues at sea—but a great adventure you and your friend, the car, a sports car, have had together.

If you have it, you'll know what I mean. If you haven't, it's just too damn bad.

Relief at Seventy

By Gordon Baxter

Car and Driver,

May 1982

'VE LEARNED SOMETHING FROM EVERY GOOD DRIVER I've ever ridden with. Stayed tuned to what he was sensing, felt the subtle shift of weight from wheel to wheel. Remembered the downshifting onrush of corners as he saw them, the braking point, the time to feed it again. I've learned, always wishing there were more. Better machines, better drivers to sit beside. I always hunger for the limits. "Works of art are indeed always products of having been in danger, of having gone to the very end in an experience, to where man can go no further."—Rainer Maria Rilke (1875–1926), *Letters*.

I am not ashamed of the times I have made a fool of myself. I once tried to learn four-wheel drifts at low speeds on glare ice. I brought out the neighbors, shouting, and paid for the shrubbery. But I've never had a car over on its back. Never hurt anyone.

I have never driven in real competition, so I have no idea of how good or bad I may be. In midnight drags back in my salad days I had a full-house Ford tudor that looked stock except for the 800-16s on the rear. I could leave its driveshaft lying hot and smoking on the pave any time I wanted to. But by careful milking I could devour those first-year Olds 88s and Hudson Hornets, which had six pistons, big as syrup cans. That was back when those cars were the devourers.

Fiftyish and bifocaled now, but the tiger still alive, I drive pussycats with good handling. My frontal lobe holds the whip over the tiger, who still pads to and fro in the dark back caves of my mind. A reasonable man must bargain honestly with his years. I am a survivor more than a hero.

And yet I come before this company of good drivers, men the age of my sons, and offer to you something that may be of value: a driving technique, if not invented by me, at least being first told by me.

My native state of Texas is embarrassingly big. Not so big as Alaska, true, but Alaska is not paved with tens of thousands of miles of straight, flat asphalt that sometimes notches both horizons, the one before you and the one behind you, without a curve or a side road to surprise you. There are deer, both buck and John, to test you. A John Deere tractor on the road in transport gear appears to be standing still when suddenly uncovered in a low valley from a rise that has lifted your car on its springs. But Texas farm-to-market roads are cut to a 50-foot right-of-way instead of the usual 35, and with a steady hand and good steel radials a combine can be taken on either side. Do not go back, however, to help him find his hat. He will kill you, and tell God you died.

I drive to Dallas a lot. It's five hours at a steady 70, if you do not stop to eat. A long way. You could fit the entire troubled Middle East into central Texas.

We respect the Texas State Highway Patrol. DPS, we call them—Department of Public Safety. Trained in driving academies, the trooper in his broad-brimmed hat is mounted in a black-and-white Plymouth that shudders when it idles. Do not contest him. But he is fair, and unspoken is the belief that the DPS will allow you 9 mph over 55 if you look sane and sober and are not crowding the weather or the traffic.

Texas plants wildflowers along the beautiful, loping miles. A Texas trip is a car tester. Along the endless open miles you see fan belts, twisted and blown treads, and many "last chance" signs at desolate little wayside stops: "Last chance for fuel, for coffee, or whatever needs may be pressing you."

We plan a Texas cross-country as carefully as any pilot would. We figure time, distance, fuel, and many of us carry a thermos of hundred-mile coffee.

The coffee solves one problem, creates another: to ride on into the pain and pressure, or to make an average-destroying pit stop. This is how I discovered, may have invented, the 70-mph relief.

At 70, even at 60, there is sufficient slipstream around a slightly opened car door to create a powerful low-pressure area. A localized venturi effect. Do not be encumbered. All lower garments should be down around the knees; farther down hogties the ankles, and the feet must be apart. The right is positioned steadily on the accelerator, the left slightly drawn back to provide a strong knee brace against the open door without distraction. Serious concentration is vital to this operation.

The seat harness must be removed, of course, in order to roll one's body to the left, hips thrust as far as possible toward the rush at the door. Pick light traffic—the novice may swerve or veer a little at first. Then have confidence in the venturi effect.

It is here that my experience in aeronautical matters has proven to be so valuable to me, although this feat is not possible in light cabin planes so far as I know. The problem in planes is that the door can't be closed again against the extreme low-pressure area at that point of the fuselage curve. Also, the 100-mph-plus speeds tend to empty the cabin of vital navigational charts, loose items of clothing, small pets, etc. An open door in most

general-aviation aircraft is not a control hazard, but there usually must be a landing to close it, and in the interval all communications will be in sign language.

In aviation there are devices available from pilots'-accessory stores that will aid a pilot in matching the five-hour endurance of his aircraft. But we are not speaking here of airplanes, we are speaking of sports cars. A sports car is any car that is driven in a sporting manner.

I learned of the venturi effect through flying, and with enough passage of air you may count on this phenomenon with utter certainty. There is a vacuum, a funneling and channeling effect, on the downstream side of a venturi. Your partially opened car door provides the venturi. Experience will teach you the optimum speeds and the best door-opening angle.

The two primary elements here, other than the driver's individual nervous system, are a solidly braced knee at the open door and close attention to driving with one hand. Keep your eye on the road, trusting that everything else is going according to proven scientific principles. Do not keep glancing away from the road with an overconcern about neatness. The partial vacuum and centered wind pressures will direct everything for you with only the most casual aim. Drive the car.

Out of social courtesy, avoid populated areas. But insofar as I know, only the speed laws are being violated here. Avoid tailgating, so as not to have sudden need of your left foot for braking. Even if you are a skilled right-foot brake man, braking will cause an unwanted drop in wind velocity. A sudden deceleration might cause the open door to swing forward and cause eddies and burbles in the slipstream and a reversing of the venturi effect.

Swerving or hard braking might also upset your own delicate balance. There is some element of chance in this system of relief, but there is no truly flawless scheme. In this case your door is open and you are leaning toward it—braced, balanced, but with no seatbelt. A mishap might leave you to be found on some desolate stretch of highway, pants down around your knees, and the wreckage of your car perhaps miles on down the road. Friends, relatives, county officials, and the local press would forever be at a loss to explain how you did it.

In this age of elevated awareness of time and energy management, we think the 70-mph-relief concept might be of value to some. The idea is not without historical precedent. During the great age of steam, the then carefully managed railroads provided at intervals a long, shallow trough of water between the rails, and a signal board to tell the engineer when to deploy the scoop beneath his mighty, rushing locomotive to fill the tender with boiler feed water without the costly and time-consuming tank stops.

What we have here, in essence, is the same concept with reverse flow. Slightly hazardous, yes. But so is space flight, and man's reach should always exceed his grasp.

CHAPTER 4

The Racing Bug Bites Fast

1971:
The Race
That Shook
the World

By Brock Yates

Cannonball! World's Greatest Outlaw Road Race,

2002

T HE DRIVERS' MEETING WAS BRIEF. I outlined the Rule once again, noting that we would start from the Red Ball in one-minute intervals. The team arriving at the Portofino Inn in Redondo Beach in the briefest elapsed time—to be documented by the electronic time clocks at the Red Ball and at the Portofino's registration desk—would be the winner. Beyond that, everybody was on his own.

The cars had been parked on the main floor of the Red Ball, lined up under the light of the bare ceiling bulbs. There was the Little Rock van, with its spectacular red, white, and blue paint work; the red and white PRDA van, its flanks covered with sponsors' decals and large type proclaiming: "THE POLISH RACING DRIVERS OF AMERICA GO COAST-TO-COAST NONSTOP!" By contrast, *Moon Trash II* had been painted, bumper to bumper, in a murky coat of flat black. Crouching beside it was our Ferrari Daytona, its mirror-polished, Sunoco blue paint glinting in the raw light, its elegant finish highlighted by a masterful network of yellow pinstriping, and its fenders amply covered with decals from sponsors that Kirk White's staff had attracted to help defray expenses. Gurney's and my names were displayed in neat lettering under the windows. It had been the first time I'd seen the car up close. "It's been cunningly disguised as a racing car!" I gasped.

Wind was kicking up litter on 31st Street as the midnight starting time approached. While the first four cars departed, Gurney and I went off to gather up some provisions at an all-night delicatessen.

We rolled the Ferrari out of the Red Ball and onto the dark street. As a cluster of friends stood by, Gurney and I fitted our gear around the seats and wound ourselves into the elaborate seat belts and shoulder harnesses. We were set. Already the PRDA, the Cadillac, the MG, and the Little Rock van were on the road. *Moon Trash II* would leave half an hour after us, while Broderick's motor home and the Bruerton brothers would depart later in the day.

Dan would drive the first leg. He cranked the engine over, and a potent, whirring rumble rose out of the Ferrari's long hood. He flipped on the headlights, and the black leather cockpit glowed with the soft, green luster of the large instrument panel. A friend stamped out tickets on the Red Ball time clock—our official record of departure—and amid a tiny chorus of windswept cheers, we accelerated away, roaring down 31st Street toward the Lincoln Tunnel and California. We went about 200 feet. The stoplight at the corner of 31st and Lexington winked red as we approached, and we sat there through its full cycle. Every cross-town light then conspired to stop us, and we were immobilized at seven intersections before reaching the tunnel.

Our route was to be different from the others'. While most planned to cut directly westward to the Pennsylvania Turnpike, I'd decided that a more northern route across Interstate 80, with a subsequent cut south to Columbus, Ohio, was fastest. It was a trifle longer, but I-80 had less traffic and fewer patrols than the Turnpike and appeared to permit higher cruising speeds. It had to be reached via a series of two-lane roads in the daytime. However, in the deep of night and with Dan driving with relish, we traversed the slow section with an average speed that approached 60 miles per hour.

Gurney began to hit his stride as we reached the broad expanses of Interstate 80. He was cruising the Ferrari at 95 miles per hour—a virtual canter. At that speed, it was so positively in contact with the road that Gurney complained it was boring to drive. To understand the excellence of a machine like the Ferrari, one had to have driven a thoroughbred sports car. There is no other way.

Lights appeared behind us. Thinking it might be the highway patrol, we backed off slightly and let the car overtake us. It was a Camaro with a man in his early 20s at the wheel. He was cruising at about 100 miles per hour. Gurney watched him sail past, then accelerated to keep pace. I knew he wouldn't let the Camaro stay ahead. He opened the throttle plates on the Ferrari's 12 carburetor throats, and the big car clawed ahead, gobbling up the distance between it and the Camaro. We rocketed past. The engine noise increased slightly, but hardly to objectionable levels. The Camaro's headlights dwindled in the distance. "That's 150, just as steady as you please," said Gurney. Then he laughed.

Dan eased back to an indicated 120 miles per hour, and we cruised down the deserted road, cutting over the humpbacked Allegheny Mountains of central Pennsylvania without effort. Gurney was driving with one hand and drinking coffee with the other when he sighted a dim pair of taillights far ahead. Again, it could be the police, so he slowed to about 100 and approached cautiously. I had 20/20 vision. I saw well at night, yet I was still trying to get some rough identification of the vehicle ahead when Gurney announced, "It's OK, it's only a Volkswagen," and got back on the throttle. Sure enough, it was a Volkswagen lumping along there in the dark, and I silently pondered the power of Gurney's eyesight. It is said that most great drivers possess uncanny eyes, but I had never taken that seriously. Now I was a believer.

I napped sporadically while Dan sailed onward, running for an hour in excess of 100 miles per hour and increasing our trip average to 81 miles per hour. That was exceptional time, but neither of us expected it to hold up across the country. Three hundred miles from Manhattan when we stopped for gas, I had leaped out and stuffed the pump nozzle into the tank before the sleepy attendant had gotten out of his chair. Dan, in the meantime, had lifted the hood and was making a routine check of the oil. This pit stop procedure would be repeated for most of the trip, with me concluding the stop by stuffing a wad of dollar bills (brought specifically for that purpose) into the startled attendant's hand, leaping into the Ferrari, and spurting back onto the highway. In this manner we were able to keep most of our stops under five minutes.

Again Gurney's miraculous eyes identified another pair of taillights. This time it was a Pennsylvania Highway Patrol Plymouth, and we slowed accordingly, falling obediently into his wake at 65 miles per hour. It felt like we were walking. We reached Columbus in six and a half hours. We were one hour ahead of the time I had run with *Moon Trash II* and were averaging 81 miles per hour. We presumed we were far ahead of the rest of the entrants.

Dan had been at the wheel nearly 12 hours when we reached St. Louis. He claimed he felt fine, and I believed him. After years of being around automobiles, one can sense a change in the reactions and movements of a driver—his very cadence with the car alters—when he becomes fatigued. Gurney was in excellent shape. As the traffic got slightly heavier west of St. Louis, we backed off our speed to about 85 miles per hour, keeping a steady eye open for the law. We passed three pimply youths in a GTO, and they tried to race us. Gurney, racer to the end, responded. The Ferrari shot ahead and, witnessing that awesome burst of acceleration, the boys gave up.

I took the wheel for the first time in mid-Missouri. Dan had driven 14 hours and 35 minutes. A long time, to be sure, but with the near-mystical ease with which a Ferrari gobbles distance, the time becomes less amazing.

"This thing is a whole new dimension in driving," I said as I accelerated onto the deserted Interstate.

The sun dropped behind a thick bank of clouds in the west, luring us into our first full night on the road. I drove for eight hours before Dan took over. We were maintaining our average speed at 83.5 miles per hour. As we reached the New Mexico border, a nasty thunderstorm lit the sky with orange fireballs and sent sheets of rain pelting against the windshield. It turned to sleet, and thickets of fog lurked in the dips of the highway. But I slept. With a man like Dan Gurney at the wheel, I think I could have rested if we'd been traversing the South Col of Mt. Everest.

We reached Albuquerque in the 24th hour of our trip, convinced that not one of our competitors was within three states of us. As we stopped at Gallup, New Mexico, we spotted several approaching cars with their grillwork smudged with snow. We had just crested the Continental Divide and were heading for the high country of eastern Arizona. If we were to encounter ice, it would be in this dark and desolate stretch. I called the Highway Patrol from a gas station, while the attendant leisurely filled the tank and Gurney sipped a can of hot soup from a vending machine. We were getting cocky, and the urgency of our earlier gas stops had given way to a kind of relaxed elegance reserved for big winners. The phone operator at the Highway Patrol was vague: some snow squalls, some fog, perhaps a little ice, but nothing alarming. With the temperature sitting somewhere in the low 30s, I took the wheel and headed for the mountains, knowing that conditions were perfect for hellish weather.

I might as well have talked to the Highway Patrol in Honolulu. The lights of Gallup still winked in the valley below when the highway became sheathed in a thick layer of slush, punctuated by long stretches of hard ice. First came the fog, then fat lumps of wet snow that flung themselves into our headlights, cutting visibility to zero. The Ferrari was slewing all over the road. It was nearly uncontrollable, and we couldn't understand why our wonderful machine had become so inept in the face of this nasty but hardly unusual squall. Dan figured it out. He recalled that the Kirk White crew had increased the tire pressure to 40 pounds for added safety and efficiency in the high-speed dry stretches. Apparently they hadn't anticipated snow. The tires, of course! As we were debating whether or not to stop and cut the pressure to perhaps 26 pounds—which would mean a double

penalty with more time lost when we hit the desert reinflate—a quartet of headlights blazed in my mirrors. A car was overtaking us at a high speed, seemingly navigating the ice without difficulty. It disappeared in a patch of fog, then surged alongside and swept past. It was a cream-colored Cadillac. Gurney and I paid it little attention, still engrossing in strategy talk about what to do with our slipping tires.

"Jesus Christ, wait a minute!" I yelled as Dan was in midsentence. "That Cadillac. That thing had New York plates! That couldn't be the those three guys from Boston!" Or could it? Stunned, even horrified that any other competitor could be that close, we pressed on, trying to narrow the distance between us and the fleeting Sedan DeVille. "If those guys are with us, where are the PRDA and some of the others that left earlier?" Gurney wondered. "In the lead, hell, we may be dead last!" I said bitterly.

The lights of the agricultural inspection station on the New Mexico–Arizona border loomed out of the fog and snow. A car was stopped under the canopy. Its trunk was up. A smiling man with a heavy shock of black hair was standing beside the machine—a cream-colored Cadillac with New York plates—while a uniformed official probed through the luggage.

"Oh, shit, that's Larry Opert," I moaned. "Those are the guys, and they're blowing our doors off!" They squirted away into the night as we stopped for our inspection. Realizing there was precious little room for any dangerous quantities of wormy peaches or infected chickens to be stowed on board the Ferrari, the officer let us pass after a few routine questions. Our cockiness of a few miles back had given way to shocked despair. Our only comfort lay in the knowledge that the Caddy had started about 20 minutes earlier and was, therefore, still behind us on elapsed time. But what about the others? Surely *somebody* was in front of the Caddy. "Us cruising across half the damn country figuring we were hundreds of miles ahead, what a bad joke that was," I mumbled as I rushed through the black, fog-shrouded night. Fortunately, the roads were improving, and while they remained wet, the ice was disappearing. The fog lifted for a minute, and we saw their taillights, perhaps a mile in front. As the road and visibility cleared, we began to gnaw at their advantage, although the Cadillac seemed to be running in the neighbor-hood of 100 miles per hour on the straight stretches. Mile after mile we traveled, losing them for long periods in the gloom, then catching tantalizing glints of red up ahead. We had them in sight by the time the outskirts of Winslow, Arizona, were breached. They pulled into a gas station. As they leaped out under the bright lit canopy, I gave them a blast of the Ferrari's air horns.

We were fully awake now, vibrating with the idea of the newfound competition. We had not sought it out; in fact, we would have been perfectly contented to putter on toward California at a leisurely pace. But now that the Cadillac was surely thundering down the road behind us, its gas tank topped off and set to run for hours, we readied ourselves to play our trump cards. That meant Dan would take over at Flagstaff, in preparation for a run down our secret shortcut—a pair of moves that might put us back into the lead. My earlier run with *Moon Trash II* had revealed that by taking Arizona Route 89 south to Prescott, then cutting toward the desert and Interstate 10, we could trim at least half an hour off the trip. To our knowledge, everyone else would take the conventional old Route 66–Interstate 40 network that was slightly shorter but more congested. Admittedly, our route was more dangerous. It involved negotiating the endless switchbacks on the 15-mile stretch of Route 89 through the Prescott National Forest and the murderous plunge down a mountainside south of Yarnell, where the road featured minimal guard rails and 1,000-foot drop-offs.

Our stop for gas in Flagstaff was slow, simply because the pumps of that particular station moved fuel into our tank at a rather lazy rate. By the time we got under way again, with Dan driving, the Cadillac had caught up. We immediately passed it after returning to the Interstate. Opert and Co. were running the big crock at its maximum, perhaps 115 miles per hour, and it was easy to see how they had not lost any time with their stop. Their tank was smaller, and therefore more quickly filled, and their top speed at night was only a few miles per hour less than ours. They were back in contention.

Gurney was opening gobs of distance on the Caddy as we rushed down the winding, pine-bordered four-lane. It was a lovely stretch of road, made even more beautiful by the thick layer of snow that had fallen on the trees earlier in the night. But the highway surface seemed clear, and Dan was running 125 miles per hour when we sailed onto the bridge that was part of a long, downhill bend to the left. It was covered with a glaze of ice. Suddenly Gurney was jabbering and his hands began a series of blinding twists of the wheel. "This is glare ice! Glare ice! This is BLEEDING GLARE ICE!" he repeated with increasing volume as he slashed at the steering wheel. I had been in the middle of a statement about something (I cannot recall the exact subject), and I remember that I kept on blathering throughout the trip across the bridge, as if my brain had decided that, if I did not acknowledge Gurney's alarm, perhaps the ice would go away. Thanks to the talents of Gurney, we traversed the bridge with merely a slight twitch of the Ferrari's tail. Because he so skillfully maintained control of the car, only he will ever know how far beyond the ragged edges we had traveled.

"That's enough of the shit," said Gurney firmly as he slowed down. "Race or no race, we aren't going to wipe ourselves out on ice like that. Man, that was scary, and I don't mind telling you I didn't like it one bit!"

"God, I wonder about the Cadillac. I sure hope those guys get across the stretch all right," I said. We cruised onward, our speed reduced to a modest 70 miles per hour. I was relieved to see the Caddy's lights pop up behind us. They had slowed, indicating they, too, had encountered a few thrills on the bridge.

"That would have been a helluva crash," I mused. "And just think, not a soul within miles to see it. Most of your crashes take place in front of thousands of people. What a switch this would have been."

A tactical problem was arising. With the Cadillac cruising behind us, it was possible that they would trail after us on our shortcut. The turn to Route 89 was only a few miles ahead at Ash Fork, and we somehow had to get the Caddy out of sight before then. Outrunning them was impossible, considering the treacherous roads. Our only choice was to let them pass, then drop back and make our turn as they sped ahead.

"Hey, slow down and pull over on the shoulder," I told Dan. "Maybe they'll just drive past and we'll let 'em get out of sight before restarting."

Gurney stopped the Ferrari on the roadside. The Cadillac pulled over, too, drawing alongside as it came to a halt. We switched off our engines and sat there in the still, clear mountain night. The three men in the Cadillac looked haggard and hollow-eyed, obviously fatigued from the run.

"How'd you guys like that icy bridge?" Dan asked through his open window.

"Bad shit. We thought we'd had it," said a voice from inside the Caddy.

We chattered for a few minutes about the various adventures we had encountered. They reported that so far they'd been stopped by the police four times. Gurney started the Ferrari's engine, preparing to leave. The Cadillac hesitated, as if to follow us onto the road in the original order. "Go ahead. You guys go first," said Dan casually. "After all, we've got a 20-minute lead on you." Taking the bait, the Cadillac scurried away and rushed down the road.

We followed at a discreet distance, letting them get a half-mile ahead. By the time we reached the Route 89 turnoff, they were out of sight.

Thanks to the lower altitude, the road to Prescott was bare and clear of ice or any evidence of precipitation. It was a wide, level stretch of two-lane, virtually deserted, and Gurney ran the entire 51 miles with the speedometer needle glued to 130 miles per hour. Whisking through Prescott and not seeing a soul on its streets, we plunged into the National Forest. Mile after mile of tight mountainside switchbacks whispered underneath us. Gurney's masterful times and discipline became apparent with each passing yard.

The nasty cut beyond Yarnell was traveled with similar ease, and suddenly we were on the desert floor. Flat, open road lay between us and Los Angeles. Dawn lit the way, and Gurney upped the pace to 140 miles per hour across the desolation. Not even a stray jackrabbit or a tumbleweed was moving in the morning stillness; only the rounded, bullet-shaped Ferrari shrieking southward toward Interstate 10 and possible victory.

HE CAUGHT US ON A BACK STREET in Quartzite, Arizona. I had spotted his car, a mud-brown Dodge Highway Patrol sedan, parked in front of a run-down café at the roadside. The car had been empty, indicating that he'd been having his morning coffee when we'd ripped past, doubtlessly rattling the windows in the little place. I'd told Gurney about the car, then kept my eyes focused on the café, watching for movement. I saw headlights flick on. "He's coming. He's chasing us."

"He'll never catch us," Dan said firmly.

"He's gaining. He must be running 140 miles an hour!" I reported.

We sat there, speeding along in limbo, trying to figure out what to do. There was no sense trying to elude him on the side road. There were no side roads; outrunning him was out of the question. A short distance ahead was the Arizona-California border on the Colorado River. He could easily radio ahead and stop us at the agricultural inspection station. We drove onward, as if in a trance, letting him close the gap. "We'll turn off in Quartzite and get some gas. Maybe he'll miss us," said Gurney. He sailed onto an off-ramp and scuttled down a back street. Sighting an empty self-service gas station, he braked the Ferrari to a stop. Perhaps our pursuer in the mud-brown Dodge hadn't seen us get off the Interstate.

He had. In fact, we had barely shut off the Ferrari's engine when the boxy form of the Dodge, its twin gumball roof lights flashing crazily, skidded to a halt in the gravel beside us. A tall patrolman in a starched khaki uniform leaped out. He was wearing a crash helmet. His glands still pulsing from the pursuit, his feathers ruffled in a kind of cock-rooster triumph, he marched over to Gurney and curtly demanded his license and registration. Little more was said as he strode back to his car and removed a pad and pencil. We stood there, the silence broken only by the furry, electronic jabbering from his radio and the hushed background rumble of an occasional passing truck. He obviously recognized Gurney, and for a few minutes hope rose in us that he might issue a stern warning and send us on our way. But he kept on writing. A summons was being issued and a hardness crept across Dan's face.

Ripping the ticket off the pad and handing it to Gurney, the highway patrolman, as if to signal the end of official business, turned to regard the Ferrari for a moment, then asked rather affably, "Just how fast *will* that thing go?"

"C'mon out on the highway, and we'll let you find out," Gurney snapped.

Fortunately, the officer chose to take Dan's crack as an attempt at humor and let us go. Although he had spared us the agony of being dragged off to a justice of the peace, which would have consumed perhaps an hour, the incident had used up at least 10 minutes. "That does it, we've probably lost for sure," I said dejectedly as we pulled back on the Interstate.

An evil smile spread across Gurney's face. "He was wondering how fast this thing will go. Let's find out." The Ferrari began to gain speed, whisking easily at 150 miles per hour. The car felt smooth and steady. There was not much wind noise, considering the velocity. "There's 170!" said Gurney. The needle pushed its way around the big dial, then stabilized at 172 miles per hour. Gurney laughed. "This son of a bitch *really* runs," he said in amazement. "And it's rock steady." He took his left hand off the wheel, and we powered along toward Los Angeles, the Ferrari rushing through the desert morning at 172 miles per hour.

"You think we ought to turn back and answer the cop's question?" I asked. But our amusement from the 172-miles-per-hour run was only temporary. As we slipped back to a more normal cruising speed, we both decided that the delay from the arrest had ended our chances of winning the Cannonball. "Those other guys have to be miles ahead by now," I grumbled. We stopped for gasoline in Indio, California, where our general discouragement led to more torpor and lost time. Once on the road again, with the end in sight, we managed to perk up, drawing on our final reservoirs of energy. "Listen, at least we ought to try to make the trip in under 36 hours," said Gurney. "If we can do that, we can't shame ourselves too badly."

We were back in it again, running hard. To reach our goal, we had a little over two hours to run about 130 miles—practically all of it over heavily patrolled Los Angeles freeways. "You watch out the back for the Highway Patrol, and I'll run as fast as I can," said Dan. I turned in my seat, scanning the off-ramps and the passing traffic for the familiar black-and-white California Highway Patrol cruisers. Gurney drove through the building traffic with incredible smoothness, seldom braking and never making severe lane changes. We turned off at the Western Avenue exit and bustled through three miles of heavy urban congestion, heading for Redondo Beach and the Portofino Inn. The masts and spars of the yachts moored in the Redondo Beach marina appeared, and Dan accelerated the Ferrari the last few yards into the Inn's parking lot. I was out of the car before it stopped moving and sprinting into the lobby, where a pair of mildly shocked bellhops looked up to see an unshaven, grubby form rush up to the desk. The clerk punched our ticket.

Our elapsed time was 35 hours and 54 minutes. What's more, no one else had arrived. We were the first car to finish.

Lady Driver

In Which Our Intrepid Girl Reporter Is Sent to the Shelby School of High Performance Driving to Learn How to Race— and, Incidentally, How to Drive

By Chris McCall

Car and Driver,
April 1967

NOTHING LIKE STARTING OUT BRISKLY, I thought, as we pulled out onto the track. I was still figuring out the shift pattern.

"I guess you know the clutch, brake and accelerator," says Timanus. "The shift pattern is an 'H'—pretty standard. Go through the gears a couple of times and get familiar with them." It's Monday morning at Willow Springs Raceway in California's high desert country. The car is a GT 350 belonging to the Carroll Shelby School of High Performance Driving. The instructor is John Timanus, well-known West Coast racing driver and Shelby employee. Timanus has his work cut out for him. He has exactly five days to teach me the fundamentals of racing. That part is fairly routine. But there's a catch. Somewhere in those five days—preferably at the outset—Timanus also has to teach me how to drive a car.

FRIDAY

"Have you ever driven a race car?" Timanus asks on the phone.

"Uh, no, John. I thought you knew."

"Knew what?"

"Well, I don't drive. At all."

There's a dead silence while the long-distance wires crackle and buzz.

"Not at *all*?" he finally manages.

I tell him no, that in New York a car is more trouble than it's worth, and somehow I just never learned. I tell him it seems like a fascinating experiment to begin learning how to drive by learning how to race, before I pick up a lot of sloppy, bad habits. He agrees, a little ruefully, to do it, and I make arrangements to meet him Monday morning in Los Angeles. I get plane and hotel reservations so fast it'd make your head spin because I don't want to start thinking about it and change my mind.

MONDAY

A red, white and blue Ford Econoline with ridiculously small mag wheels pulls into the parking lot. It's Timanus. He looks about 35, has sandy-reddish hair, a high forehead, is tall, tanned, and wears glasses. His face, up close, is scarred and somewhat creased, but these are the only clues to his actual age—46. He seems shy and he talks and moves slowly and deliberately. He's a nice guy, and I enjoy the hour and a half it takes to get to Willow Springs.

189

I'm a little apprehensive when he tells me the school car is a 1965 GT 350. I've heard you have to be Charles Atlas to steer it and have the leg muscles of a high-jumper to stop it. Timanus grins and says that's only at low speeds—I won't have to worry. I worry. We pull into a rutted, dusty lane, and jounce up to the Willow Springs pit apron. There's the car, blue and white, nasty-looking, with big, fat tires, no trim, and a gutted, stripped interior. Timanus says it has 25,000 miles on it, and is virtually stock, except that the side windows have been removed for safety. It looks hairy to me.

The course is two and a half miles long, and is set partially on a hill and partially on the flat. It's ideal for teaching, because you can see the whole circuit from almost any point on the track. We get into the GT 350 and Timanus fires it up. Oh-oh, it sounds like a racer; this whole project is suddenly getting serious. We move off to see what the track is like—the beginning of a long learning process.

Timanus proceeds to pour it on, meanwhile telling me about lines, shifting, and apexes, and although I'm convinced we're out of control most of the time, I get a glimmer of what he's talking about. He makes it look easy.

We pull off to a gravel pit apron and begin with the basics. When I know the gears, Timanus tells me to drive up and down the apron. I'm very proud of the fact that I don't stall the car, but this is immediately dispelled by my shock at how heavy the car feels. It's a pig, I think. I suggest this and Timanus says it'll get lighter the faster I go. I don't believe him. After dodging around some scrawny, dried out trees (an impromptu slalom course, so I'll have an idea how to aim the car), we pull onto the track. Nothing like starting out briskly, I always say. I've been driving less than an hour and I'm on a race track. Save me, somebody!

Once we're off the gravel, the car does feel easier to drive, but I'm startled at how sensitive the accelerator is, how stiff the gearbox feels and—holy cow!—how intractable the steering seems. But I'm actually driving, and I do several laps in third gear, finding out what the course looks like from the driver's seat. *Me! Driving!*

Gradually, Timanus gets me up- and downshifting. Ha! I can't downshift. My upshifts aren't all that hot either, but I'm really bombing out on the downshifts. I never manage to blip the throttle and keep the revs up while I'm shifting, and we go lurching around each turn with something less than flair. I despair when I see how much I have to learn, but the narcotic of being able to *drive* faster than I've ever been *driven* before is tantalizing. I start noticing the apexes John says I must clip, and I understand—intellectually, at least—why the lines Timanus points out are the fastest way around the corners. Now all I have to do is learn to drive.

TUESDAY

It's obvious that I'm going to have to learn to downshift properly before we do anything else. Timanus tells me to run up and down the pit apron by myself (*myself!*), practicing until I can shift automatically. I'd gone to sleep last night flexing my feet, trying to make the brake-clutch-accelerator sequence into a rhythm, and—eureka!—this morning it seems to have settled into place. I can *do* it! Oh, not beautifully, mind you, but I'm getting better every time. I work and work at the downshifts, driving back, and forth, back and forth, and when I've done this for half an hour, Timanus hops in and we take to the track.

There I am with my newfound skill, and the first time we come to a corner I do it and it works! I stomp and blip and shift and accelerate, and the revs stay right up there and fourth gear becomes third. So much for Turn One. At Turn Three, I need to go from third to second, and the going gets interesting. I fail to keep the revs high enough to prevent the car from lurching around and chirping the tires as I let the clutch out, and moreover, I'm so busy shifting and looking at my feet that I'm taking a ridiculous line through the corner. By the time I'm at the top of the hill, my arms are all twisted around each other (I'm steering like a grandmother), and Timanus is wearing a broad smile. Well, finesse is for later, I tell myself. At least I'm still on the road.

After a spell of this, Timanus takes over and does it right. He also does it at about 5,000 rpm, while I've been hovering around 3,000. He is smooth, relaxed, and collected, and I want to learn how he does it.

After lunch we go round and round, me driving, and he tells me I must get smoother. I can't imagine how anybody could seem smooth in this car—unseen things rattle on the bare sheet metal insides, the wind drums through the side window area, and the engine thug-thug-thugs, growls, and whines. Timanus starts telling me to accelerate here and there, and when I do, it feels great. I don't get sideways the way I thought I would, and the car is suddenly 500-pounds lighter. Some of the choppiness is gone. I inch up to 3,500 and stay there for awhile, and John tells me, at the broad, sweeping righthander called Turn Two, that I can easily do it at 4,000. Disbelief again, but I try. Hey! It's easy. I accelerate all the way up and around the turn, and it all feels light and slippery and I realize that the rear end was hanging out all the way. I learn at a fantastic rate in this session, and eventually I'm doing 110 on the straight, 70 in Turn One, and 75 up Two. We decide to call it a day ("Always knock off when you start getting careless and ragged."), when I start into the esses at Three, get really out of shape, and overcorrect and fishtail madly up the hill, whooping and laughing. I sputter, "Oh, sir-*sir*!" Timanus guffaws and tells me exactly what I was doing wrong, why I got into trouble, and how the apex is something I've got to learn about, now that I'm going fast enough to get into trouble. I am purely exhilarated.

WEDNESDAY

We start out by walking around the track, with Timanus explaining shut-off points, lines, and apexes. Each corner has several pairs of black skid marks going off the road in various directions. Every one represents a mistake, where someone lost it, and it's sobering.

The tour over, Timanus says, "Today you can solo." Until now, I've always had Timanus with me, and I decide that somehow his presence in the car is indispensable—he makes it go. But Timanus has been a riding director, telling me what to do at every point around the course. He's said the same things at the same places so often that I'm doing them automatically anyway, so I tell myself it isn't really going to be any different to solo. But when I start off, my palms are all clammy, my legs are shaking, and my heart is thumping away like heavy artillery. Off I go, with Timanus standing by the side of the road, receding in the rear-view mirror. I make it through the gears to third, and settle down for a nice, slow tour. I'm nervous all the way around—I can't believe that I'm actually driving—but by the time I pass Timanus, my anxiety is giving way to pure euphoria. I know I can go faster and stay out of trouble. I drive for three-quarters of an hour, and although I don't hang the car out much, I do get smoother and more aggressive with my driving—before, I was passive, responding to instructions. When I come in, I'm over my nervousness completely. Besides being the most patient man in the world, Timanus must also have a degree in psychology.

He gets into the passenger seat and we go off to learn some more. As the tachometer inches up, a number of things start becoming clear. Again, I'm smoother, a rhythm is developing, and Timanus tells me I can go faster here, can brake later there, can accelerate much sooner on Nine, and always, always, can get closer to the apex.

I finally catch on to what he's been telling me about Turn Five. Two apexes, cut in sooner because I've been wide, clip the first, back on the throttle, wide again and drifting, clip the second, and accelerate all the way around. After about eight tries, I finally get it right, and it's a fantastic sensation.

Same thing with Nine. Timanus keeps telling me to hang on until the "200" marker, and then cut down to the apex, but I consistently chicken out and dive down too soon. But it gets better and better, and at last I'm on. I rack into Turn Eight at a little over 4,000, hold it all around that broad, sweeping turn, shift to third at one apex, go wide and fly around the decreasing-radius right. The two yellow stripes come up, and it seems impossibly late, but we dive in, and I accelerate just as I near the marker pylon. True to John's predictions, the car drifts through using all the road, and straightens itself out at the last minute, pointed correctly down the straightaway. Beautiful. Timanus says, "Good." Oh, gosh, sir.

THURSDAY

Aha! Now I know what Timanus means about the importance of hitting the apex. Trust me to discover a mortifying way to get the point. There I am, assimilating like crazy, and having a great time working at it. I'm still messing up Turn Three but I'm finding out how the car reacts at speed, how it's important to get the suspension set up properly for a corner because braking, accelerating, or any sudden twitch when the car is heeled over is going to get very squirrelly. Being set up means being properly aimed and in the right attitude *before* you get into a corner, not after you're in. Which, in turn, means the right line through the preceding corner. I find that if I'm off the line in one place, I'm still out of shape for the next turn. The faster I go, the more obvious this is. You start linking corners together and eating up the straights between them faster, and you learn in a hurry that you need to be right from the beginning. I also find out that the correct line is not only the *fastest* way around a corner—after you pass a certain speed, it's the *only* way around a corner, if you want to stay on the road.

I know I've knocked several seconds off previous times, and Timanus tells me I did a 2:05. That's 15 seconds better than yesterday! It was a ragged 2:05, but it felt great to me. We go a little slower now, trying to get smooth before we inch up to speed again, and that's where I make my dumb mistake.

I'm accelerating along the straight to Turn One. Cloudless day, empty track, a few gusts of wind rippling the hood as we bound along at 4,000 in fourth. Shut-off points coming up, throttle feathered, brake, clutch, shift, tap gas, complete the shift, more power, and—oops! I'm high; I can't make that apex. I'll keep trying anyway. Ah . . . uh . . . no. Goodbye, apex. Car's light—too light—the rear end is out and trying to pass me. Steer into skid. Too much. Overcorrect, undercorrect. It's no good, I'm sideways and slipping off the track at a terrible rate of speed. Timanus is yelling for me to get off the gas as we swap ends and hit the shoulder of the track. We bounce along broadside, achingly slowly now. A wire fence is looming up on John's side, and gravel and rocks are raining on the windshield.

The car lurches to a stop facing the way we came, and Timanus bursts into whooping laughter. Dust settles all over the windshield, the interior, and us. I am truly, horribly embarrassed. Not frightened, although I was sure for a moment that we were going to hit a ditch and roll. I'm humiliated. John says, "Well, let's go back and look at the skid marks and see what you did." How can he be so calm? I might have broken his neck. (I learned afterwards that almost every student spins, but I can't help but feel sorry for John—he must see it coming awfully early.)

We go back, Timanus chuckling over the great, broad tire marks, and he shows me that I was maybe a mile from the apex and that I kept cranking the car into the turn anyway, and no wonder the rear end broke loose. I also stayed on the gas much too long.

I help him clear the stones and rocks off the track—they're all over the place—and we go back to the pits to check the wheels and tires before continuing.

The car is fine, so I set off by myself, just to be sure I get over any trauma. I tip-toe around One several times, and realize that I'm having trouble putting my foot on the gas with any authority. But I gradually inch up to where I was on Wednesday, and I stay there. I have learned about line the hard way, and probably the best way.

FRIDAY

I start off slowly, as usual, and because of my idiocy yesterday, it takes me awhile to reach 4,000 rpm and hold it around the entire course. I swing around Four better, and am shocked to find that, without knowing it, I've learned to handle the steering wheel without getting twisted up and moving my hands a lot. I no longer think about it. I just do it right, and I'm amazed at how necessity has forced this adjustment. In fact, I'm doing everything almost automatically. Timanus says I'm getting through the corners at close to the maximum, and the way I can pick up seconds is to put my foot in it earlier, and keep it there all along the straights. I'm about to start working on this when the brakes start locking up and grabbing.

The car isn't unmanageable, but it puts me off, so Timanus changes the pads on the front discs. The car still doesn't feel right, so he gets in and invites me along.

What an education. We tool around, picking up speed, and brake for Three. Nothing. No brakes, and I wonder how he's going to get us out of this one. "Ho-ho-ho-ho-*hoho-HO!*" says John and tracks the 350 around the outside of the corner. We stay on the road—just barely—and I'm terribly impressed. A few more tries, and the brakes are back, but locking. He removes a wheel and finds that the brake seals are leaking, and that's all for my racer. We stand around kicking stones and talking quietly, and it seems to be all over, when Chuck Cantwell shows up.

Cantwell is Shelby's production racing manager, and he's testing the '67 racing Mustang. He climbs in and starts the beast. Wild. Makes our car sound like a motorbike. I wander off to watch him, and really get my eyes opened. He goes faster and faster, and I'm thinking, "Hey he doesn't even have to lift off there," and "I could probably pick up two seconds at Four, and three at Six . . . "

I stop, amazed. A week ago I wondered if I'd be able to shift. Now I'm worried about where I can pick up seconds . . . Timanus is some kind of a genius. I know 100% more about driving than I did a week ago, and I also appreciate the whole process 100% more. How did he do it? Now what I'm gonna do is, I'm gonna get about two years' experience on the road, and then I'm going to go back for another week of instruction. You hear that Timanus?

I warn you, you can't get rid of me that easily. I'm gonna find those seconds!

There Goes Tokyo

BRE's Retro Modern Datsun 510 Is a Chip Off the Old Brock

By Scott R. Lear

Grassroots Motorsports,

August 2009

BEFORE 1968, THE AMERICAN SPORTS CAR SCENE was dominated by automobiles from the U.S., Germany, England and Italy. Few people on our shores owned Japanese cars, and fewer still raced them. That all changed when Brock Racing Enterprises thrust Datsun into the spotlight in SCCA Production-class competition.

It's difficult to be concise when describing Peter Brock. For Datsun fans, he's the guy who put the company on the racing map with BRE. Corvette nuts know him for his work on the design of the iconic Sting Ray. European racing fanatics and Shelby enthusiasts revere his streamlined, championship-winning Cobra Daytona Coupe.

Brock is a pioneer of ultralight aviation, a Baja off-road veteran, a graphic designer, a journalist, a photographer, a husband and a father. The 73-year-old is still active in many of these circles, and he and his wife Gayle operate the multifaceted BRE organization out of Redmond, Wash. Wearing so many hats at once would lead to spinal compression in the average person, but Brock is able to shoulder still another insatiable passion: He's an old-school hotrodder. Spare moments are rare in his hectic schedule, but for the past several years he's been using his free time to create the Datsun of his dreams, a dramatically altered V8-powered 510.

Ahead of His Time

Peter Brock has lived so many different automotive fantasies in his day that it's difficult to keep them all straight. When he was an eighth grader, his first job was sweeping floors and cleaning up tools after school at a hotrod shop in the San Francisco Bay area. "That's really where I learned about the art of building race cars," Brock recalls.

As a youth, Brock was also strongly drawn to Ken Purdy's 1952 book *The Kings of the Road*, which details the automotive masterpieces of engineering and style that defined prewar Europe. "The performance he describes was just fabulous," says Brock of Purdy's tales of early race cars. "Today [their performance] would be nothing at all, but for its day it was pretty inspirational."

Imports were an early part of Brock's life, and his first car was a 1949 MG TC. In high school, he was already demonstrating a superior knack for design and fabrication; his daily driver was a chopped and channeled 1946 Ford hotrod called *El Mirage*, and the machine won a prize at the

Oakland National Roadster Show. Unfortunately, he sold the car and it has since vanished from the public eye. "I wish I could find it today," he laments. "It exists somewhere."

Eager to Race

Brock wanted desperately to be a road racer, but at the time the SCCA had a minimum driving age of 21. To position himself for that eventual racing seat, he headed to Stanford University to study engineering. However, he never really clicked with his classes. He left the school mid-semester to investigate the automotive design program at the Art Center College of Design in L.A.

"On my Easter break I went to the Art Center and asked them how I could apply to get into school," he recalls. "I didn't know that it was a school for people who were already professionals." When they asked to see his portfolio, Brock admits that he was absolutely clueless; someone at the school filled him in. Unwilling to walk away from the opportunity, Brock went to his car, dug up his high school binder, spent a couple of hours sketching, and returned to the admissions office. His doodles earned him entry to the prestigious school.

Brock recalls his time at the Art School fondly, as he was surrounded by gifted model builders, designers and artists. "The guy that was sort of the inspiration for [me and] about 90 percent of the guys in the world was Strother MacMinn, head of the transportation division of the Art Center," says Brock. "Talk to any car designer from the '60s on back; most came out of the Art Center."

Designing for the Best

Though he was learning a great deal about design, the Art School was very expensive and Brock had trouble finding the funds to stay enrolled. Luckily, a connection he'd made with Chuck Jordan of the GM Styling Division panned out. Brock left school, and at age 19 he became the youngest designer ever hired by General Motors.

Brock's first in-depth project at GM was to create a car—the Cadet—for students about his own age. His microcar design made it as far as the Styling division's internal VIP show, where GM president Harlow Curtice nixed the idea on the stance that GM didn't make small cars. In late 1957, Brock penned a design that became the template for a future Corvette—the 1963 split-window Sting Ray. He also worked closely on a prototype Stingray Racer that was shelved due to the Automobile Manufacturers Association's ban on racing projects in the early 1960s. Due to a lack of racing projects at GM, Brock left the company in 1958 and headed back to California to race his Climax Cooper.

In California, he found work running parts and cleaning up shop at Hollywood Motors. There he learned all he could about racing cars from Max Balchowsky, whose Old Yeller Buick Specials were at the top of their game. Through a bit of luck, Brock was in the right place when Carroll Shelby decided he needed to hire somebody to instruct at his new driving school. The young Brock became Shelby's first paid employee.

Brock's time with Shelby is well documented. In addition to designing much of the company's visual elements, he finally got a chance to shape a full-on race car: the Cobra Daytona Coupe. The Coupe took an FIA championship against the likes of Ferrari, and aerodynamics were the key to its success. "'When I was working at GM I spent a lot of time reading," says Brock. "They have a very good library that nobody uses; you go in there and it's like a tomb. I happened to discover a little sheet of mimeographed paper that had been recovered after WWII by the Allied forces. [It covered] anything of value to American industry."

Among these documents were drawings and test results from aerodynamics engineer Reinhard von Koenig-Fachsenfeld, who was responsible for the legendary Kamm tail—Koenig-Fachsenfeld was an understudy of Wunibald Kamm at the time. "They had built prototypes called the K models: K1, K2, K3. They were built on chassis by BMW and Adler. Of course all this stuff got bombed flat, but the drawings remained," he continues.

"I couldn't read the German, but I could understand the numbers and the coefficient of drag. I applied that formulaic knowledge to make an efficient shape," he says of planning the Cobra Coupe. "Once you determine the hard points of the chassis, the body pretty much designs itself."

"Fortunately, there was no money to hire a real designer at Shelby, so they left me alone and I could do exactly what I thought would work," he laughs. "In spite of the resistance [to the radical shape], we got it done to the point where we could test it, and it turned out to be really, really fast. People started understanding that [aerodynamics] was good."

The Rise of the Japanese Sports Car

In 1965, Brock left Shelby and started his own team, Brock Racing Enterprises. At first the team raced Hinos, but when that company was absorbed by Toyota, BRE was expecting to get the contract for the new, highly advanced Toyota 2000GT. At the last minute Toyota yanked the contract from BRE and gave it to Shelby, leaving Brock high and dry—and with more than a bit of steam to blow off.

Rather than bury his head in a pillow, Brock figured he could get even by beating Toyota and his former employer on the track. "You had Toyota, Nissan and Honda," he says of his options. "It was the same thing as Ford versus Chevy—who was Toyota's biggest rival?" He was rebuffed by Datsun's American branch, but a former Hino connection happened to be friends with the president of Nissan in Japan. "You just need to have the red phone that goes to the president," he chuckles.

With Brock at the helm, BRE's relatively low-tech Datsuns embarrassed Shelby's Toyotas in SCCA Production racing, and instantly Datsun was a major player in American club competition. The BRE Datsun Roadsters and later 240Zs earned SCCA championships from 1969 through 1971.

BRE also took a run at the Trans-Am 2.5 Championship in 1971. His team was so dominant with their Datsun 510s—they won the 1971 and 1972 titles—that the other teams dropped out. The series had lost its appeal, so Brock gravitated toward other venues, including Baja and drag racing.

Without Brock and BRE to provide their big breakthrough, Japanese cars might never have ended up on the map in the U.S. racing scene, or be appreciated as old-school racers today. Brock attributes the success of BRE to his team members.

"The collection of guys we had, they were—every one of 'em—the best." he says. "They were all innovators. When you're talking about three different marques of cars within one hundredth of a second, it's the crew that really makes it work in the pits when the chips are down."

Brock's exploits could fill a book. Thankfully, Peter and his wife, Gayle, both have a knack for writing, and many more details of his life can be found at the Brock Racing Enterprises Web site, bre2.net. Flipping through their archive photos and reading more on his unique journey through racing's history is an enlightening way to spend an evening.

Behold Datzilla

When he was working on the all-conquering BRE Datsun 510s, Brock had been tinkering with an idea: Why not perform a V8 engine swap on one of the diminutive sedans? He figured that an aluminum Buick or Pontiac V8 would be the way to go.

"I ended up doing that particular conversion on a VW Bus," he recalls. "It was such a great combination, but after I got it all done I was worried about the weight distribution—but it didn't matter. I [realized] I could have put a Chevy V8 in it and it would have been a lot more practical."

Those plans eventually started to take root, and over time the 510's appeal has only grown. "It's a modern '32 Ford, a car you can build into a hotrod," Brock explains. "I had bought the tub to do a father-son thing, but my youngest boy didn't really have much interest in it. It continued on at a slow pace; I'd hand it off to friends or acquaintances when I had a little extra money to do something."

Brock is still keen on perfect weight balance, and his solution was straightforward: "Really, you just go, 'God, this is going to be a big lump.' If you want to get the weight where you want it, you shove the engine back." Brock relocated the engine, dash and other components about 18 inches back, and he now sits where the designers originally placed the rear seat. "You're taking a four seater and stretching it out. It makes a great two seater, makes it really comfortable."

Brock Approved

V8-powered Datsun 510s have been done before, but Brock built his 510 to please himself, not others. The man has known many incredible automotive experts through the years, and the 510 showcases their impeccable work as well. This car is a rolling yearbook, one that's thick with the mechanical comments and signatures of good friends.

"The big V8 doesn't necessarily create the most horsepower, but it has a sound that resonates with my original desire for a hotrod," states Brock. "I love the American V8."

Connecting Highway

By Joe Oldham

Muscle Car Confidential,

2007

THE CONNECTING HIGHWAY. In New York in the sixties, this was where it was at in terms of big-time street racing. The Connecting Highway is actually a short stretch of roadway that connects the Brooklyn–Queens Expressway to the Grand Central Parkway in Queens, New York. All the big money runs took place at "the Connecting," as we called it.

All the real street racers knew this and so did the cops. In addition to holding the record for most street drag races in one night, the Connecting Highway also held the record for the place where the most tickets were given out in any one night and also the record for most arrests of street racers in any one place.

In fact, Fred Mackerodt, managing editor and later Editor-in-Chief of *Cars* magazine, was arrested at the Connecting Highway one night while watching. He wanted to see the spectacle with his own eyes. He didn't believe it.

Even with all the police hassles, on a good night, you couldn't beat the Connecting for great racing. One of the reasons it was so good is that it was all packed into one little quarter mile, from one underpass to the other. You could see everything. Granted, it was easier for the cops to see, too. But if you wanted to street race right, you did it at the Connecting.

I used to go there regularly to watch and to hear the stories. I got a lot of good article ideas there, and you would not believe some of the stories. Like the time they towed in a Double A/Fuel Dragster, rolled it off the trailer, fired it up, smoked the whole length of the highway, then popped the chute as it went under the second underpass. Right there on a public highway! It was a common sight to see '55 Chevys and Willys gassers being towed into the pits at the Connecting.

The "pits" were the two elevated service roads that flank each side of the highway itself. I saw outlandish things there, like transmissions being changed, slicks mounted, and shifters adjusted. Tuneups were common and didn't even rate a second look, while a transmission or rear-end change usually gathered a crowd, because to change a transmission or rear end right out on a public street was a class move.

Spectators looked down onto the highway from the two guard rails that ran along the elevated service roads. The rails kept cars, girls, and other debris from falling down onto the highway. It was common to see a bunch of guys standing on the sidewalk along the pits only to be interrupted by the screech of burning slicks and open headers bellowing up from the highway. A run! Everyone immediately ran to the rails to look down at the action taking place on the highway below.

There were always some drive-in *poseurs* making burnouts in the pits. But this was frowned on by the real racers because it attracted the cops and gave them a reckless-driving excuse to bust everybody.

A lot of guys used to bring their chicks to the Connecting Highway to watch the races and make out between runs. And there was always a plethora of babes there on their own, looking to pick up guys. This was something the serious racers had to put up with. With so many people around making out, watching, and cluttering the pits, it was a hassle to work on your car. But it was a happening place.

At one point, because of the popularity of the Connecting Highway with non-serious racers, the 114th Precinct of the New York City Police Department staged a drive to shut down the Connecting once and for all. The real racers moved to other, less intense street racing venues, returning to the Connecting only for the most serious of money runs well after midnight. By that time of night, the hokey people had left and there was money to be made.

Before midnight on any given night, the less formal venues thrived. Sounds from the Clearview Expressway near Union Turnpike were a clear indication of where the action was on that night. At Clearview, the scene was a little different. The area under the bridge where the expressway passed over Union Turnpike served as the pits. The runs took place up on the expressway itself. Runs went from Union Turnpike to the next exit.

If you passed the White Castle at Parsons Boulevard and it was empty, you knew you had hit a good night for racing at the Clearview Expressway up ahead. And when you pulled up to the bridge, if you saw two cars making a left under the sign that said "Throgs Neck Bridge," you knew you had gotten there just in time to see a run.

It was harder to watch runs at the Clearview because you had to follow the racers in a car to see what happened. There really was no viewing area, as there was at the Connecting. This was good for money racing because the cops weren't around constantly to clear out the spectators. There were no spectators.

There was one spot out in Queens that was the granddaddy of all street racing venues (except, perhaps, for a few blocks in downtown Los Angeles): Cross Bay Boulevard. Today, Cross Bay is totally developed with strip malls and tract housing running its entire length from Southern State Parkway all the way to Rockaway Beach. In those days, Cross Bay was a deserted strip of highway with nothing but marshland stretching for miles on each side of the roadway—and a legend.

Trouble was, it got so big and so popular that the cops just shut it down. By the end of the sixties, no one raced there anymore. Oh, you'd see some dumb clams throwing powershifts around the Bay and hanging out in the pits just past the first bridge. And there was always some goon doing a burnout out of the Pizza City parking lot. But by 1970, the cops had shut down Cross Bay and it was never again to be the scene of intense street racing, as it was in the late fifties and sixties. Then, the pits were full every night and the racing was just about nonstop, the parking lots of Pizza City and the Big Bow-Wow packed with guys on the prowl. By the late sixties, you couldn't even breathe loud on Cross Bay without getting a ticket. The racers even staged a protest one night, complete with posters, signs, and hundreds of cars slowly going the speed limit up and down Cross Bay, protesting the harsh treatment and "police brutality" being meted out to street racers.

Every so often in New York City, there was a crash and some guy died street racing his muscle car. Naturally, the *New York Daily News* and *New York Post* covered the incident in detail, with close-up shots of the crushed GTO or the splintered fiberglass remains of a Corvette. Then the politicos would decry the state of today's youth and call for harsher police crackdowns on the street racers who were threatening the life and security of all the good citizens of New York City.

But a few weeks later, I'd be back at the Connecting Highway and, inevitably, some guy would pull into the pits in a jacked up Goat or a Hemi Road Runner, roll down the window, and say something like, "I'll run anybody here for any amount."

And Wally Parks got mad at me.

Beardsley Travels 1500 Miles in 14 Days on 14 Charges

Author Unknown
The Automobile, July 1915

Los Angeles, Cal., July 13—Traveling more than 1500 miles in 14 consecutive days on 14 charges, a stock model Los Angeles–built Beardsley electric has completed one of the most remarkable electric runs ever held in the West. On the entire run, the average was 107 1/2 miles to the charge.

The announcement was recently made by the Beardsley Electric Co. of this city that a stock model brougham would attempt to run 1000 miles in 10 days on 10 charges. To show the ease of operation, Mrs. V. S. Beardsley was appointed pilot for the test and the press appointed 10 observers, all women, to accompany the car on each day of the run.

In 10 days Mrs. Beardsley had run up a total of 1066.3 miles, every day's run exceeding the 100-mile mark.

An Endurance Run in Truth Was This

Terrible Experiences of Men and Machines in the Remarkable 1,000-Mile New York to Pittsburg Test

Anonymous

Popular Mechanics,

1903

NARROW ESCAPES FROM DROWNING, thrice barely saved from being dashed down slippery mountain sides, exhaustion from hunger, sleepless nights and inhuman exposure—this is the story of the 1,000-mile automobile endurance run given by the National Association of Manufacturers. It was "endurance" almost beyond "endurance" throughout the remarkable expedition. Such another was never experienced before and will never be experienced again by those who escaped the hazards, so they declare.

The run was from New York to Cleveland and thence to Pittsburg, over a route specially selected by the promoters for its perils. Floods, thunderstorms, washouts and numerous unlooked for catastrophes added to the distress of the men and vehicles. "The automobiles at times were forced to abandon the road and take to the tracks; they had to be hauled out of the flooded districts by horses. Often the automobilists were up to their necks in water. The men proved to possess more endurance than the automobiles, as when the perils were at their height the automobiles stalled in the middle of streams, and the men had to wade out in the water and pilot them across. In one of the cars a can of carbide was ignited in a flood which nearly swept the vehicles from their path near Binghamton.

The flames burst all over the car, creating almost a panic and seriously injuring the operator, who in consequence was forced to abandon the run.

These extracts from the *Automobile*'s description of the run may give an idea of some of the other "endurances" encountered: "The jolting over the railroad tracks had loosened every electrical connection. Again our engine stopped, and for four hours we were looking for a spark. During this four hours the writer availed himself of the first opportunity in the last 48 hours to lie down by the side of the road under a tree and get nearly two hours' sleep. We covered 447 miles in 47 hours, with only six hours' sleep on the part of the operator, and no sleep from Saturday until Friday night on the part of either passenger or observer in our wagon, except such as we gained while sitting in the wagon.

"Horses refused to draw in our efforts to get out of the flood near Binghamton. For an hour and a quarter the operator, in water up to his waist, and sometimes above his shoulders, tugged away with the second horse. A rope 200 feet long was secured, and finally bystanders on the railroad track succeeded in pulling the car back to its original starting place. From there it was towed back five miles to Binghamton. There new batteries and new coil were secured, and we obtained dry clothing, having traveled in wet clothes for 96 hours."

Zora's Detour to Tours

Adventure at the Wheel of a 1952 Allard

By Zora Arkus-Duntov

Road & Track,

July 1995

Many readers automatically link the name Zora Arkus-Duntov with the Chevrolet Corvette, and in fact he was instrumental in transforming this car into the world-class sports car it has become. But before Corvette, there was an absolutely storming British sports car known as the Allard. Its V-8 engine often had Ardun heads, as in Arkus-Duntov; *and Zora was often at the wheel.*

THE 1952 24-HOUR RACE OF LE MANS WAS IN PROGRESS for 2½ hours. An incredible pace of the first hour had taken its toll, broken machinery on the road and in the pits bearing testimony to this.

The rev counter, oil-pressure gauge and temperature gauge on my Allard's instrument panel had already failed. Then came the clock. It seemed not to move—not appreciably, that is—though I was probably getting tired.

We were due for a driver change soon.

Hasty work had left holes in the firewall, and I had been breathing hot air, exhaust and acrid oil fumes for almost three hours now. I needed relief if for no other reason than to get some fresh air.

I must not miss my pit signal! Miss a "COME IN" sign and the car might run out of fuel. Almost as bad, come in at random and it causes commotion in our pits, especially if car No. 4 is already there for its refueling and driver change.

But I have been out of touch with the pit since the beginning of the race. Ours is almost the last one in a long row, just where I aim the car into the 125-mph Dunlop Bend, and an abbreviated glance is all I can afford. Half a hundred signs tell their respective drivers what to do in half a hundred coded languages. To pick the right one, it has to be conspicuous—and mine isn't. The driver has a limited picture of a race; the pit, seeing all of it, directs him. We had our original battle plan for the first hours: No. 4 was to maintain contact with the leader; No. 5, my car, was to take an easy pace.

However, this plan is discarded in the 1st lap. I mess up the start, but my Allard No. 5 helps me make up for this. Doing so, I pass our own No. 4 so effortlessly that I assume something is wrong with the other car.

The strategy absent, unable to see any instructions from the pit, I make a mental deal to have the best man in the business direct my race. This man, Alfred Neubauer, manager of the Mercedes-Benz team, is unaware of the transaction.

When the first Mercedes creeps up to me on the Mulsanne Straight, I let it pass and pull my Allard into its slipstream. The turbulent air violently jerks my helmet, the car picks up 6–7 mph and I ease the throttle so as not to ram the Mercedes.

I continue and, after a while, two more Mercedes appear in my mirror. Letting them pass, I exchange greetings with Karl Kling and Hermann Lang, both of whom I know very well.

I repass one at Tertre Rouge. Seeing that my Allard can out-accelerate them, I remain in contact with Herr Neubauer in charge of my strategy—at least for now.

Overall, the picture is fine. With power to spare, I am pacing the team that is going for a win. If only these fumes would not make me dizzy. It's good to know I am soon due for relief.

Passing the pits, I fail to pick up the sign yet again. I decide that I will pull in on the next lap.

The Mulsanne Straight is 3½ miles long, though to speak strictly, it is not that straight; there are bends at its beginning and end. The latter one is taken at 145–150 mph, but without reserve power at this speed, the car drifts wide. Within 500 yards of the 30-mph Mulsanne Corner, I take my foot off the accelerator, coast for 100 yards and then onto the brakes.

There's only the slightest resistance and the pedal goes limp to the floor.

The fumes must have me! I am asleep at the wheel at Le Mans and having a nightmare!

No. It's real. Downshift into 3rd, but it's not slow enough. Try for 2nd, but it can't be done—the speed is too high. I know I am going to crash at 140 mph. A hundred yards ahead is a fence and a mass of people. I wave both hands and scream at the top of my lungs.

The Allard hits the fence, gray planks covered with cheap white water-paint are flying over the hood and my helmet. For me, the people are frozen in grotesque attitudes of running and jumping out of the way.

This horrific photoflash lasts but a second.

Then I am shooting down a straight and empty road. No, not quite empty. It is the public highway to Tours, beyond the escape road. I am still doing more than 100 mph and I'm coming up all too quickly on ordinary road cars.

No matter. A miracle has happened. Nobody was hit. Nobody was killed. I am alive. It's glorious.

But I must avoid these cars on their way to Tours. The first moves left to overtake, but thankfully wide. I pass between the two with nothing to spare. I judiciously apply the handbrake and come to a stop in a village a mile from Mulsanne Corner. The villagers are popeyed, but they urge me on. I shout at them not to touch the car. To do so would mean disqualification, and at least mentally I am back in the race again.

The engine is still running. I make a U-turn and return to the circuit. As I reach the debris of the fence, the throng of spectators moves aside. Faces are solemn and a woman crosses herself. I am back on the track again.

When I reach my pit, there is a sign: "ZORA COME IN."

Rick Hendrick
Changes
the Game

By Humpy Wheeler and Peter Golenbock

Growing Up NASCAR,

2010

KNEW OF RICK HENDRICK BEFORE I EVER MET HIM. He came from southern Virginia. He and his father, a drag racer, were very close, and so Rick had started out as a drag racer. He also raced big boats. He started selling cars up in Raleigh back in the days when automobile companies were looking for young guys to come in and sell a lot of cars. Rick got into Chevy's dealer development program, and he ended up with a dealership in Bennettsville, South Carolina. That's where he was when I first heard about his boat racing.

City Chevrolet in Charlotte for years had been one of the premier Chevy dealers in the state of North Carolina, and when it came up for sale Rick bought it. I remember the shockwaves that went through the business community that a guy as young as he was—Rick was about twenty-eight—and someone not from Charlotte was buying it. Charlotte was a traditional, conservative southern town where most of the businesses were owned by Charlotteans. And here was a young guy from Virginia coming in and buying one of the most successful franchises around Charlotte.

I became aware Rick had moved to Lake Norman because one day I noticed a cigar boat running very fast on the lake, and when I asked who owned it, I was told it was Rick's. We ran into each other somewhere, and he said, "I'd like to talk to you about NASCAR. I'd like to get into it."

That was in 1983, a time when single-car owners without a whole lot of money could still get into racing. That's not possible today. Rick came to my office, and little did I know that sitting across from me was one of the most interesting, engaging, complex characters I would ever get involved with. I was embarking on a friendship with an extraordinarily bright and intelligent person and also one of the most caring and giving people I've ever known.

Rick wanted some information from me. I have learned that Rick is very good at asking people's opinions on purpose. He wasn't just looking to get my opinion so I could feel good. He actually wanted my opinion. I told him the pitfalls of getting involved in racing. I talked about getting in bed with the wrong driver or the wrong employees. We talked about playing the NASCAR game. Usually I'm not so frank with strangers, but I just felt so good around him I figured I'd tell him everything I possibly could.

"You don't jump in with both feet flying," I said. "You don't tell NASCAR what to do. You have to come along slowly and gain everyone's confidence."

It takes time for people to even talk to a rank stranger. People have to get to know you, and you have to prove yourself. There are no open arms in NASCAR. My guess is he realized this anyway.

We talked about drivers and crew chiefs and about finding a place to operate.

Rick started his race team, and he did everything just right, which is the way he does things. He is the most forceful unforceful person I know. He never acts aggressively. He never acts like he wants it all, needs it all, and he's going to get it no matter what. He is kind to a tee, just a person you enjoy being around.

For me this was really refreshing, because I had been around so many people who were the other way, who felt they had to steamroll you to get their way. Rick was so good-natured, I started to ask myself, *How in the world is he going to get results?* Little did I know how brilliant his approach would be—putting together the right chemistry to have the most phenomenal operation in the history of NASCAR.

ONE OF RICK'S MOST IMPORTANT HIRES was crew chief Harry Hyde. No one had been able to handle Harry, who was cantankerous and had all the diplomacy of 80-grit sandpaper. (That's a grinding sandpaper.) Harry was really tough on drivers. He was a tobacco-chewing guy, a World War II veteran who came out of Kentucky. His brother was police chief of Louisville. Harry didn't put up with anything or anyone.

Before Harry went to work for Rick, Harry and I didn't get along. He had had a huge run-in with J. D. Stacy, which led to all kinds of allegations. J. D. owned a coal mine, and Harry had once worked in the mines. Stacy was from West Virginia, and Harry was from Kentucky, and the two weren't but a sixteenth of an inch from being the Hatfields and the McCoys. The final end was that they parted ways, but Harry, the guy in the fight who didn't have any money, ended up losing most of what he had. Stacy even had the garage padlocked so Harry couldn't get to his tools.

What saved him was that Harry was a close friend of Nord Krauskopf who owned K&K Insurance, one of the three major companies that insured racetracks. Harry had been Nord's crew chief when Bobby Isaac won the championship in 1970, and when Nord was dying, he called Harry and several other friends to his death bed and bequeathed them each a substantial amount of money.

During the row with Stacy, I defended Harry in the press, and that's how Harry and I got to be friends. I didn't believe what Stacy was saying about Harry. I knew he was honest, and I defended him. One day he walked up to me and told me how much he appreciated my support. He was very gracious.

Of course, that didn't stop Harry from being Harry. After Rick came into racing, he and Harry had set up shop in a building owned by the Speedway. They were renting it from the Speedway, and when their lease was up, the Speedway needed it back and asked Rick and Harry to move. Harry had put a wall up inside without asking my permission, typical of Harry. I said something to Harry about the wall that ticked him off. He didn't like having to leave anyway, so he took a front-end loader and knocked the wall down.

I confronted him on the phone.

He said, "I ain't taking crap from you."

"Well, I'm not taking it from you either," I said. "You're off base, and I ought to . . . "

We decided we'd meet out on Highway 29 and duke it out. That's the way people up in the mountains like to fight, by the side of the road. But something happened, I don't remember what, and the Duel of Highway 29 never did happen. Eventually, Harry and I resumed our friendship.

At the time Rick was thinking about hiring Harry, he and his nephew, Tommy Turner, were building race cars for whoever hired them. Harry had bought a piece of property about a mile away just off Highway 29. He put up a mobile home and a garage, and he moved in. That led to Rick Hendrick buying land from Harry and locating where he did. A lot of people don't know that.

When Rick asked me about Harry, I said, "I think Harry will get the most out of a driver. He's going to make sure things are done right." I'm sure Rick asked quite a few others for their opinions, and then he hired Harry.

With Harry, Rick began to have success. He hired Tim Richmond to drive for him, and in 1986 Tim won seven races and came in second four times.

TIM RICHMOND WAS THE NEW JAMES DEAN. He looked like him. He acted like him. He was handsome and debonair, and the girls loved him. He was completely reckless, a total daredevil in everything he did. Tim was the only son of a wealthy Ohio industrialist. He went to prep school. In short, Tim did none of the things a stock car driver in those days did. He even went to college for a while. He was quite an athlete—a football player and a track man.

Tim's father didn't bring him up on road courses. Rather, he started him out on oval courses in Ohio, running their weird kind of race car called a Super Modified, one of the most powerful oval race cars ever built. It was very lightweight and had loads of horsepower. And right from the start, everyone knew Tim Richmond had it. Guys who were there say that very few people who ever got behind the wheel of a car were as good as he was. We have a standing joke that Curtis Turner must have been floating around Ohio somewhere back in the 1960s because Curtis and Tim drove so much alike it was incredible.

I didn't know him when he was running Sandusky and made the jump to Sprint cars where he was so prolific on the track. People who saw him said he was Curtis Turner, A. J. Foyt, Mario Andretti, and Parnelli Jones all wadded into one. He was a rebel, a James Dean rebel.

He showed up at the Indianapolis Speedway, and he astonished everyone his first year by finishing high. He was the IndyCar rookie of the year. His car conked out on the last lap, and he jumped on top of Johnny Rutherford's car and rode around the track sitting on top of the car, and of course the photographers ate it up. I can remember seeing four different angles of it.

The next thing I knew, people kept telling me, "You gotta meet Tim Richmond. He's just what stock car racing needs." We had Harry Gant, Cale Yarborough, and Darrell Waltrip, but none of those guys were going to play Hollywood.

Meeting him turned out to be one of the best and the worst decisions of my life.

I first met him when he came to Charlotte looking for a ride. I knew right away Tim was just what NASCAR needed, though I felt like someone had thrown me a K-bar knife, and both sides were razor sharp. He was something else. He dressed Mod—like no one in stock car racing had ever seen. He looked like he had just come from a store on Rodeo Drive. He reminded me of Jackie Stewart on steroids.

We talked and talked. I explained to him how different NASCAR was from Indy racing, and said these cars weren't easy to drive. He acted like he was paying attention, but he probably wasn't. It wasn't long before he got a ride, and right off the bat he was something else.

Tim Richmond was really the first driver to come in from the outside. Oh, Tom Pistone had come from Chicago much earlier, and there was David Hobbs and Ennis Ireland and a few others, but most of them were long in the tooth when they came in. Tim wasn't. He had left Indianapolis to come to stock car racing full tilt, and that had not been done before. He got in the cars and he took off. He impressed everyone from his first ride.

He began racing for Raymond Beadle, a drag racer from Texas who also liked to have a good time. Tim drove like the dickens. In fact, he drove exactly like Dale Earnhardt—and those were two of the most opposite people in NASCAR at the time. Sooner or later you knew those two would be getting into it.

I started working with Tim in every way possible. I could tell, number one, that he was spoiled rotten. Every time he messed up, his mother came to the rescue. His mother really loved him dearly, but she kept him from god knows what. And although his father, Al, was a tough-looking guy, he wasn't tough on Tim.

That needed to be corrected. I knew if I didn't straighten him out, he was headed for a big oak tree. Like James Dean, I had the feeling that something was going to happen to this guy. And it was not going to be good. Because he was so reckless in the way he acted, the way he drove a car, and the way he drove a motorboat.

One time we had a party at my lake house with just the guys. The only non-racer I invited was a tough-guy game warden from the state of North Carolina who I liked. I noticed during the party that Tim was sitting out at the entrance to my cove in my boat with another guy. I couldn't figure out why he wasn't coming back to my party. I sent my brother-in-law, Joe Williams, to go and get him. When Tim returned, he was three sheets to the wind, to put it mildly. I don't know how he got that way. I was never any good at mixology.

As soon as Tim saw the game warden, he went ballistic and acted like he was going to attack him. Tim couldn't lick a postage stamp, so I'm quite certain the game warden would have beaten him to a bloody pulp. Joe grabbed Tim, and I led him back to the boat. We sat him down, and I proceeded to chew his butt out. Fortunately, the game warden showed tremendous patience and restraint.

"That son of a bitch," said Tim. "He pulled me over." Tim owned a cigarette boat. Many a night after a race I could hear Tim crank that thing up. He didn't care what time of night it was. He'd crank it up and take it out into the main channel. It sounded like something out of the bowels of hell. I thought I was at the Bonneville Salt Flats again. Over and over I told him not to take it out on Lake Norman. I told him, "That boat is for Miami Beach, not Lake Norman." Tim said, "I was just going down the lake minding my own business and he pulled me over." I asked him, "How fast were you going?"

"About a hundred."

"He should have given you eight tickets," I said. He started letting me have it, and I just blistered him. He left in a huff.

Two days later he called me. He wanted to meet. I told him to come over to the Speedway where we had a father-son-type talk. Now he was playing the role of the penitent. I said, "Tim, you can't act like that. You have to get rid of that damn boat." Of course, he didn't get rid of the boat. Tim only did what Tim wanted to do.

About three weeks later, on a Saturday morning, he called me in a panic. He said, "Humpy, you have to come over here. My boat is ruined." I went over there, and as soon as I got there, I knew what had happened. He had the boat on a lift, and someone had snuck over there and poured sulfuric acid into the hatch. It melted the fiberglass and got down into the manifold and heads. Tim's boat was pretty much ruined, and he was livid.

"Tim, I hate to tell you this, but I knew this was going to happen," I said. "They are just not going to put up with this bullshit." Tim got really mad.

Tim wasn't intimidating as far as banging people around, but he could just drive the heck out of a loose race car. That's what really makes them go fast. Dale Earnhardt was never particularly good at qualifying, and at Charlotte one time he went out first and ran fairly well, and Tim said, "I'm going to beat that by a half second." He went out, and he came off that fourth turn, and I've never seen a car as loose as his coming off that turn. His right rear quarter panel just barely touched the outside wall. Anyone else would have wrecked big time, but he didn't. It was a fabulous run, and with that run he got the pole.

BY THIS TIME TIM HAD DONE SO WELL in racing that he was being acclaimed as the next great race driver. The media loved him because he had that gleam in his eye. The women loved him. There were rumors floating around about some unsavory habits off the track—staying up all night, partying with prostitutes. At the same time Rick Hendrick, who had a wonderful eye for talent, started talking to me about Tim. Sooner or later he said, "It would be great if we could get Tim and Harry Hyde together."

I said, "Rick, if you could pull that off, we'll put an eighty-foot bronze statue of you on Highway 29, because that will never work."

Harry Hyde, who was from Kentucky, was the most cantankerous human being who ever has been in the garage area. On his best day Harry was in a terrible mood. He put up with nothing from race drivers. Absolutely zero. He would have been better off if he had remote control equipment and a transmitter and a receiver rather than a race car driver. And he was totally old school. He wore stiff collars and high-topped brogans. If you had gone to Central Casting and said, "Give me a man from Kentucky in 1918," Harry would have showed up. He still used Brylcreem.

Rick, being much smarter than me and everyone else, put that deal together to everybody's astonishment. No one in the industry believed they could work together. But they did. Harry gave Tim a whole lot more room than I thought he would. All of a sudden under Harry, Tim blossomed and began to finish races, began to stop knocking walls down, and started to lead races.

Around this time, Tim got into it at Daytona with David Pearson who was long in the tooth by then. It happened after the race when Tim got too close to David and bumped him. I heard people talking about what happened. David, being from a mill village, wasn't going to take crap off anybody, especially a "long-haired Yankee," as he would say. Tim walked up to him and said something nasty and called him an old man. The next thing you know, Tim was lying flat on his back in the garage area. David dusted off his hands and walked away. Tim learned not to mess with David Pearson any more.

Tim continued driving great, and by this time he was driving for Folger's coffee for Rick Hendrick. He was winning races, but the dark rumors kept circulating.

As good as he was doing, I could tell something wasn't right. I went to the banquet in New York in 1986 and saw him at a reception. He looked absolutely awful. Two weeks before that he looked terrible. He told me he had the flu. I said, "You have to go to the doctor." I got him an appointment with a doctor in Charlotte. He went to my doctor, and then he absolutely disappeared off the face of the earth. No one knew where he was. No one heard from him, so I began to worry. I called his mother, and she wasn't saying anything. I began to suspect the worst. I suspected he had AIDS.

He wasn't gay, but he had described his symptoms to me so extensively, and I was a guy who read everything medical I could read. I'm a nut about that. His symptoms shouted AIDS. This was when it was rampant. I thought, *How could he have AIDS?* He was dating a girl who used to work for me—a gorgeous girl by the name of LaGina Lookabill. She had been in and out of Little Theater in Charlotte and had left for Hollywood, where she was a young actress. She flew back and forth to Charlotte because she knew a lot of people in racing and a lot of people knew her.

Rick didn't know anything and neither did Harry Hyde. His mother wouldn't tell me anything. But they thought he had pneumonia—pneumocystis pneumonia—that's what you get when you get AIDS. He was from Ashland, Ohio, and I figured that if he was getting medical help it would be at the Cleveland Clinic. I called there and asked for Tim, and after they gave me the runaround, I figured he was there. I was flabbergasted. I came very close to flying up there.

Then one day out of the blue Tim called me. He said he was in Ohio and said he felt okay, but I could tell he wasn't.

"What's wrong with you?" I asked. He repeated that he was okay.

He then called Rick Hendrick and told him the illness was going to keep him from racing at Daytona. He didn't run for several months, and then in May he called me again. He said he wanted to come down and watch the World 600 at Charlotte with me.

Around seven o'clock the morning of the race he showed up at my house, and we rode to the track together. He didn't look good, but he was okay. He acted very nicely. I got him a pass so he could go wherever he wanted at the track. I told him if he got tired, he should come up to my office. After the race he said he was going to hang around the Speedway Club.

"How are you going to get home?" I asked. He said he'd find a way. I had left the keys to Tim's truck in the ignition at my home. When I got up the next morning, Tim and the truck were gone.

I didn't hear from him again. By this time rumors were really flying around, especially the one that he had AIDS. Then one day he called Rick and told him he was ready to go racing again.

"I want to go to Darlington and test," he said. He ran like he had never been out of the race car. And he won the race, which was incredible.

I needed to ask him point blank what was going on with him because I was baffled by how well he was running. And he ran again and won another race. But Watkins Glen wasn't a pretty scene. Before the race he fell asleep. The other drivers were very concerned about him. And just like before, Tim disappeared again. Nobody knew where he went.

I found out he was in Miami. But I couldn't locate him. I called a buddy of his in Miami, and he didn't know where Tim was. When the Daytona 500 came up, Tim decided he wanted to run it. Because AIDS had become so rampant, NASCAR was concerned about what would happen to the rescue workers if he got hurt and was bleeding. Bill France Jr. told Les Richter that Tim couldn't run unless he took a blood test.

Tim and I were staying at the Hilton on Daytona Beach. Bill France Jr. invited Pat and me to dinner Saturday night with him and Les Richter. The whole conversation centered on Tim Richmond. Tim wouldn't submit to a blood test, and he threatened to take NASCAR to court if he couldn't run the race.

I told the others that I had talked to Tim a couple of times but that Tim wasn't talking. Then Sunday night, after the Busch Clash, Tim called me. He said he needed to talk to me. I went up to his room. Visiting him were the weirdest bunch of people I had ever seen in my whole life, including his girlfriend and a far-out motorcycle guy.

He said, "I'm going to race. I'm going to do whatever it takes to get this done. I'm going to have a press conference."

"Are you going to take the blood test?" I asked.

"No," he said. "I'll take one only if everyone else takes one."

He held his press conference. I attended. He announced he would either race or go to court. There was a showdown. NASCAR replied by saying he couldn't race without a blood test.

Then as fast as he had arrived, he left, and that was the last I ever saw of him. Not long afterward I got a call from Carolyn Rudd who told me that one of the girls Tim had been dating had died of AIDS.

He called me on the phone one time from Miami. When I asked him how he was, he was evasive. A month later, I received a call he had died.

It was a tragic story that didn't end there. A few months later I got a call that LaGina Lookabill was coming out with a story on the front page of the *Charlotte Observer* that said Tim had infected her with HIV. It had happened in New York, and she was telling her story because she wanted everyone to know.

60 Minutes picked it up, and LaGina called me and asked if I would be on the show. People were very reluctant to talk about it, mostly because at the time it was regarded as a strictly homosexual disease. But LaGina had recently gotten married to Danny Green, an actor I knew, and out of respect for her, I went on the show. And that was the end of the chapter on Tim Richmond.

Looking back, I often thought of what might have been had Tim not contracted AIDS. He would have lasted up until the early 1990s when racers started getting killed again, starting with Kenny Irwin and Adam Petty and ending up with Dale Earnhardt himself. Could he have made it that long? I don't know. Frankly, I don't think Tim would have raced that long. What he really wanted to do was try Hollywood. He had been out there, and he was enough of a ham and an actor that I believe he could have pulled it off. But we'll never know.

Phil Hill

By Robert Daley

The Cruel Sport,

2005

OR TWO AND A HALF HOURS the Grand Prix driver is cooked by heat, dulled by fumes. The wind tears at him, the noise batters his brain. His body is subjected to frightful pounding, and his mind, if he has one, usually has been pounded numb too. Hour after hour the trees rush by, the road slides sideways under his wheels. The car fights to get away from him, as if it has a life of its own.

At the end of the race, the driver's clothes are soaked through, his face is slack, his eyes unfocused. He is close to exhaustion. This is Phil Hill, second by 1.3 seconds in the 1962 Monaco Grand Prix, as he climbed from his car.

Race driving is a métier for hard, sure men. A driver cannot be stupid and survive, but introspection will ruin him just as fast. The Grand Prix driver must be hard physically and hard mentally, unable to imagine what will happen if he hits a tree at 160 miles per hour.

If he is to win often, the driver must have no thought except to beat down other drivers, to demoralize them with conversation off the course and tactics on it, to smash them.

Most—not all—of the top drivers are like this. But Phil Hill is a thoughtful, gentle man. "I'm in the wrong business," he said once. "I don't want to beat anybody, I don't want to be the big hero. I'm a peace-loving man, basically."

In sports cars Hill won the 24 Hours of Le Mans three times, the Sebring Twelve Hours three times, the 1,000 Kilometers of Buenos Aires, of the Nürburgring, and of Venezuela. In Grand Prix cars he was world champion in 1961; in seven races he was first twice, second twice, and third twice. He won the two fastest races of the season, the Belgian Grand Prix at 128 miles per hour, and the Italian Grand Prix at 130. He did not make a mistake all year.

Behind him are many track records, notably at the Nürburgring. There are 175 curves per fourteen-mile lap of the Nürburgring. They are curves of all sizes, shapes, and speeds, some at the bottom of long, steep downhill runs, some just after humpbacked bridges which send the car aloft, wheels dangling, reaching stiff-legged for renewed contact with the road. Worse, the road is narrow and alternately bordered by forests, by stone walls, by precipices and impenetrable hedges. If a car leaves the road, its driver almost certainly will be badly hurt, perhaps killed.

For thirty-five years it was said that no man would ever lap the Nürburgring under nine minutes. The great Fangio had not come close; his best was only 9:13. But in practice in 1961, in a car powered by an engine forty percent smaller than Fangio's, Hill lapped in 8:55, and in the race itself, with the course littered by slower machines, in 8:57.8.

HILL WILL TELL YOU HE IS NOT A BRAVE MAN, but the evidence is to the contrary. He won his first Le Mans in 1958 by stomping on the gas instead of the brake in the middle of the night in a blinding rainstorm. More prudent drivers slowed, and when the storm eased, Hill was too far ahead to be caught.

He won once at Sebring in another blinding rainstorm.

"When you passed me, I was horrified," said the Swedish driver Jo Bonnier after the race. "You were laughing. I didn't see how you could stay on the road at such speed. What were you laughing about?"

"It amused me the way the rain was running down your beard," Hill replied. "You looked so uncomfortable."

At times like this Hill sounds as racing drivers are supposed to sound: aggressive, insensitive to peril. So he does when he says he is not very friendly with other drivers: "How can you be friends with a racing driver? You try to beat them all day on the circuit, and then at night you're supposed to forget all that? I think all racing drivers secretly hate each other anyway."

BUT THEN THE HARD VENEER DISAPPEARS and he adds morosely: "Racing brings out the worst in me. I don't know what would have become of me if I hadn't become a race driver, as a person, I mean, but I'm not sure I like the person I am now. Racing makes me selfish, irritable, defensive. There are thirty other guys trying to get where I am. I have to be on my guard all the time. I even have to hang around the cars when I could be doing something useful, in order to make sure the mechanics are doing what I have asked them to do. We're not allowed to touch the cars. I don't hang around the cars all the time because I like to, but to protect my interests. If I could get out of this sport with any ego left, I would."

Hill pauses, then observes: "Life is a struggle whatever work you do, but at least in any other business you don't have to risk your life."

It is clear that the strain of the permanent danger weighs more heavily on Hill than on most other drivers. Drivers are always talking about death, often outrageously, as when Stirling Moss remarks: "Racing is a kind of Russian roulette. You never know when the chamber will come up loaded." The listener is always shocked, perhaps awed, and Moss basks contentedly in this reaction. Many drivers enjoy the danger, or say they do. Not Hill.

As he struggled to win the world championship, Hill was handicapped precisely because he did think of it, and because (as he says) his ego no longer needed the glory it once had sought. Certain risks he accepted. Others he would not accept.

In May of that year he dueled lap after lap with Jim Clark's Lotus, the two cars at great speed never more than a few feet apart. "There was a very fine ethical line which both of us recognized," Hill remarked afterwards. "Certain tactics were okay. Others were too dangerous. Some drivers would not have recognized this ethical line. There is one driver, for instance, who has a reputation for imprudence and who now uses this reputation as a weapon to scare other drivers out of his way. I think that's evil." The implication is that Hill would refuse a dice with a driver he could not depend on, as he refused to dice with Trips in the British Grand Prix that same year.

Hill had gone directly from the French Grand Prix to Aintree, England, where he spent days walking, driving, studying the course. Suddenly a telegram arrived from Enzo Ferrari.

Ferrari wanted to know why Hill had not returned to the factory to test cars. Ferrari threatened to send no car for Hill for the British Grand Prix.

Ferrari harries his drivers, undermines them, perhaps feeling that a shaken driver will race faster than a confident one.

Now Hill worried until race day. Would his car come? He was shaken, all right, but into driving slower, not faster.

"Ferrari pressured Peter Collins like this just before Peter was killed," Hill muttered when he saw his car unloaded at last. "Now the same thing is happening to me."

The race began, Hill was still upset, and then rain poured down. On a tight turn in the rain Trips nipped in front of Hill. Neither driver had much traction, neither could see. Hill started after Trips, but was unsettled, had no confidence in himself nor in his machine in the blinding rain. Abruptly he dropped back.

"I'm not going to kill myself just to be world champion," he mumbled to himself. He finished second to Trips that day.

PHYSICALLY, HILL IS AN ALMOST PERFECT racing machine: keen eyes, strong hands, heavily muscled arms and shoulders. He has never had a serious accident in fourteen seasons of racing. He has rarely even slid off the road, and he cannot remember the last time he overstressed an engine.

But mentally Hill is different from most other drivers, for he is basically a gentle man in a profession devoid of gentleness. Motor racing is noise, speed, danger, crowds, constant travel, living often in seedy hotels out of suitcases jammed with dirty clothes. Many of the people in it tend to be callous, if not cruel at times.

Hill cannot seem to be cruel to anyone. Hordes of hangers-on, many of them rich, follow the races from country to country, buttonholing Hill and other drivers incessantly, begging for conversation, a ride out to the circuit, a cup of coffee on the terrace perhaps. "Where do these people come from, what are they doing here?" cries Hill. He resents them because "they make me see the phony side of all this," but he is polite to them nonetheless.

Interviewers plague him, often with stupid questions, but if he is driven to show annoyance, he will usually apologize contritely a few moments later. People attach themselves to him and he worries for days about how to get rid of them without hurting them.

Race day is an ordeal for him. "It is always the same," he says. "I'm asleep in a warm bed, the sun is shining in the window, and I start to wake up and I'm lying there all warm and secure. And then I start to think: this is not just any day. This is race day. Then in an instant all the warmth and security is gone, the bed is cold, and I sit up wide awake."

Hill genuinely dislikes the limelight, keeps no scrapbooks, sometimes refuses to read articles about himself, and, instead of displaying all the dozens of trophies he has won, he stores most of them in barrels in his cellar. When he wins a race he seems embarrassed as the flowers and trophies are heaped upon him; he tends to hang back in the crowd of officials and also-rans who are also part of the ceremony, and he will strike none of the triumphant poses the photographers beg him for.

There is gentleness also in the way he speaks of the danger he has faced for so many years: "I would so love to get out of this unbent. I have a horror of cripples. Even when I was a little boy I couldn't bear to look at anyone who was deformed, could not bear to see them suffering. I guess I've always worried about ending up that way myself. I want to get out of this in one piece. Do you know, I've never been hurt in an accident."

Ask him why he races and he will reply: "Because I do it well." What he means is that this is the only thing he does that well, meaning brilliantly. How can a man not do something which he knows how to do brilliantly?

No other driver I know of doubts the worth of racing. Most adore its glamour and excitement, and do not ask further questions. But Hill wonders all the time about the "intrinsic value of what I do. Does it have any intrinsic value? I have become a cynic. I no longer believe that driving race cars is so important." He would like to believe he contributes to the world, but his case is complicated by the risk he runs. If he crashed tomorrow, what exactly would he be dying for? The $20,000 or so he earns each year? Hardly.

PHIL HILL STANDS OUT AS A VULNERABLE human being in a trade where nearly everyone else pretends to be invulnerable. Most others are surrounded by the mob and love it. At times, Hill also seems to enjoy the pressure and excitement, but mostly it just makes him nervous.

Periodically during the season he will sneak away between races and drop out of sight for days at a time. He never tells anyone where he has gone. He has many acquaintances, but very few friends and no intimates, male or female. When not preoccupied by a race, he is a very warm person. He invites close friendship, but when it is offered to him he backs off. No one can get close to him.

He loves music. He buys tickets to the opera outdoors in August in the Roman arena at Verona or to hear Joan Sutherland at La Scala in Milan. He invites the Gendebiens or the Ginthers to drive up with him, and they enjoy the performances, but not as much as he.

Between races he lies in his hotel room at Modena listening to symphonic music on a hi-fi rig which he has brought in and put together by himself.

Sometimes he says he hates racing.

What he really likes to do, and what he seems much better suited for temperamentally, is to restore old cars. He has ten of them at home in California: Pierce Arrows, Packards, an Alfa Romeo, all thirty years old or more, all gleaming and new as if built only yesterday. Hill has rebuilt them all with his own hands, starting usually with rusted hulks and decayed interiors, many parts missing or ruined. He has worked on one car for months at a time, sanding away the rust of decades, finding or making missing parts, polishing old chrome till it shines again like silver, restitching interior leather, cleaning, painting, perfecting down to the last ashtray. When working on a car he can go weeks without seeing anyone, without eating a proper meal, or getting a full night's sleep. When he has finished, the car looks and runs like new, a little bit of the luxury and elegance of the past lives again, and Hill himself feels a satisfaction which few races have ever given him.

Certainly this is an art form, and temperamentally Hill seems more of an artist than a race driver. He is as alert to sounds as any musician and his eye is as keen for detail as any painter's. He is forever noticing details others don't notice: a certain color, a certain view, someone else's inconspicuous habit or attitude. Hill can put a little artistry, a little perfectionism into racing—to take a corner on precisely the same line lap after lap after lap at 128 miles per hour is not easy—but not too much. Because in racing the primary thing is not perfect technique but winning.

It is significant that Hill likes sports car racing better than Grand Prixs, endurance better than sprints. In a sports car race, if a man drives perfectly for twelve hours or twenty-four he will win—time will destroy his opposition for him. But in Grand Prix racing a man must harry his opposition from beginning to end and somehow, at the crucial moment, get past it. Grand Prix racing demands what in sports is called "killer instinct," and this Hill lacks. He is not mean enough. He understands too well that others would like to win, to be champion, just as much as he. This robs him of the ability to work up a consuming (if temporary) hatred for his rivals, without which a really superior performance is impossible.

WHEN HILL WAS MUCH YOUNGER, and fighting for a place on a factory team, he was, by his own admission, aggressive and a fool. He drove frantically, and rivals gave way out of fear. The years dulled that aggressiveness, but sharpened his skills until he was, in 1961, at the age of thirty-four, as fast as, or faster, than any driver except, possibly, Moss. He was certainly faster than Trips most times. But in some races Trips would nervously hound him, pressure him, until Hill became nervous himself and feared being forced, or forcing Trips, into some ghastly mistake. He would feel a kind of panic; not trusting Trips' judgment in a race car, he temporarily did not trust his own, either. The stakes were too high to take a chance, and so he would give way to Trips.

In the end, the ghastly mistake Hill feared indeed occurred. Trips plunged into the mob and killed fifteen people, himself included. Hill drove on very, very carefully, very, very fast, winning that race and the world championship at an average speed of 130 miles per hour.

He had driven that whole season like a single long sports car race—preferring to race too cautiously, rather than too fast. A bundle of nerves inside, he made no mistakes; his rivals did make them, and so he won the world championship.

But in the tumult and gloom of the Trips tragedy, it went unnoticed that Phil Hill was champion of the world. Worse, the sentimental preferred to believe that Hill had not won, poor Trips had merely lost. Phil knew this. There was no pleasure in his victory. He felt empty and a little bitter. He had won the prize, and it was worthless. He took his trophies and went away, hoping that some day the world championship would mean something to him. But so far it has not.

When he came back to race for Ferrari again the next year, he was a different man. Much of the spirit seemed to have gone out of him, and after the first few races he did not really seem to care about his job.

"I no longer have as much need to race, to win," he said in a sad, puzzled way. "I don't have as much hunger anymore. I am no longer willing to risk killing myself."

He had raced for Ferrari exclusively for nine years, but at the end of that long, slow season Ferrari and Hill parted.

His friends did not know whether to weep or applaud, and apparently Phil Hill didn't either.

CHAPTER 5

Law Makers, Law Enforcers, and Safety... or Lack Thereof

Another Day, Another Convertible . . . & Another Hotel Full of Cops

By Hunter S. Thompson

Fear and Loathing in Las Vegas,

1971

HE FIRST ORDER OF BUSINESS WAS TO GET RID OF the Red Shark. It was too obvious. Too many people might recognize it, especially the Vegas police; although as far as they knew, the thing was already back home in L.A. It was last seen running at top speed across Death Valley on Interstate 15. Stopped and warned in Baker by the CHP . . . then suddenly disappeared. . . .

The last place they would look for it, I felt, was in a rental-car lot at the airport. I had to go out there anyway, to meet my attorney. He would be arriving from L.A. in the late afternoon.

I drove very quietly on the freeway, gripping my normal instinct for bursts of acceleration and sudden lane changes—trying to remain inconspicuous—and when I got there I parked the Shark between two old Air Force buses in a "utility lot" about half a mile from the terminal. Very tall buses. Make it hard as possible for the fuckers. A little walking never hurt anybody.

By the time I got to the terminal I was pouring sweat. But nothing abnormal. I tend to sweat heavily in warm climates. My clothes are soaking wet from dawn to dusk. This worried me at first, but when I went to a doctor and described my normal daily intake of booze, drugs and poison he told me to come back when the sweating *stopped.* That would be the danger point, he said—a sign that my body's desperately overworked flushing mechanism had broken down completely. "I have great faith in the natural processes," he said. "But in your case . . . well . . . I find no precedent. We'll just have to wait and see, then work with what's left."

I spent about two hours in the bar, drinking Bloody Marys for the V-8 nutritional content and watching the flights from L.A. I'd eaten nothing but grapefruit for about twenty hours and my head was adrift from its moorings.

You better watch yourself, I thought. There *are* limits to what the human body can endure. You don't want to break down and start bleeding from the ears right here in the terminal. Not in this town. In Las Vegas they *kill* the weak and deranged.

I realized this, and kept quiet even when I felt symptoms of a terminal blood-sweat coming on. But this passed. I saw the cocktail waitress getting nervous, so I forced myself to get up and walk stiffly out of the bar. No sign of my attorney. Down to the VIP car-rental booth, where I traded the

Red Shark in for a White Cadillac Convertible. "This goddamn Chevy has caused me a lot of trouble," I told them. "I get the feeling that people are putting me down—especially in gas stations, when I have to get out and open the hood *manually*."

"Well . . . of *course*," said the man behind the desk. "What you need, I think, is one of our Mercedes 600 Towne-Cruiser Specials, with air-conditioning. You can even carry your own fuel, if you want; we make that available. . . ."

"Do I look like a goddamn Nazi?" I said. "I'll have a natural *American* car, or nothing at all!"

They called up the white Coupe de Ville at once. Everything was automatic. I could sit in the red-leather driver's seat and make every inch of the car *jump*, by touching the proper buttons. It was a wonderful machine: Ten grand worth of gimmicks and high-priced Special Effects. The rear-windows leaped up with a touch, like frogs in a dynamite pond. The white canvas top ran up and down like a rollercoaster. The dashboard was full of esoteric lights & dials & meters that I would never understand—but there was no doubt in my mind that I was into a *superior machine*.

The Caddy wouldn't get off the line quite as fast as the Red Shark, but once it got rolling—around eighty—it was pure smooth hell . . . all that elegant, upholstered weight lashing across the desert was like rolling through midnight on the old *California Zephyr*.

I handled the whole transaction with a credit card that I later learned was "canceled"—completely bogus. But the Big Computer hadn't mixed me yet, so I was still a fat gold credit risk.

Later, looking back on this transaction, I *knew* the conversation that had almost certainly ensued:

"Hello. This is VIP car-rentals in Las Vegas. We're calling to check on Number 875-045-616-B. Just a routine credit check, nothing urgent. . . ."

(Long pause at the other end. Then:) "Holy shit!"

"What?"

"Pardon me . . . Yes, we have that number. It's been placed on emergency redline status. Call the police at once and don't let him out of your sight!"

(Another long pause) "Well . . . ah . . . you see, that number is not on *our* current Red List, and . . . ah . . . Number 875-045-616-B just left our lot in a new Cadillac convertible."

"No!"

"Yes. He's long gone; totally insured."

"Where?"

"I think he said St. Louis. Yes, that's what the card says. Raoul Duke, leftfielder & batting champion of the St. Louis Browns. Five days at $25 per, plus twenty-five cents a mile. His card was valid, so of course we had no choice. . . ."

This is true. The car rental agency had no legal reason to hassle me, since my card was technically valid. During the next four days I drove that car all over Las Vegas—even passing the VIP agency's main office on Paradise Boulevard several times—and at no time was I bothered by any show of rudeness.

This is one of the hallmarks of Vegas hospitality. The only bedrock rule is Don't Burn the Locals. Beyond that, nobody cares. They would rather not know. If Charlie Manson checked into the Sahara tomorrow morning, nobody would hassle him as long as he tipped big.

Safety Measures— Who Needs Them?

By Jeremy Clarkson

Clarkson on Cars,

1996

I N A LITTLE OVER A HUNDRED YEARS, THE MOTOR CAR has killed more people than every single war that has ever been waged.

Stacked up against the car's adroitness at wholesale slaughter, the Somme begins to look like a Sunday School outing.

In India alone, where cars haven't even caught on properly, nearly 50,000 people a year are killed on the roads. In just one state, 16 people are killed every single day, and 97 are injured. Out there, one in every 42 cars on the roads, at some stage, will be involved in a serious accident. It's so bad that in the 5 to 44 age group, car accidents rate as one of the biggest killers.

In the West, the car is still a murdering blaggard but at least the picture is a little more rosy. Indeed, while the number of cars on the roads goes up every year, the number of people they kill is falling.

But I fear that this statistic is about to be filed under 'history'. I fear that within the next five years, the number of people being killed will rise sharply all over Europe and North America.

And I blame the air bag.

Earlier this year, Mercedes-Benz unveiled a new concept car which is basically a bouncy castle on wheels. Hidden away, in little recesses all over the interior, are no fewer than seventeen air bags.

Quite apart from the usual places like the steering wheel, they're located under the dashboard to save your parts, in all four doors, between the front seats, in the roof and in the headrests. There is even an air bag in the back of each front seat so that should the driver crash while you're in the back, working on a laptop computer, you won't emerge from the wreckage with qwertyuiop[] stencilled on your forehead.

At the moment, this is at the concept stage but we can rest assured that something along similar lines will soon find its way into ordinary cars for the road.

Volvo is already advertising its seat-mounted air bags which pump themselves up should anyone be foolish enough to drive into the side of one of these Swedish tanks.

Now you must remember that Volvo already has its Side Impact Protection System (SIPS) which transfers all the energy of a crash into the roof and the floor, and away from the poor souls in the car.

Then there's Audi with Procon Ten. Run into something bigger than you are—a Volvo for instance—and at the same moment, the seatbelts are tightened as the steering wheel is pulled forward, away from your head.

This is the cutting edge of safety in cars, and it comes on top of anti-lock brakes, rigid safety cells, traction control and any number of other devices to keep you alive, should everything turn pear-shaped.

And therein lies the problem. Very soon, people are going to realise that they can have huge crashes, at any speed they choose, and walk away.

They'll be careering into buildings, pedestrians, lamp-posts and people in older, less-well-protected cars, knowing that they are immune from injury. This won't do.

So if car manufacturers are really interested in promoting safety on the roads, rather than introducing new measures about which their marketing departments can crow, they should ditch all the new ideas.

Rip out the air bags, and in their place, fit titanium spikes which, in the event of a crash, will leap out of the centre of the steering wheel, and impale the driver on his seat.

And hey, Mr Audi, instead of pulling the steering wheel forward in a crash, why not give us something which shoves it back into the guy's face—hard.

And Volvo, forget SIPS. Better to fit a small nuclear bomb in the back of the child seat which is triggered to go off should the car receive a significant jolt. Crash and your baby is blown into such tiny particles, you won't even need a coffin.

With these sorts of features in all cars on the road, I think it's safe to assume that the number of deaths on the road would fall, in an instant, to zero.

Right now, people are quite happy to hurtle down the outside lane of a motorway, in thick fog, at 100 mph because their anti-lock brakes will keep them out of trouble—they'd better go too—and that even if they don't, everything else will.

Well, they'd think twice if the car was nothing more than a series of booby traps.

To make sure this was fair, and that all cars are equipped with the same menacing array of death traps, the government needs to introduce legislation. But this is where it all gets sinister. The government won't do this, because it wants us to drive fast and dangerously.

They know that if they ban seatbelts, rip down all crash barriers and douse all roads with a mixture of diesel oil and washing-up liquid every morning, people would never dare drive at more than 10 mph.

And this would remove one of the most iniquitous taxes ever dreamed up—the speeding ticket.

It's all so obvious. By forcing car makers to give us safer vehicles, and by making the roads less dangerous, they are encouraging us to drive faster and faster. Couple this with ridiculous vigilant police patrols, and they have a small fortune.

People are dying out there, to pay for the National Health Service.

Winter Driving Made Easy

Everything You Always Wanted to Know about Surviving the Snow Season (But Were Too Cold to Ask)

By P. J. O'Rourke

Car and Driver,

December 1982

THE GREAT THING ABOUT DRIVING A CAR IN THE WINTER is that it's so convenient. Compare what it's like, being inside a car in December, with what it was like a hundred years ago, being inside a horse. This was much less comfortable and couldn't have been good for the animal. Another convenient thing about winter driving: if you have an attached garage, you can start your car, leave the garage door down, and kill yourself and your entire family. That is, you can achieve the same results as you'd get from a gigantic flaming wreck on the highway without the bother of leaving your house. But the most convenient thing about driving a car in the winter is that you often can't. This is a perfect excuse for staying home and not going to work, and what could be more convenient than that?

If you have to drive during the winter months, it's important to own the right car. Jeeps, Eagles, Blazers, and Subarus won't do. When your brand of automobile is shown delivering Sherpa food to Sir Edmund Hillary during every NFL timeout, it won't be convincing to tell your boss that you can't get out of the driveway. Buy something with no ground clearance instead, like a Corvette or a Ferrari. Probably the best I-can't-get-there winter-driving car ever is the old Austin-Healey with the original exhaust system in place. You can get hung up driving one of those across your front yard in August, if you haven't mowed the lawn in a week.

Be sure to get a car that has no traction, either—something big, with rear-wheel drive and all the weight in the front. Don't get a rear-engined car or a front-wheel-drive car. A car with good traction will go fast on ice-covered roads, and it's obviously dangerous to go fast on roads like that. Also, if you have poor traction, you might go off the road and wind up in a soft snowbank; if you have good traction, you might make it to work and wind up in a hard job. Winnebago motorhomes are huge and have all the weight in the front. Get one of those, and when you get stuck in a snowbank, you'll have a bathroom and a kitchen and it will be almost like staying home in the first place.

But if you really have to get to work in the winter, make sure your vehicle is properly prepared. Don't worry about maintenance, though. Cars are like vegetables: they'll keep indefinitely at freezing temperatures. Especially don't go hosing out your wheel wells because of road salt. Salt causes rust. Water causes rust. So you can imagine what the saltwater

you're making with that hose will cause. You do, however, have to make a decision: whether to use your regular tires, which have hardly any tread, or whether to use your snow tires, which also have hardly any tread because you were driving around on them all summer. A lot of people are going for the new all-weather tires because you can let them get bald without feeling guilty about not changing them every spring and fall.

Of course, the best choice would be studded snow tires, but the tow-truck and ambulance lobbies have made them illegal in many states. The next-best thing to studded snow tires is tire chains, except it's impossible to attach tire chains unless you are physically able to lift your car and you have prehensile feet to put the chains on while you're holding the car aloft. The only other way to attach tire chains is to drive your car up on a stump so that all four wheels are off the ground. Then wait for a glacier to come along and knock the car off. If you can't get the chains on and are forbidden by law to have studded snow tires, you can use four cement blocks to improve winter driving. Put your car up on the blocks and fly someplace where the weather is warm. You can rent another car when you land.

One other possibility is to turn your car into a snowmobile by tying a pair of cross-country skis to the front tires. This has not actually been tried yet, but it sounds interesting. The skis will probably go around a couple of times inside the wheel wells and make a terrific racket, but once you get moving, your car should behave just like a snowmobile. Which is to say, it will get stuck in a snowbank.

Preparation, of course, is only part of the winter automobile problem. Getting a car started when it's ten below can be even more difficult than getting it off the stump after you've put the chains on. Some people leave a light on all night in the garage on the theory that it will generate just enough heat to keep the crankcase oil from congealing. This does not work. During a bad cold snap last winter, I left my headlights on all night in the garage and the car wouldn't start for shit the next morning. It is true, however, that congealed crankcase oil makes a car hard to start, so use a lighter-weight oil in the winter. Johnson's Baby Oil, for instance. Rub this all over somebody cute, stay home, and forget about starting the car.

Turning the engine over frequently works, too. When the weather gets extremely cold, you should get up in the middle of the night and start your car. Keep it running long enough to get to the airport, and fly someplace where the weather is warm. Proper use of antifreeze can also help. Alcohol is effective as an antifreeze. Gin has alcohol in it. So does vermouth. Mix eight parts gin to one part vermouth, call your boss, and say you can't get out of the driveway.

You really *shouldn't* get out of the driveway, either. Once you're out of the driveway, winter driving requires all sorts of complex, special techniques. One of these is the foghorn technique, such as ships use in bad weather. When visibility is poor, drive very slowly straight ahead and beep your horn three times every ten seconds. This worked for the *Andrea Doria*. Actually, come to think of it, it didn't.

Anyway, the first rule is to go slow. Get up late, have a big breakfast, take a nap, have a second breakfast, call the boss, and tell him you can't get out of the driveway after all.

The second rule is to steer into a skid. This is a difficult rule for a lot of people to understand, and I'm one of them. What's that mean, "steer into a skid"? Is it a command? Are you supposed to go someplace and have a skid? Is it a general observation? Does it mean, if you steer then you'll skid? And who's being fooled anyway? If you're able to steer where you want—like "into a skid"—then you're not skidding anyway. So forget this rule. Learn the Bob Bondurant technique for skidding instead. Bob's technique is to fly someplace where the weather is warm, start a driving school, and get other people to pay to learn how it's done. (He tells them to steer into a skid.)

You don't actually have to go to the Bondurant school. You can teach yourself many of the techniques of winter driving. Just cut the brake lines on your car, remove the tie rods, put ice down the front of your pants, and accelerate full speed into a crowded shopping-center parking lot. This will exactly simulate driving in the middle of winter on icy roads in heavy traffic. What it will teach you is not to do any such thing.

You may call this an expensive lesson, but that shows your lack of consideration for others. Think how amused the rest of us will be when we read the newspaper story about how you cut your brake lines, removed your tie rods, and drove full speed into a shopping center with a Fudgsicle in your shorts.

Many other winter-driving situations can be practiced beforehand, too. To practice operating the accelerator, brake, and clutch pedals in a great big pair of Sorrels, play the piano in oven mitts. To practice starting cars with dead batteries, take a Sears DieHard into the grocery store, lean over into the meat freezer, and thaw a Butterball turkey by running a twelve-volt current through it with jumper cables.

One type of practice for winter driving doesn't require any physical activity. It's strictly a matter of mental preparation. After all, driving on icy roads has a lot to do with how you think about them, so conceive of a metaphor for icy roads and you'll know how to behave. Think of icy roads as politicians, for instance—crooked, slippery, and treacherous. If you hit a politician on the nose (equivalent to hitting the brake pedal on an icy road), you'll go to jail. If you kick a politician in the ass (equivalent to putting your foot into the accelerator), you'll go to jail also (going to jail is the equivalent of getting stuck in a snowbank). Using the politician metaphor, wintertime is one long election day. Do what any sensible person does on election day and stay home.

The remaining winter-driving techniques don't have anything to do with driving, because you're stuck in that snowbank. When stuck in a snowbank, use the "cradle" method of rocking the car: rock back and forth, back and forth, back and forth, then stick your thumb into your mouth and cry.

Remain inside your car when you are stuck in a snowbank. This will make your body easier to find later. However, if there is a telephone available within safe walking distance, maybe you should call the AAA. Anybody who does any winter driving should belong to the AAA. Non-AAA towing services are expensive and often don't come. AAA towing services are free and often don't come. Actually, that's not true. The AAA is a very good organization, and they'll come get you as soon as they can in the spring. As good as the AAA is, what's really needed is an AAAA or an AAAAA; instead of helping you get home in bad weather, it would help you stay home in bad weather by bringing some drinks over to your house or would call your boss and say your driveway is a snow-emergency area and the Red Cross has flown you someplace where the weather is warm.

Meanwhile, as long as you're stuck in a snowbank, this is a great opportunity to jacklight deer. Build a fire in your car so the game warden will believe you when you say you thought you were going to have to stay there all winter. Jacklighting deer, of course, is only one of the many outdoor winter activities that can be enjoyed with your automobile. Ice fishing is another. Drive your car right out onto the ice. It will fall through, oil and gasoline will seep out into the pond, and in the spring all the fish will be lying there right on top of the water and you can scoop them out with your hands and not have to fuss with expensive poles and lures. Cars are great for skiing, too. The point of skiing is to pick up girls, and you can pick up a lot more girls if you tell them your car is a Porsche 928. It's all covered with sleet and ice and probably stuck in a snowbank, so they can't tell.

But the very best automotive winter sport is just going for a ride in the country. Make that country Australia. It's summer down there now. And the boss will never find you in Sydney.

Auto Theft
Is Big Business

By J. Edgar Hoover, Director,
Federal Bureau of Investigation

Motor Trend,
December 1952

INCE THE CLOSE OF WORLD WAR II, more than one million automobile thefts have been reported to law enforcement agencies throughout the United States. The prey of amateur and professional criminals alike, automobiles now are among the largest items on the nation's ledger of annual losses due to theft.

The magnitude of the automobile theft problem is shown in reports which have been received by the Federal Bureau of Investigation from law enforcement agencies in 381 U.S. cities. These reports reveal that the value of automobiles stolen in the 381 cities totaled more than $95,000,000 during 1951, while all other property taken by robbers and thieves was valued at little more than $61,000,000.

Over the entire nation an estimated 196,960 automobiles, valued at more than $190,000,000, were stolen last year. Even when it is considered that an estimated 180,810 stolen automobiles were recovered during 1951, the citizens of the United States still suffered a net loss of $15,600,000 through theft of automobiles alone in that 12-month period.

Statistics such as these certainly do not adequately portray the true picture of the losses suffered by law-abiding citizens through the theft of automobiles. Each of the 196,960 cars which were stolen resulted in police investigation, financed by public funds. In addition, many of the owners of these cars were dependent upon them in their vocations. Others suffered severe inconvenience which cannot be estimated in dollars due to the loss of their automobiles.

Statistics showing the total estimated value of automobiles stolen in the United States demonstrate that car theft is a major law enforcement problem. Aggressive action has been taken in the past to combat the auto thief, and such action has been stepped up to further combat this menace. Like all criminal acts, automobile theft is not solely the concern of the police or of the person who suffers the loss. It is also the concern of the public and must be met with vigorous and constructive action.

Armed with Federal legislation which makes illegal the inter-state transportation of stolen motor vehicles, the FBI has been active since 1919 in smashing auto theft rings which have operated on a national or international basis. The investigative jurisdiction of the FBI is limited to those cases in which the stolen automobile has been transported from one state to another; however, through cost-free services provided by the FBI Laboratory and Identification Division, the FBI has been able to assist state and municipal law enforcement agencies in identifying and convicting numerous auto thieves whose operations have not extended across state lines.

Each year it has become increasingly more obvious that the challenge presented by automobile thieves can be adequately met only through united action. As a first step in effecting a more concentrated offensive against automobile thieves, the FBI called upon state and local law enforcement agencies to meet with its agents in regional conferences which are now being held throughout the nation. Also participating in these conferences are state motor vehicle bureaus, the National Automobile Theft Bureau, and other interested agencies. Devoted solely to open forum discussion of car thefts, the conferences are meeting everywhere with interest and enthusiasm. An encouraging number of fine solutions to this problem have already been proposed at these conferences, and there has been universal agreement that an alert, educated public is the greatest asset available to the law enforcement officer in coping with this type of crime.

There are, in general, three types of car thefts. The first is committed by amateur thrill seekers who steal automobiles for "joy rides." This type of crime is responsible for an untold amount of needless grief each year since the overwhelming majority of amateur "joy riders" are able to steal only those automobiles which thoughtlessly have been left unlocked.

One such theft was committed by a "gang" of four boys whose "joy ride" in a stolen automobile came to an end when they collided with a gasoline pump and ran into a store building. The oldest of these boys was nine years of age, and certainly none of the four had the criminal skill to steal a securely locked automobile.

Numerous other cases have been brought to my attention in which motorists have left their cars unoccupied and with engines running while they stopped to attend to minor business matters. Finding their automobiles missing upon their return, these persons have learned too late that carelessness is a close companion of the auto thief.

The amateur automobile thief must rely upon the negligence of motorists. He has neither the training nor the tools to enter a securely locked automobile and drive it away. Although the overwhelming majority of automobiles stolen by "joy riders" are recovered soon after they are taken, each such theft requires the investigative time of police officers and the expenditure of public funds which might have been saved had the motorist thought to lock his car.

A second type of automobile thief is the person who steals a car for immediate transportation or for use in another crime. Although these persons fundamentally are not professional automobile thieves, they generally are hardened criminals who are well trained in the art of breaking into locked automobiles and starting them without the use of ignition keys.

John Dillinger was one such criminal. While Dillinger and his gang were plundering the Midwest, they frequently stole automobiles for use in their holdups and for transportation purposes. The FBI first was able to enter actively into the search for Dillinger when he stole an automobile in Indiana in March, 1934, and transported it to Illinois. Dillinger's 15-month flight from justice was ended when he was killed while resisting arrest in a gun battle with FBI agents and the East Chicago, Indiana, police in July, 1934.

Although the majority of automobiles stolen by this type of criminal later are recovered, many of them are badly damaged or completely demolished in efforts to prevent their being identified or linked to other criminal acts.

Professionalism in the theft of automobiles reaches its ultimate peak in the operations of the gangs which are organized in a business-like manner to steal cars for resale. Over the years FBI agents have cooperated with local police in smashing auto theft rings which were so highly special-ized that the function of each member of the ring was narrowly defined. These rings, tightly organized and composed only of skilled professionals, recognize no state boundaries in carrying out their criminal activities.

A typical auto theft ring employs a "spotter" who locates automobiles to be stolen, often having instructions to find cars of a particular make and model. Another member of the ring steals the car and delivers it to a garage where the automobile may be repainted and such identification marks as engine and serial numbers altered or removed.

In addition, these rings have employed persons who specialize in obtaining false registrations and bills of sale, using still others to drive the cars to various points throughout the nation to be sold.

One such gang which was composed of 10 men recently was smashed by the FBI in cooperation with several municipal and state law enforce-ment agencies in the South. This ring was engaged primarily in the theft of 1949 and 1950 models of one type of automobile. Included among its members were persons who were skilled in changing engine and serial numbers. In addition, they often replaced the transmissions and locks on the cars before selling them. The expenses incurred by such auto theft rings are high. Their continuation in "business" is dependent upon handling a large number of stolen cars.

In another case, the FBI joined with the Royal Canadian Mounted Police in rounding up a ring which specialized in stealing automobiles in the U.S. and transporting them to Canada. Here again was a ring which amassed huge profits despite expenses.

At the professional level, automobile theft is highly organized, encom-passing the nation and extending even beyond national boundaries. On the amateur level it presents a critical problem to the citizen and to the law enforcement officer, all too often serving as a springboard from which the criminal neophyte is launched into a life of underworld activity.

In addition to adhering to the practice of securely locking any automobile which he leaves unoccupied, the average citizen can greatly assist in coping with the car theft problem by reporting any persons whom he sees tampering with automobiles or prowling in parking areas. An alert, observant public is a necessary element for the most effective law enforcement.

A woman in the West wrote to the FBI revealing that her neighbors had aroused her suspicions by parking automobiles in the surrounding woods in such a manner that she felt they might be attempting to hide them. Based on this information, the FBI launched an investigation which identified this woman's neighbors as a gang which had stolen 58 automobiles!

Each year thousands of stolen automobiles are bought and sold by innocent citizens throughout the United States. Before buying a used car, it is the prospective owner's responsibility to carefully inspect the title and the motor and serial numbers. If it appears that efforts have been made to alter these numbers, or if doubt arises concerning the authenticity of the title, the police should be notified immediately.

The auto theft problem can be met adequately only through the full cooperation of all law-abiding citizens. The rules are simple and sensible to follow: Protect your own car; report suspicious activities; and be certain that you aren't duped into buying a stolen car.

WILL YOUR CAR BE STOLEN?

IT MIGHT BE, IF YOU . . .

. . . leave your engine running while you

jump out to run into the store

. . . leave the keys in your ignition lock

. . . leave your car unlocked

. . . don't report prowlers in parking areas

. . . don't report persons tampering with automobiles

Frontline

By Rowan Atkinson

CAR Magazine,
February 1993

THERE ARE NO GERMAN COMEDIANS. This week, I was travelling at the legal speed limit on a British road, and it felt peculiarly dangerous. The road wasn't twisty, it wasn't raining, it wasn't dark, it was just . . . that the speed limit felt perilously high. The road in question was a stretch of urban dual carriageway on which one is never supposed to travel at more than 70mph, and yet this tarmac boasted a plethora of appallingly dangerous features. It had three narrow lanes, blind crests, T-junctions leading onto it, even bus stops in the slow lane for goodness' sake, and yet there I was whisking along at the maximum speed one is allowed to drive anywhere in Britain. The same speed at which one may traverse the M8 in Scotland at 9am on New Year's Day, when you are unlikely to spot a Scottish motorist for 25 miles.

Speed limits are really a nonsense of generalisation. There are no German comedians. Sweeping statements based on profound ignorance. I am as sure that there are roads in Britain for which 70mph is a ridiculously and possibly dangerously slow speed, owing to the soporific ease with which a modern car travels at it, as I am that there is a rich bounty of Teutonic comedy. Obviously, national speed limits are generalisations perforce. It is impractical to have a speed limit sign every 200 yards, operated like a scoreboard at a village cricket match by a genial man with a flask of tea, who lowers the indicated maximum whenever it gets dark or rains and raises it again when things improve. Which is a shame, but in its absence how are we to be protected against the irrational application of laws which cannot account for circumstances? Well, that has traditionally been the job of the police—

The boys in blue
Who can take a view.

I once interviewed a chief constable, and implied that it was the job of the police to interpret the law. He corrected me by stating that that is the job of the courts: the job of the police is to *enforce* the law. He may have been strictly right, but I don't believe that I was strictly wrong. The police are constantly having to make judgments about *whether* to enforce the law, and that involves an instantaneous interpretation of the facts and the law, and its application to the particular circumstances.

The degree to which the enforcing of law depends on the whim of the individual police officer is quite frightening, or quite reassuring. Just because you have been caught breaking the law doesn't inevitably lead you to prosecution. The officer at the scene takes a view, makes a judgment which, it is to be hoped, in the case of a speeding offence will take account of road and weather conditions, possibly the competence of the car you're driving and, of course, the margin by which the speed limit has been exceeded. Having assimilated the facts, the police then decide what action to take. They may just give you a warning, they may give you a lecture, they may already have looked the other way, they may give you a ticket. In theory, you get a humane assessment of a human failing.

I know that there is a potential downside to all this, because it is not only facts which are being assimilated, but feelings and vibes. What kind of mood is the policeman in? What kind of mood is the offender in? How does he respond to being stopped and questioned? I met someone today who was caught speeding through a London park at 11pm last night, and because the police were catching so many people in such a short time, there was a wait of *an hour* between being forced to stop and being issued with the ticket at the roadside. Can you imagine the mood those people were in when the moment came to confront an officer of the Crown? What if the offender is of a different race to the officer? What if there is a sweepstake back at the station on which officer that day will deal most viciously with a pensioner?

Stranger games have been played in the professions. I knew of a game, keenly played by the cast of the Agatha Christie play *The Mousetrap* called the Brussels sprout game. At the beginning of the play, a member of the cast would take on stage a Brussels sprout. He then had to pass it to another actor at the earliest opportunity, preferably without he or she being aware of the transfer: drop it into someone's pocket when he was passing, leave it in somebody's briefcase. When the receiving actor discovered the deposit, he had to pass it on, because the loser was the person left with the Brussels sprout at the end of the play. It was all very bemusing for a perceptive member of the audience, wondering what was the significance of a cast of characters who were constantly patting their pockets, opening and closing their handbags, and glancing down their cleavages.

But I digress. Law enforcement. The business of its subjectivity and randomness has its disadvantages, owing to the potential for abuses, but I think its advantages have been thrown into relief by the legalisation of Gatso speed cameras. You have probably heard of them: they are mainly stationed, for now, on urban trunk roads, and simply photograph every passing car that breaks the speed limit by a certain margin. A prosecution can result from the photographic evidence alone.

My concern is their clinical objectivity. It's not too much of a problem at present, because on suburban roads the speed limits are usually close to what would be considered by a rational person to be a sensible driving speed. But I would be very worried if they became prevalent on motorways, where it is universally acknowledged by both those who use them and those that police them that the 70mph limit is a load of blithering nonsense. The subjective assessment of the policeman on the spot has traditionally incorporated a healthy cynicism of this speed limit, which he knows is maintained at its present level only out of political fear. He knows that 85mph is a perfectly safe speed for the vast majority of the time, as well as he knows that 70mph is insanity in freezing fog. Gatso knows nothing, other than when to go click. Where is the humane assessment? The compassionate and realistic view? We need a human being to assess the situation, as much as the Germans need a good laugh.

The Driver's Zoo

By Margaret O. Hyde

Driving Today & Tomorrow,

1965

SOMEDAY YOU MAY DRIVE A CAR THAT IS GUIDED on an electronic pathway. Your only responsibility may be setting the pattern that will take you where you want to go.

In today's cars, YOU are the power behind the wheel. For the good driver, the feel of the steering wheel in his hands and the response of the car to the touch of his foot on the accelerator mean real pleasure. He can project his thoughts ahead to prepare for the foolish moves of the poor drivers, and he is ready for defensive action against them. At the same time, the good driver enjoys taking a curve smoothly, speeding along the open highway, and being in full control of his car at all times.

Your attitude, your ability to concentrate, and your skill play a large part in determining your safety on the road. A driver's attitude and personality are so important that a study is being made in New York City by the Department of Traffic. A number of psychiatrists are searching for information in the interest of safety. They believe that many so-called accidents seem to be predetermined by the underlying emotional states of the people involved. When a driver is angry with a friend, he may transfer his hostility to the car or the pedestrian ahead of him. Even if you are a habitually cautious driver, you are more accident prone when you are angry, upset, or feeling guilty.

Some drivers have personalities which entitle them to belong to a "Driver's Zoo." As a champion of the road, you must defend yourself from the actions of such personalities. Sometime when you are a passenger in a car, see how many of these types you can recognize.

The "road hog" is easy to spot. He thinks he owns the highway, so you are the one who should move out of his way. You cannot easily predict what he will do, for he will often weave back and forth, or drive near the center of the road, making it difficult for you to pass.

Here comes a "turtle" moving along the open road at his own slow speed. He feels very righteous about his pace. When you try to pass him, he speeds a bit and moves toward the center of the road. Soon there is a long line of cars behind you, and all the drivers want you to pass the slow car. They are becoming impatient because the "turtle" is forcing them to drive 30 miles an hour in a 50-mile speed zone.

One car pulls out of line and attempts to go by a group of three cars. You are in the middle. A car comes in the opposite direction, and the driver who is trying to pass has no place to go until you drop back and allow him to slide in line in front of you. You are a defensive driver and like all defensive drivers you drive to protect yourself and others by making allowances for their actions. You have prevented an accident, but the "turtle" pokes along unaware of the tragedy he may have caused. No wonder it is often said that death drives a slow car.

"Antelopes" travel too fast. They aim to go as fast as possible and then brag to others about the time they made going from one place to another. Such drivers frequently endanger their lives and those of others for the sake of a few minutes.

You will meet many "sheep" on the road. They follow too closely in a line of cars. The one behind you is telling his passengers not to worry because he can tell when you are going to stop by watching the car in front of you. Suddenly a dog runs onto the road. The car in front of you continues, but you must slam on your brakes. You signal for a stop, but the "sheep" behind you cannot stop in the space between his car and yours, so he runs into the ditch. This "sheep" would have profited by more skillful driving.

The "goose" is a horn blower who honks if you fail to start just as the traffic light changes. Some honk at stalled cars. They jangle everyone's nerves by their noise making.

A "gawker" is a strange kind of bird who is distracted by scenery or activities along the road. He turns his head to converse with passengers in his car or just lets his mind wander to problems other than driving. When an emergency arises, he is slow to come back to the business of driving.

An "eager beaver" passes other cars without making certain that it can be done safely. He rushes full-speed ahead to a red traffic light, slams on his brakes, and then starts up again just as soon as, or sometimes just before, the light changes. This driver is punishing his car as well as himself. And the wear and tear on his car may be minor compared to what might happen during one of his hurried passes.

The show-offs of our zoo are often seen on the highway. These "monkeys" dangle their arms from car windows so that you wonder if they are planning to turn or if they are just feeling the breeze. Some hold the roof in place while they drive. "Monkeys" brag about their one-armed driving and their ability to outdrive other motorists. They think they are smart drivers, but mature people know they lack confidence and are trying to prove their abilities to themselves as well as to others. They are dangerous on the road. The skillful driver spots them and drives with greater care than ever to avoid them.

A new driver is apt to act like a "mouse." In the beginning, there is so much to think about that one can easily understand why he is timid and confused. Later, many actions become automatic.

Some drivers feel that they know everything. Such drivers are the "lions" of the road. In time, many of these drivers become skilled motorists who show consistently smooth operation.

Safety authorities are convinced that almost all accidents are preventable. With a record of over 300,000 traffic deaths and nearly 10 million injuries due to driving errors in the United States during a period of ten years, it is not surprising that many people are saying "Something should be done about it." Something is being done. Driving tests and traffic laws are being revised. Various groups of experts from insurance companies, business clubs, industries, universities, and civic organizations are studying the problem. The American Automobile Association and other automobile clubs are sponsoring and supporting safety programs. Highways are being developed and improved with safety as a goal. Driver education is a growing trend in high schools, and skillful driving is an exciting new sport at local and national teen-age Road-e-os.

Expert driving is a challenge to the young drivers of today. Everyone agrees that the problem of highway safety must be solved if our nation is to grow. Two million new drivers each year join the 50 million on the roads. With superior training and better physical equipment, young drivers may show the world true sportsmanlike driving.

Driven to Distraction

By Jay Leno

Popular Mechanics,

July 2006

Jay Leno for *Popular Mechanics* (popularmechanics.com)

AS I WAS DRIVING DOWN THE FREEWAY RECENTLY, I watched an SUV in front of me drift out of its lane, off the road and down an embankment. I stopped, ran to it and saw two young women inside, apparently okay. There was music blaring and something was on the navigation screen.

This happened on a straight road, on a sunny day, without much traffic. And I thought how much safer I was, driving in my 50-year-old Jaguar XK120—with no side windows, no radio, no distractions—than these women were in their new truck with its ABS, airbags and other modern tech.

Why? Because I was paying attention.

I read a study once that said the more potholes there are in a stretch of road, the fewer accidents people have on it. Drivers pay attention when they hit that piece of road. They drive more slowly. So the highway departments deliberately don't fix them. I think there's something to that.

Recently, I drove a new car with satellite radio. And it kept me informed of very important facts: I'm 1.3 minutes into the song. Now I'm 1.4 minutes, now I'm 1.5 minutes . . . Why do I need to know that? And why do I need to know what year Lloyd Price recorded it?

These subtle things are distracting. Yes, I know you can turn the thing off. But it becomes addictive. I don't want to turn it off.

Another time, one of my old cars broke down on the freeway. Here in California, there's hardly any shoulder on the road anymore. So I'm standing at the back of the car, waving people out of the lane. And I see people on cellphones, heading right at me. At the last minute, I see them go "*aaarrrggghhh!*" Then they swerve.

I grew up in an era when people took pride in their driving. You focused on what you were doing. Women were impressed by skillful driving. "Wow," a girl might say, "this guy is such a good driver. I didn't even realize he was shifting."

Nowadays, you're just operating a machine. A machine that happens to be a car that's probably been designed to do most of the driving for you.

It kind of reminds me of a television commercial: The family's at the airport and the father is eating his third chili dog. He's getting sick. And his family is worried. Even you're screaming, "Stop! I can't take any more of these chili dogs."

So what is his cure? It's not to stop eating. He takes an antacid. And then he eats two more chili dogs.

Rather than teach people how to drive well, we override their need for skills. How far are we from cars that drive themselves? I don't know about you, but I don't want that car. Shouldn't we be responsible for doing some things ourselves?

And not only are so many new cars full of distractions, their controls are confusing. The other day, I got into a car that was loaned to me by one of the manufacturers. The clock was wrong. To reset it, I had to get the manual out. I ended up having to turn on the radio and hold down the digit 4 on the radio while also pressing the digit 3. How are you supposed to figure that out by yourself?

In some cars with those little joystick controllers on the console, like BMWs with iDrive, it's even worse. I don't know why I should have to go through the entire air-conditioning system to turn on the radio. I just wanted FM, and now it's blowing cold air. Wha?

Don't get me wrong—not all this new stuff is bad. Navigation systems are pretty good tools. They work well, and you don't have to turn them on if you don't want to.

Some cars have systems where you can set the speed you want to cruise and select the distance you want to keep from the car in front. One car length, two car lengths, etc. Then if the system senses a problem in front of you, it applies the brakes, which can be handy.

Of course, you could just pay attention and drive.

But it seems as though a lot of this technology serves no real purpose. Take keyless ignition. You don't have to use the key to get into the car or to lock it—or to start it. My Z06 has keyless entry. One of the guys from my shop drove off in it, and I had the keys in my pocket. I thought he'd get stuck, but he didn't. Of course, if he'd turned the car off, he couldn't have restarted it. There was probably a warning light flashing, but he didn't notice. Me, I'd rather just use a key.

Then there's GM's OnStar. It can come in handy when you lock the keys inside. The OnStar crew can remotely unlock the car for you. But I don't like OnStar. I don't want my car to make dinner reservations for me. And I certainly don't like the idea that if I have an accident, all of a sudden a voice in my car is going to start saying, "Jay hit a tree! Jay hit a tree! We're calling the cops right now!" The few times I've had an accident, I dragged my car home and I fixed it.

"Jay hit a tree! Jay hit a tree!"

Shadddup.

It Ain't Summer, So Drive Accordingly

Maybe Failure to Use Winter Tires Should Automatically Assign Degree of Responsibility

By Jim Kenzie

Wheels.ca,
February 2008

SOMETIMES YOU WONDER WHAT, IF ANYTHING, goes through some people's minds. Like the dozens of people who roared past me on the eastbound 401 between Guelph Line and Mavis Rd. recently, or the drivers involved in the series of multi-car crashes on an ice-covered Highway 400.

What, exactly, did they think those (mostly) SUVs were doing slammed into the concrete median, or door-handle-deep in the snow off the shoulder? Practising for the synchronized driving competition at the upcoming Vancouver Winter Olympics?

Were images of the pileups near Bradford involving 100 vehicles plastered all over the media the weekend before just too far in the past to remain in their memories?

Were their vehicles—again, I almost hate to add, mostly SUVs—equipped with some *Star Trek*–like anti-no-grip technology protecting them from the laws of physics that had done in dozens of their fellow drivers? Did I miss the press preview for that piece of hardware?

I was gingerly ferrying my 1991 Jetta Diesel to its new home in Pickering that evening; the new owner had already paid a deposit for it, so I was taking it easy.

But surely, the presence of so many wrecked vehicles might have suggested to these other goofs that maybe they slow down a titch?

Not so you'd notice—which I guess is why there was more than one multi-car crash.

I hate to use the word *schadenfreude* because it's difficult to spell, and no one knows what it means (deriving pleasure from the misfortune of others, in case you were wondering).

But I confess that when I see some idiot speeding by me on a slippery road and see him again a few kilometres down the pike stuffed into the wall, I just can't help smiling.

Aside from cars crashed all around you, what are the clues that maybe it isn't summer out there?

One is the glare level on the road surface. If it is bright and shiny, chances are it's wet. Now, wet is obviously worse than dry, but again you have clues: there is spray from other cars, and you probably have your wipers and washers working full-tilt.

It's when the road surface has an ominous matte finish with no road spray coming off the tires of other vehicles that you really have to be very careful. That'd be the dreaded "black ice," and your coefficient of friction is approximately zero.

In this scenario, if you get a chance when there's no one around or (especially) behind you, try a brief brake test. If the car sails along like a curling stone, ABS chattering away (if your vehicle is so equipped), that's clue No. 2 (after the crashed cars). Slow the heck down, and flick on the four-ways to warn following drivers.

Not that they're likely to pay any attention, but at least you can say you did your part.

Another way to help protect yourself is to fit proper winter tires on your car. A friend of mine suggested that we publish an issue of *Wheels* at the start of each winter driving season with nothing but "*Put winter tires on your car. Put winter tires on your car. Put winter tires on your car,*" on every line of every page.

The car advertisers might not be crazy about it, but the tire retailers would love it—and it would make a point.

As John Mahler so eloquently pointed out last week in *Wheels*, as CBC's *Marketplace* showed this week, and as TV commercials have been pointing out all winter, there are summer tires, there are winter tires—and there are no-season tires.

The tire manufacturers came up with no-season tires in response to demands from the car manufacturers, the bulk of whose customers live in the United States. "All-season" in Phoenix means three rain showers a year. And who wants to change their tires twice a year for that?

This ain't Phoenix, folks.

Just as I wish the media reports of every fatal car crash were required by law to note if the victims were wearing their seatbelts, I wish they were similarly required to report if the cars in winter crashes were equipped with winter tires.

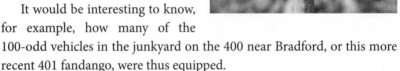

It would be interesting to know, for example, how many of the 100-odd vehicles in the junkyard on the 400 near Bradford, or this more recent 401 fandango, were thus equipped.

As John Mahler suggested, perhaps mandating winter tire use is going too far. But maybe failure to use winter tires automatically assigns you a degree of either legal or insurance responsibility for any crash you do get into.

Another point, too: put winter tires on all four wheels. It isn't just about getting traction to get out of snowdrifts (if you can't get out, you can't crash, so you're actually safer!) or to accelerate (the less you can accelerate, the slower you'll be going when you do crash).

It's because you have to steer and stop, too, and you do that with all four wheels.

Is it a bit late in the season to be telling you all this?

Did I mention the multi-car pileups two weeks ago?

Oh, and once you do get winter tires on your car? Take one of the many advanced driver training programs available in this area to learn how to drive in winter.

Because the life you save could be mine.

Traffic Court

The Diary of
an Alleged Perpetrator

By Patrick Bedard

Car and Driver,

August 1981

W hat you are about to read is the truth, so help me God. It's the story of an unplanned field trip into the criminal-justice system of the United States of America, where I found disrespect for law and order on both sides of the bench, and very little justice.

It all began at 8:40 a.m. Saturday, December 29, 1979, with a traffic ticket on the New Jersey Turnpike. Traffic southbound was light, punctuated by an occasional clump of cars. One formation had a car in the center lane; then a substantial distance ahead (perhaps a dozen lengths), one more car in the center flanked by another on the left; only the slow lane was open. Continuing on cruise control, I stayed in the left lane until well past the first car, moved to the right lane to pass the other two, then steered back to the center lane.

As I completed this maneuver, I made a routine sweep of the mirrors and saw a New Jersey State Police cruiser approaching in the right lane (the only one empty of traffic) at high speed, at least 80 mph. He was about a quarter of a mile back when I spotted him. When he caught up, he honked his horn and gestured to the side of the road.

Our conversation was brief. He asked to see the turn signals in operation. When they worked, he ticketed me for "failure to give proper signal," in violation of New Jersey statute 39:4-126.

The ticket didn't say how much the fine would be, just the number to call. My last traffic ticket was so far back I couldn't remember exactly when I got it, more than five years for sure, so my license was not in jeopardy. It would be easy to send a check and be done with this one. But I kept thinking about the charge. Is it really illegal to change lanes without giving a signal? I couldn't believe that it was. When everybody is moving along at roughly the same speed, and when there is sufficient room, a lane change in no way interrupts traffic. Signaling gives no information other drivers need to act upon. Besides, if signals really were required under those circumstances, almost every driver would be in violation.

From the standpoint of common sense, I knew I had done nothing wrong. But that doesn't count in court. There, if you are in violation of the letter of a law, you're guilty, whether the act upsets society or not. After a week of should-I-bother-or-not, I finally went down to the library and looked up New Jersey statute 39:4-126, the relevant part of which reads as follows:

"No person shall turn a vehicle at an intersection . . . or . . . enter a private road or driveway or otherwise turn a vehicle from a direct course or move right or left upon a roadway . . . unless and until such movement can be made with safety. No person shall so turn any vehicle without giving an appropriate signal in the manner hereinafter provided in the event any other traffic may be affected by such movement."

In my case, no other traffic had been affected by the movement—no question about that. And now that I knew the law, I felt a certain annoyance at having been ticketed in the first place. Clearly I was innocent. Apparently some patrolmen feel they can write up anything. So I called the phone number, pleaded not guilty, and was given a court date. The Washington Township Municipal Court is in Robbinsville, New Jersey, something over 60 miles from New York City, so I left before rush hour. The Honorable Paul Shalita seemed relatively young, under 40, and very direct in his statements. Most of the cases called before my turn were traffic-related, though some were domestic problems and one was for possession of marijuana.

The defendant in this latter instance did not have counsel; Shalita solicitously advised him of his rights and coached him on his plea so that he might get the easiest sentence—in sharp contrast to his brusque attitude toward traffic offenders.

When my case was called, Judge Shalita made sure I understood that by not having a lawyer present I was giving up my right to be represented by a lawyer of my choice. With that detail out of the way, trooper Kenneth R. Lathan was sworn in. He told the court that the defendant "made one sweeping movement from the left lane all the way to the right lane without the use of any turn signals to indicate that he was changing lanes. He passed two vehicles and then moved back into the center lane without, again, any turn signals to indicate his lane change."

Since the New Jersey statute is so specific about a signal being required only "in the event any other traffic may be affected by such movement," I feared that the trooper would say I'd cut somebody off, just to make sure his charge stuck. But he didn't. He did, however, testify that he was in the center lane when he saw the movement, which might have been true since he could have changed to the right lane before I saw him. The frame-up started with the judge's next question: "Did you have a clear and unobstructed view of the defendant's vehicle, that is to say, were there any cars between you and the defendant's vehicle when this alleged movement . . . was made?" The trooper answered, "No." This was news to me. The first car in the formation was in the center lane. I crossed over in front of it and behind the next two in making the pass. Moreover, there were several other cars even farther behind those, which caused the trooper to make his approach in the right lane. Apparently both the judge and the trooper expected me to defend myself by saying that I had in fact signaled, but intervening cars had blocked the trooper's view. To check this defense, the other cars were being testified out of the picture.

My plan under cross-examination was to establish the trooper's location as being far behind, which it was, meaning that his perception of clearance between my car and the others would not be very accurate, then ease into the subject of the other cars' not being affected. When asked, under oath, how far back he was, he answered, "Approximately ten car lengths, eleven car lengths." He was giving himself a front-row-center seat from which to view the proceedings. I was so shocked by this claim, and so unsettled by the judge's friendly tones when speaking to the trooper in contrast to his sternness toward me, that I was unable to finish the cross-examination with any finesse. The trial transcript reads as follows:

Q: Did the defendant go at the same speed or did he accelerate when he passed these cars?

A: He accelerated.

Q. The other cars, were they going at a constant speed?

A: I really can't say. I wasn't clocking them.

Q: But they didn't speed up to your notice?

A: No, not to my observation.

Q: And they didn't slow down to your notice?

A: Not that I observed.

Q. And you didn't see any brake lights?

A: No, sir.

Q: And there was no swerving from one lane to another by any of the cars being passed?

A: No.

At this point I took the stand and testified that "I very carefully checked before I made this maneuver. I saw that there was no traffic that would be affected by it. There was plenty of room." And I admitted that I passed without signaling because the law requires a signal only when other traffic is affected by the movement.

The judge responded, "Says who?"

"Well, I have a copy of the law here," I said.

Judge Shalita then summed up all of the testimony thus far, opened his law book to statute 39:4-126, and read aloud to a point just short of the statement I was counting on for my defense. Then he closed the book and began to render a judgment.

"The rest of that line is important," I suggested.

He opened the book and began where he had left off. "'Provided in the event any other traffic may be affected.' *In the event.* But I don't interpret that to mean that traffic must be affected."

After some thought, he said, "It is my position and my interpretation of this statute that when moving from lane to lane on a public highway, a vehicle is required to give signal of an intention so to do. And the failure to do so constitutes a violation of that statute. When applying the facts to the law, the defendant will be found guilty. Fine $10, court costs $15."

As an afterthought, he said, "I cannot believe that the intent of this statute is to leave in the discretion of the driver what would affect traffic."

Since, up to this point, I had shared the common middle-class belief that American courts produce justice, the outcome of this trial caused me to stop and take stock. I had been ticketed by an officer who either didn't know the law (that a signal is required only when other traffic is affected) or was deliberately making a false charge. Probably, he was ignorant of the law. If he was willing, under oath, to move himself to a more favorable position on the roadway, I suspect he would have also said I had affected traffic if he had known that was necessary for conviction. But of course it wasn't in this case, because the judge refused to act upon the law as written, thereby compounding the injustice.

Upon my return to Manhattan, I called my friend John Nicholas Iannuzzi (of the New York law firm of Iannuzzi, Russo and Iannuzzi), a criminal lawyer fueled by a seemingly bottomless reservoir of idealism, and asked him if I had grounds for an appeal. Absolutely, he said, and volunteered to coach me through the procedure.

An appeal, in essence, is a re-examination of the case based solely on evidence introduced in the original trial. New testimony of fact is not heard. To proceed, the appellant must file notice of appeal and obtain a transcript of the original trial. The transcription fee was $30 in advance, $12 of which was refunded later.

The Superior Court of New Jersey responded by issuing notice of the hearing on March 20. It arrived, along with the necessary transcript, in my mail on Saturday, March 22. The appeal was scheduled to be heard April 3, seven working days away, and I was required to file a letter brief in advance. Since the court was in another state, that seemed an impossibly short time. Iannuzzi told me to request an adjournment (a postponement). I called the judge's assistant, explained the problem, and was told the Honorable Paul G. Levy did not give adjournments on such cases.

So we went to work on the brief. It's a wholly logical document in which the appellant states what he thinks went wrong in the first trial, and how he thinks it should have gone, and supports these opinions by citing previous court decisions that agree. But the form is stilted, and the research necessary to build a good argument is beyond the capabilities of someone who has not had some legal training. I could not have done it without help. When finished, the brief ran six typewritten pages; it was served through the mail three days before the trial. Iannuzzi said my oral argument would be based on the brief but I would not be allowed merely to read it. So I spent another day memorizing it and trying to prepare logical responses for whatever way the judge might zig or zag.

As I walked into the courtroom in Trenton, New Jersey, the cost of the appeal was running into four days of my time, the transcription fee, a round-trip train ticket to Trenton, and what surely would have been several hundred dollars' worth of Iannuzzi's time had he not donated his services. The Honorable Paul G. Levy was conspicuously surprised to see me. The cost and red tape scare off most people who would appeal a traffic ticket.

A young woman named Patricia Bowen Atkins was acting as prosecutor, and she began reviewing aloud the proceedings of the lower court. When she came to Judge Shalita's interpretation of the law, Judge Levy interrupted: "He was wrong. Let's skip what he had to say."

I was beginning to see how the court system works. Judges can be terribly wrong, and nothing happens to them when they are. But the cost to you of gaining access to a higher court so a wrong judgment can be reversed is incredibly high; and yet when you get there, the lower court's logic may be so obviously faulty that the appellate judge dismisses it without even hearing your argument. They didn't tell us in civics class that the system was so capricious.

Judge Levy rejected Judge Shalita's interpretation of the law, but he did not reverse his decision. Instead, he began sifting through the transcript to find some other way of hanging me. He decided that moving back into the center lane at the conclusion of the pass—in front of the passed car in the center lane—actually amounted to affecting that car. I reminded him that there was no testimony whatever establishing that traffic had been affected. There wasn't even the suggestion that traffic had been affected. In fact, the trooper never even mentioned the possibility. He just testified that I had changed lanes without a signal, which of itself is not against the law. But Judge Levy found me guilty anyway. So much for the fundamentals of American justice, which are *innocent until proven guilty* and *proof beyond a reasonable doubt*.

At this point I was thoroughly depressed. For years I've been hearing radicals and minorities complain that they couldn't get justice in the white, middle-class courts. But I'm as white and as middle-class as they come, and I couldn't get justice either. Had I been a raving maniac accused of an ax murder, I could perhaps have understood a judge erring on the side that would protect the citizenry. But my suit was pressed, my shoes were shined, and I was accused of not giving the proper signal. Why withhold justice on such an inconsequential matter?

Could it be that civics-book justice is no longer available? Or is it more a matter of court procedures being so technical that a citizen, even a well-informed one, has no hope of successfully defending himself? Once again I called Iannuzzi, this time asking him to take over the case, to handle the next appeal in the best professional manner. Then we would find out if a lawyer could make the right answer come out of the court where a citizen had failed.

Since he is not licensed in New Jersey, Iannuzzi said he would do the work but the brief would be filed by Stephen Russo, a partner in his firm who is a member of the New Jersey bar. This would be the major leagues, an appeal to the second-highest court in the state, and the costs were commensurate: $50 for a transcript of the first appeal ($25 refunded later), $20 to file a new notice of appeal, and $305 to print a new brief in the manner required by this superior court and have it served in Trenton. Remember that this sum had nothing to do with the research for and the writing of the brief. Iannuzzi did that for nothing: nineteen pages of argument punctuated by citations of precedent, a job that has to be worth a week's pay for most of us.

The court gave the prosecutor one month to answer our brief. The deadline was not met. After another week, we petitioned the court to bar the prosecutor from taking any further action. Iannuzzi said that was just a formality to get things moving, because if the prosecutor's office asked for an extension, even after the deadline, it would surely be granted. As predicted, Patricia Bowen Atkins woke up and asked that she be allowed to come in late. Iannuzzi okayed that on the assumption that the court would rule her way anyway if presented with the request.

In her brief, Atkins homed in on the word "may" in the part of the law that reads "in the event any other traffic may be affected by such movement." She said, in effect, that there are all manner of traffic patterns on the road that *may* be affected by a lane change; you can't tell in advance.

To show after the fact that no traffic was affected is an invalid test. The word "may" requires prior determination. And since that can't be made, giving a signal is the only way to comply with the law.

That's stretching logic past the breaking point, in my opinion. But in any case, the trial transcript—which is all that may be considered on appeal—contained my testimony that I had checked carefully in advance to ensure that other traffic would not be affected, so we were covered. Iannuzzi's contention was that the law meant exactly what it said in plain language. If the lawmakers had intended for a signal to be given at all times, they certainly would have written it that way. They did not, since they foresaw times when requiring a signal would be unreasonable. So instead of saying "every time," their determinant for when a signal must be given is "in the event any other traffic may be affected by such movement." This was left to the driver's discretion, just as the response to a yield sign or a flashing yellow is left to the driver's discretion. It is common to elect that appeals at this level be heard without oral argument. Both sides submit written briefs on the law; the judges read them over and render a decision. To keep the cost down, we chose this alternative.

And we lost. The verdict handed down by Judges Fritz and Joelson, Appellate Division, Superior Court of New Jersey, said, "There was ample credible evidence in the record to support the finding of the judge [Shalita]."

"Bang," went the gavel.

"Next case," said the court.

Of course Iannuzzi had anticipated the possibility of the verdict going against us and had salted the brief with constitutional questions that would allow us to slide the next appeal into federal court. But what's the point here? Certainly not burning up half the GNP just to put the court system through all its contortions. I'm pretty well convinced that when three layers of jurisprudence hear the evidence and all of them fail to act in the manner required of them by the Constitution, there is something fundamentally wrong, something that climbing up another layer is not going to fix. Moreover, I don't think this case is unique in any way, except for the length to which it was pursued. Correspondence from readers on their experiences confirms that traffic court has become largely a formality. If the police say you're guilty, you're guilty. The court just rubber-stamps the charge.

How did the system get distorted in this way? From this case and others, I've made the following observations:

1. Judges subconsciously feel that traffic cases are not entitled to due process. Compared with real criminal cases, penalties for traffic violations are small. Erring on the harsh side, it is assumed, will throw fear into drivers, which can only make them safer.

2. Judges are pressured to back up the police. While a citizen may appear before a given judge only once in his life, each policeman in the division may have five cases before the same judge every week. Everybody whines when he loses, but scattered citizens don't whine as effectively as the entire police force. Also, many judges feel it's their responsibility to maintain police morale. They can't give pay raises, so they dole out convictions instead.

3. Judges generally subscribe to the peculiarly American view, sponsored by the government and the National Safety Council, that there should be no creativity—indeed, no thought—in driving. Each motorist should stay on his side of the dotted line, follow in procession behind the car ahead, and keep the pace slow. That way nobody will get hurt. If accidents still happen, well, nothing can be done. But woe be to those who deviate from the procession by exercising their discretion and judgment. Independent thinking will be punished.

4. Judges forget they are judges. They start acting like prosecutors. When Judge Shalita examined trooper Lathan, it was in the same patient and protective tones a district attorney would lavish on his star witness. Judges aren't supposed to produce law and order. They are meant to be independent umpires who decide cases on their merits. Judges, and the population at large, frequently lose the distinction between these two missions.

5. Judges fall into disrespect for the law just as citizens do. The mood of society is tilting toward "whatever I can get by with," and judges are a part of society. They disregard the Constitution when other interests seem more compelling. Constitutional freedoms are no longer sacred.

SO WHAT ARE WE GOING TO DO? We can't accept a separate standard of justice for traffic offenses. Moreover, we can't assume that the cavalier attitude shown toward traffic cases doesn't also creep into the handling of more serious criminal matters, because, after all, they are frequently lumped into the same courts. More important still, we must remember that the first exposure most citizens have to the judicial system is a traffic charge. If there is to be respect for the law, we have to see that the courts set a good example right from the beginning.

All of this is easy to say, but how do we get there from here? I have observed that most issues of public dispute are settled in favor of whoever has the best PR. Whether it's the windfall-profits tax, or where to build the nuke plant, or gay rights, the side that applies the most pressure usually wins. In traffic cases, judges feel pressure only from the police. To counteract that, we must know our rights under the Constitution and demand that the courts safeguard them. Tyranny, after all, is tyranny, whether at the hands of a Communist dictator or a biased judge. When the courts fail, we must apply pressure, both in the higher courts and in the public forum. The free press can be an effective watchdog, but you have to do your part. Local judges respond to local pressure. You have to inform the local media when judges do not live up to their responsibilities. It's very much harder to deny civil rights when the whole community is watching.

America will be as good as Americans demand it to be. The next time you're issued a bum ticket, you have a choice: take the easy way and mail in a check, or fight it to discourage the system from making the same mistake again. Fighting is expensive. Against a $25 ticket, I've now invested more than six days and over $500, not to mention a great deal of a friend's time for legal help. And even though I lost, if another circumstance arises, I'll do it all again. Because that is the cost to a citizen of keeping the system honest. Nobody ever said that living in a free country would be cheap.

Speed Limits Waste Life

They Are Just a Tool of Repression

By L. J. K. Setright

The Independent,
November 2003

HOW FAST IS TOO FAST? I shall not wait for an answer; there is none. All speed limits are implausibly arbitrary, but only once did a former Minister of Transport admit speed limits were for political rather than practical reasons. Speed laws are like all laws: they are a codification of yesterday's practice, and an expression of yesterday's prejudices.

Our basic 30mph limit for built-up areas was introduced in 1935, the year in which Germany opened its first real autobahn. Then, most of the popular cars on our roads would never reach 60, many had no brakes on their front wheels, tyres were made of natural tree-rubber naturally skiddy when wet. Most of our roads were surfaced with glassy bitumen or polished Bridport pebbles and coated with a mix of spilt oil and horse-droppings, which made them like a skating-rink.

If the physical conditions then are irrelevant now, what about the attitudes? In those days, one in 55 Britons owned a car; seen as a luxury of the wealthy, it was treated with the same resentment as its owner.

Wherever individualism tends towards anarchy, somebody will try to drive faster than everybody else; wherever democracy tends towards mob rule, everybody will see to it that nobody goes faster than anybody else. To drive at your own comfortable speed, irrespective of how everybody else drives, would mark you as dangerously anti-social.

Speed limits are a tool of repression. That was why the Minister of the Interior for the Grand Duchy of Baden directed Karl Benz, whose first four-wheeler was being readied for the market in late 1893, that it would be subject to a speed limit of 12kph on the open road, half that in towns or around sharp corners. Matters were no better in Britain, where the notorious Locomotives on Highways Act had been so maliciously compounded as to subject the most innocuous of lightweight motor cars to the same costive restrictions (red flag and all) as were applied to the elephantine traction engines of the 1860s. That Act scuppered the steam stagecoach trade, too, all because a lot of our Members of Parliament had strong and profitable interests in the railways.

A century later, our politicians devised and controlled a Road Research Laboratory, which enabled them to say there should be a blanket 70mph limit through Britain. The RRL dutifully produced statistics purporting to show the limit saved lives. But the statistics were manipulated and falsified. The result was that the cost to the nation caused by traffic delays was three times greater than the total cost of all motoring accidents, which caused an annual death toll similar to nephritis. Does Government campaign against nephritis?

Speed limits cannot be justified. Logically, there should be only one motoring offence, dangerous use (which covers parking as well as driving) of the highway. Morally, it should probably be an adequate defence if the accused could show that he had endangered none but himself.

The rabble-rousing rant of the politicians is not to be trusted. Speed does not kill. Speed saves. It saves life by saving time, which amounts to the same thing. Alas, there can be no law-abiding driver today under 55 who can have any idea what it was like to drive at over 70mph on British roads. It was practical, sensible, and pleasant. If you can forget Big Brother watching you, it still is.

The **Ferocious** Animal Is **Tamed: Roaring** and **Pitching** Inhabitant of the City's **Wilderness** of Walls Submits to **Complete Control**

Author Unknown
Popular Mechanics, 1902

The automobile is becoming tamed. It was formerly believed to be something like the zebra, the lion or other wild animals of the dark continent that defied the efforts of man to effect its subjugation. Like a wild bronco of the Texas plains, it would buck and lunge and pitch until few had the nerve to tempt its ferocity. Sometimes it would charge backward when the chauffeur tried to make it go forward and sometimes it darted forward when he wanted it to go back. It would switch around sideways, jump upward and endways, and in fact it was a hard matter to tell which way the "mechanical beast" would go when the lever was touched.

But now all these troubles of the automobilists are over. Automobile trainers have become expert in their work. They have so completely subjugated the former wild, rearing, untame thing that it is now as docile as a work horse. No longer does it tear down a crowded street, despite the chauffeur's efforts to stop it; nor does it plunge into street cars at the crossings or suddenly take a notion to make a speed test run when the chauffeur has left it to stand for a while. To demonstrate the abject submission this once proud, ferocious creature has undergone, it is but necessary to glance at the front page illustration. Here is a chauffeur making his automobile climb on top of a house. He is running up an inclined track, 42 78-100 per cent grade, the wheels on either side being supported by wooden rails but little wider than those of a railroad. This feat was performed in Chicago and is considered the most remarkable ever attempted by a motor vehicle in any country. It was done by its manufacturers to demonstrate its complete control, wonderful power and grade climbing ability.